Betrayal of North-East

The Arrested Voice

Attention Authors

'We Convert Fighters into Writers'. That's the motto of Manas Publications for more than four decades. Our message to the world is that India can win the battle not only by bullet but also by the pen. There is no dearth of intellectuals in our country, but their knowledge is confined to them only. No sincere effort has been made by any other publisher to channelise their knowledge in national interest. That is why the talent of a large number of intellectuals remains latent. An author transforms his knowledge into a manuscript, and it is our job to spread his/her knowledge by converting it into a beautiful book. For over four decades, Manas has been motivating the intellectuals by publishing their manuscripts and would like to publish your manuscript too. If you or your colleagues have any manuscript ready for publication or are working on it, kindly contact us with detailed synopsis and list of contents. We will transform your work into a valuable publication. If you wish, we can also suggest you the suitable subjects for writing the books related to your area of expertise. Manas is known for its publishing quality and commitments. We take utmost care in production and give wide publicity to the book as well as its author through our national and international distribution network.

Betrayal of North-East

The Arrested Voice

Hiranya Kumar Bhattacharyya
IPS (Retd)

(Foreword by Bertil Lintner)

Manas Publications
(We Convert Fighters into Writers)
New Delhi-110002 (INDIA)

MANAS PUBLICATIONS
(Publishers for IAS, IPS, IFS, IRS, Defence, Press, Judges etc.)
(Publishers, Distributors, Importers & Exporters)
4402/5-A, Ansari Road (Opp. HDFC Bank)
Darya Ganj, New Delhi-110 002 (India)
Off: ✆ 011-23260783, 23265523, Res: 011-23842660
Fax: 011-23272766
E-mail: manaspublications@gmail.com
manaspublications@yahoo.com
Website: **www.manaspublications.in**

2015

ISBN: 978-81-7049-505-5
₹ 795/-

Designed at
Manas Publications

Printed in India at
RK Print Services, Delhi
and published by Mrs Suman Lata for
Manas Publications,
4402/5-A, Ansari Road, (Opp HDFC Bank),
Darya Ganj, New Delhi-110 002 (INDIA)

To

Dr. Hiren Gohain

Foreword

India's oldest and longest-lasting ethnic conflict is not in Jammu and Kashmir, which gets most of the attention of the domestic and international media — but in the remote northeastern states. Connected with the rest of the country by a narrow stretch of land called the Siliguri Corridor, or, more colloquially, the Chicken's Neck, it seems a world apart from what many people in the northeast often refer to as "mainland India." It is sometimes hard for me as an outside observer to understand this neglect because no part of India is as strategically important as the seven northeastern states. Nepal and Bhutan are one side of the corridor and Bangladesh on the other. Further to the east, India's northeast borders China and Myanmar. India's first ethnic insurgency broke out in the 1950s — in the then Naga Hills of Assam. The Nagas received support from Pakistan in the 1950s and early 1960s, and later, in the 1960s, from China. When a rebellion broke out in the Mizo Hills in the late 1960s, both Pakistan and China provided sanctuaries — and weapons — to the Mizo rebels as well. Manipur and Tripura have been in a state of turmoil since the 1970s.

But the most crucial ethnic conflict in the northeast has been, and still is, in the most populous of the northeastern states: Assam. As Hiranya Kumar Bhattacharyya states in this excellent account of the troubles in his home state: "Assam is India in miniature, but very few national leaders are in a position to claim to have appreciated this intricate situation." Since his childhood, Bhattacharyya has been a witness to the tumultuous events in Assam, and how the hopes and aspirations of the people of the northeast have been dashed by ongoing conflicts and the inability of people in power to understand the roots of the troubles.

But no one should get the impression that Bhattacharyya is some kind of rabble-rousing, local agitator. In 1958, at the age of 24, he joined the Indian Police Service and has always had the best interests of his country at heart. During the freedom struggle in what was then known as East Pakistan, he trained 250 Mukti Bahini guerrillas for which he in March 2013 was awarded the "Friend of the Liberation War" honour by the government of Bangladesh.

But even so, he was arrested and detained twice, in 1981 and 1983, under the National Security Act on what he asserts were fabricated charges. This as at a time when many local people in Assam stood up for their rights. During his first stint in jail, he was dismissed from his post in the police force. In 1995, however, he was rehabilitated by India's Supreme Court — but that order came after the age at which he should have retired from the IPS.

In more recent years, Bhattacharyya has played an important role in facilitating peace talks between the Government of India and leaders of the United Liberation Front of Assam, or ULFA. He has also written thirteen books, including two in English, as well as more than 200 articles in different newspapers and journals — all about the troubles in Assam, and how society could move forward towards a lasting peace while at the same time fulfilling the hopes and dreams of the people of the Northeast for a better and more prosperous future.

This book, his fourteenth, is more autobiographical in nature — but all set in the context of the troubles in the northeast. It should be required reading for anyone who cares about what undoubtedly is, and remains, the most troubled part of India. Hopefully, it should also prompt policymakers to pay more attention to a region that for far too long has been neglected and, at best, misunderstood by people in power in the centre.

Bertil Lintner
Chiang Mai, Thailand

Acknowledgment

Though I have depended mostly on my fast fading memory while writing this account of my life's journey, I must admit that this book would never have seen the light of the day but for the active assistance rendered by Shri Jayanta Goswami, my youngest son Shri Rajeev Bhattacharyya and Shri Pradip Nath, the designer. My heartiest thanks to all of them.

My special thanks are also due to the legendary journalist Bertil Lintner who took the pain of going through the manuscript of this discourse and wrote the foreword. I am further thankful to Shri B G Verghese for having given me some important tips for making this book publication worthy. Also, I thank Manas Publications for undertaking to publish this book.

Introduction

With dark cloud hovering low and rain playing hide and seek, the day was not certainly conductive to any creative ventures. Even then, I decided to go ahead with the project as I felt that the time would otherwise run out.

After good deal of thoughts, interaction and deliberations with others, I have ultimately decided to be myself. Doubts, skepticism, apprehensions and even, at times, optimism of uncertain magnitude have completely dominated my mind. What I am presenting below will be mostly from the fast-fading memory and the lasting impression left on me by the time. Accounts of various events and analysis thereof may not be in chronological order but nonetheless, their relevance is of immense measures in respect of the time I have left behind. Let it be very clear from the very beginning that what I am submitting below is not out of any inclination to authorship or for any literary achievement; but out of strong urges to let the future generations know the changes Assam has undergone or suffered during the last century and half.

The entire north-eastern region of the country is a geographical and economic unit – a phenomenon that has been continuously ignored by New Delhi until recent times. The geographical isolation, coupled with New Delhi's step-motherly attitude towards the region for decades, contributed volubly to the growth of a sense of alienation among its denizens. Very few persons have cared to know about the composite nature of Assam's socio-political and economic life. In fact, Assam is India in miniature; but very few national leaders are in a position to claim to have appreciated this intricate situation. It can hardly be gainsaid that some of the hill tribes of the region were brought into the Indian fold by the British rule only. In fact, Assam was also never politically a part of India or of any of the pre-British empires ruled from Delhi, although religio-cultural links contributed to cultivating affinities with the Indian mainstream. The advent of the British facilitated the inclusion of Assam in the political map of India. Even then, the sense of national oneness could not be driven home very deep and the geographical isolation did not help matters either after Independence. The tardy pace of development despite her rich natural resources, as compared to the rest of the country, also engendered a feeling of deprivation in Assam; thus, the sense of alienation coupled with the sense of deprivation ultimately degenerated into militant secessionism. Howsoever lately it may be, in the wake of the changes in the international scenario and the secessionist activities, New Delhi realized the strategic importance of the North-East and the ongoing massive developmental programmes have given a new direction to the hopes and aspirations of the people of the region.

Since my childhood, I have been a witness to tremendous changes all over—some of these beneficial and some others causing sheer consternation and loss of confidence in the system prevailing today. However, various doubts fortified by apprehensions galore, clouded my mind during my school days.

Contents

Foreword		7
Acknowledgement		9
Introduction		11
1.	Nalbari Days	15
2.	What Ails Assam's Economy	24
3.	Allahabad Days	34
4.	IPS Days	45
5.	A New Chapter of Life & New Challenges	54
6.	Dhubri Days	65
7.	The Days of Turmoil	75
8.	As DIGP Border	101
9.	Demands For Three Ds	104
10.	Assam Movement	107
11.	Detention and Dismissal	132
12.	In Uncharted Waters	181
13.	Election of 1983	185
14.	Glimpses of a New Venture	217

15. Assam Accord: A Stillborn Baby 220
16. Two AGP Governments 230
17. The Rule of Law 253
18. BJP Days 255
19. Little Digression 264
20. Back to BJP Days 266
21. Retirement and Back to Public Life 274
22. Trip to Bangladesh 299
23. Discernible Social Changes 303
24. Envoi 306
Index **311**

1

Nalbari Days

I had my schooling in three different places because my father's was a transferable job. However, the major portion of my schooling was at Gurdon High School, Nalbari where I had the fortune of being taught by some teachers of extraordinary eminence. On the other hand, my father, late Devendranath Bhattacharyya, was himself a renowned educationist as also an eminent litterateur. (We have already published all his literary works in 10 big volumes.)

I have a mixture of both pleasant and unpleasant memories of my school days. Unpleasant because in the early years of my schooling days, my mother, Chandraprabha Devi, was taken seriously ill, confining her to bed for months on end. Such occasions were quite frequent. Even after partial recovery, she was no more the same active housewife capable of looking after the entire household all by herself. The gap had to be filled up mostly by us—the children. In the long run, as I look back, the years of her ailment turned out to be very educative for us. Because, circumstances compelled us to do most of the house chores with the lion share falling to my lot. In fact, the only helping hands used to be the cook and my younger sister Anupama Devi, six years younger than me. Unfortunately, the services of the cook were not of uninterrupted nature. As such, cooking responsibility had also to be undertaken by Anupama and me. As if, that was not sufficient, laundering for myself, cleaning the utensils and the likes, had turned out to be daily routine, with no regrets though. No regrets because this ultimately made me not only self-dependent but also very self-confident with the result that I never fell a victim to the unmanly habit of shirking responsibility.

Though Nalbari in the 40s of the last century had an elected town committee, it would have been an exaggeration to call it a town in real sense of the term. It neither had electricity nor a system of water supply. (Not that it has full benefits of these services now in 2014.) It might have been well-described as a big village with a semi urban making. However, it had the advantage of being in a position to boast of a vast and rich hinterland, both economically and culturally. In fact, Nalbari was known as the Nabadweep of Assam because of its rich heritage of producing, the erudite Sanskrit scholar like Mahamahopadhyaya Dhireswaracharya of all-India fame. His creative genius in the field of Sanskrit prosody in the shape of his "Brittamanjory", has been acknowledged all over India for a century now as unsurpassable. He was a cousin of my grandfather and my father had inherited his legacy to considerable extent and despite being a science graduate he had cultivated the ability to deliver speeches in Sanskrit amongst well-known Sanskrit scholars. Anyway, I mention this only to lament an irony of fate: Notwithstanding my literary association and legacy, my understanding and attachment to the study of Sanskrit left much to be desired. The resultant tragedy is that Veda Vyas, Balmiki Kalidasa, Bhababhuti, Sriharsa (our ancestor), Banabhatta, Sudrak and many others continue to be Greek jargon for me in their originals. What a misfortune! Now in the evening of my life, the grim realization has dawned on me. What an unworthy descendant I have been of worthy ancestors! Even then, I was immensely benefitted from the academic atmosphere created during our childhood and adolescence by our parents. It was due to my mother that epical characters like Rama, Sri Krishna, Bhisma and the whole lot are still very much alive in my memories. On the other hand, my father, very anxious to educate his children properly as also to cultivate in them undying devotion to Indian heritage, took recourses to various ingenuous but ingenious strategy. As for instance, he compelled me to memorize Tagore's

"Gitanjali" when I was a student of Class VII. Not that I understood everything, but Tagore's "Bharat Tirtha" ignited in me a deep desire to understand the significance of Indian heritage. This apart, he used to recite for us some of Tagore's most famous poems like *Dui Bigha Jami, Puratana Bhritya, He Mor Durbhaga Desh, Devdasi* etc., etc. Beside rousing my curiosity, some of these poems had cultivated my concern for human sufferings, socio-economic complexities and a deep attachment to my own country. Which is why, one of Walter Scott's composition continues to be my most favorite:

Breathes there the man
With soul so dead
Who never to himself hath said
This is my own – my native land

Above all, our father cultivated in us the habit of reading books, particularly biographies and historical accounts of many revolutionary events of the world history. In fact, he started a library within the family and named it after his father as Damodar Library. "Damodar Library" played a great role in rousing our interest far beyond the classroom. My father had his own armour of pride and self-esteem, very proud of his heritage and uncompromising in his conviction, almost verging on conservatism. Even then, he was a liberal man in the sense that he never pressurized our tenants to pay their dues. Rather he used to be very kind even to the extent of forgoing his legal dues in case of hard-up tenants. In fact, he wrote off a large chunk of his land in favour of some peasants and one of his younger brothers.

My mother was also very enthusiastic about the library and she used to read all the Assamese and Bengali books collected for the library. If anything, this library was instrumental in dissociating us from the "gossip club" which used to crop up amongst all growing children. Above all, this library is mainly responsible for cultivating my reading habit which has outlived most other interests both indoor and outdoor. Not that this adolescent period was free from various aberrations which might better remain unsaid lest one be branded as a mini edition of Khuswant Singh. However, the "summum bonum" was that we, all the children in the family, were ushered in an atmosphere of academic exercises which sustained me all through my life.

Then came the days of Nalbari College. Those were the days of great exhilaration, escapades and what not! Despite being the "Best Man" in two consecutive years, the college authorities did not take to me very kindly, only because I, with my father's approval, refused to participate in the electioneering campaign of 1952 and the rancour caused thereby continued till I left the college. However certain undeserving deprivations did create some bitterness in my mind and this engendered a critical attitude towards my surroundings. This critical attitude, at times, used to be swayed away by emotional outbursts much to the detriment of stability in life.

However, this critical outlook did give me an insight into the bane of India's national life and its deficiencies as my analysis led me to consider. In ancient India, as I considered, the academic domain was confined only to the Brahmins and the Kshatriya, the ruling oligarchies with the result that no system of elementary education followed by any arrangement for higher pursuits was available to the common man, the purpose obviously being to perpetuate a servile feudal system as well as to monopolize the political and economic powers. This is how the talents of Ekalavya and Data Karna were not allowed to intervene in the traditional set up. Certainly the Brahmins appeared to be very active for perpetuating their stranglehold not only on the masses but also on the ruling class which had to depend on the lords of the academic world for sustenance. The common man thus had practically no role to play in the administrative affairs, a great tragedy of Indian heritage. True, artisans were there but hardly their names were available excepting the epical names of Viswakarma, Moidanab, etc. Indian masses were kept spellbound by the shrewdly cultivated tradition of Bhakti (devotion) to the authorities that were. The exposure came with the advent of the foreigners who threw open the gates of education to the common man. But still restrained by tradition and devotion to authorities, he could not imbibe the healthy traditions and conventions necessary for a democratic way of life and living. Which is why, even after more than six decades of Independence, healthy democratic traditions, conventions and practices were yet to grow deep roots in our administrative system. No wonder that there have since been countless cases of misappropriation of public funds with Assam not being an exception. The absence of stability and a moral purpose encompassing contemporary life has been thus agitating my mind for last few years.

Digression has throughout been the bane of my organized thinking and writing despite some benevolent critic ascribing such trend to the stream of consciousness or virginian style of depicting contemporary times. So back to Nalbari days:

My days in Nalbari College, as hinted upon earlier, were not of unmixed ease and bliss. The main reason being that I was not amenable to tow a particular political line— much to the dislike, if not annoyance, of the leadership predominantly not only bias in favour of a particular political philosophy but also some partisan leaders who were college teachers by profession. This, somehow did not fit into my concept of pursuing a purposeful academic career.

Nalbari of those days was a hot bed of RCPI activities, so much so that not less than 700 RCPI activists were rounded up between 1948 and 1951 and tortured mercilessly. As I look back and analyse, it transpires that the grassroot level leadership of RCPI was totally neutralized as was done by SS Roy, the CM of West Bengal while dealing with the Naxalites. However, the fallouts of the general elections of 1952 witnessed the emergence of a rich crop of socialism oriented activists in Nalbari area. In this context, late Hem Barua, the famous MP, principal TN Goswami, Prof Umakanta Sarma, late Lakshyadhar Choudhury, Viswadev Goswami, etc., were the torch bearers. To cut a long story short, it may be pertinent to mention that even now, Nalbari continues to be breeding left-oriented, dissenting voices. Needless to mention that Nalbari turned out to be a very fertile recruiting ground for ULFA. However, it is tragic that Nalbari could not reap any rich harvest from such a people-oriented background.

It was during my Nalbari days that I cultivated my love for dogs, flowers & gardening and undying addiction to angling. Dr Jatin Babu, the famous angler of Nalbari area, had introduced me to the mysterious world of angling, a very innocent and painstaking sport which offered me the best means of recreation even during so many crises of my life. Also, it was through angling that I cultivated some life-long friendships. Dr Jatin Babu, who was our house physician and a lifelong bachelor, died in 2010 at the age of 103. His selfless devotion to the treatment of our ever-ailing mother kept her active even with her agonizing chronic rheumatism. No wonder he became a great favorite with all the children. Though a bachelor, his only undying attachment was to angling only and no other vice. But as I look back, his expertise was limited to only close-water angling and not ever flowing torrential rivers which in subsequent years, captivated my heart and soul. In fact, one of my books, captioned "Fagunar Kopili" has been acclaimed as the first Assamese book on angling coupled with accounts of adventurous, if not risky, journeys through hills and dense forests depicting Assam's rich potentials for developing international tourism. Anyway, I must inform my readers that this addiction to angling survives in the closing years of my life's drama, although wanton and unabated devastation caused to Assam's hills, forests, and rivers, the scope for angling has been reduced to a unbelievably low level. On the other hand, the joy of pitching one's tent and camping in the wild on the banks of rivers like Manas, Jiyabhoroli, Kopili, Buroi, Subansiri, etc., is becoming a thing of the past, thereby impoverishing the quality of one's outdoor life and close contact with the nature. These days, only memories of the past keep on haunting.

To focus on the contemporary life in Assam, before delving into my Allahabad days, may be very much in order. By the time I left for Allahabad in early 1954, the first general elections were held in the country in 1952. The sudden and sad demise of Bharat Ratna Gopinath Bordoloi, the first chief minister of Assam in independent India, was a rude shock to the entire North-east. The foundation laid by Bordoloi for integrating all the ethnic groups into a composite whole was shaken with divisive forces taking full advantage of the vacuum created by Bordoloi's death. Bishnuram Medhi took up the mantle of Assam's governance in place of Bordoloi. Medhi was also a staunch freedom-fighter and a keen watchdog of Assam's interests. His uncompromising devotion to Assam's cause had, on occasions, irked Pt Nehru. Nehru had failed, even from pre-independence days, to appreciate Assam's apprehension of losing her distinct identity. He betrayed total apathetic attitude towards Sadulla's "grow more Muslim" policy and was prepared to handover Assam to Pakistan in the wake of the notorious "grouping scheme". Thanks to Mahatma Gandhi's blessings, Bordoloi could stave off the dark cloud looming large in the horizon. Because of such insensitive attitude on the part of the Congress's central leadership, Bordoloi had even threatened to think in terms of an independent Assam, seceding from India. Though he could stave off the crisis with blessings from Mahatma Gandhi, bad blood had already been brewed, a legacy surviving throughout the tenures of late Medhi, late Bimala Prasad Chaliha and late Mahendramohan Choudhury. It is now possible with the help of hindsight to discern such an uneasy ambience until the assumption of power by late Sarat Chandra Sinha whose ascendency to chief ministership ushered in an era of total submission to New Delhi and during the national Emergency of 1975-77, the submissive attitude degenerated into a servile state of affairs, thereby totally divesting the country of its federal character. More about it in due course.

Until the late 50s of the last century, Assam did not witness the emergence of a strong opposition party with Congress being the only well-organised political party worth the name. Even then a rich crop of socialist leaders did emerge. The election of late Hem Barua in 1957 to the Lok Sabha from Mangaldoi. Lok Sabha constituency was a big shot in the arms of the young socialist activists, who also succeded in returning another socialist MLA from Nalbari, namely, late Badan Chandra Talukdar in 1972. As mentioned earlier, Nalbari in those days used to be a hot bed of anti-establishment, Left-oriented politics. In fact, immediately after Independence, entire Nalbari area was crisscrossed by militant RCPI activists. The state government was so much exercised over this development that it had to start, as hinted upon earlier, a full-scale operation in 1950 against the RCPI activists who were sent in their hundreds to the temporary jail set up at Nalbari. Leaders like Bishnu Prasad Rava, Chhatrasingh Teron, Tarunsen Deka, etc., went underground and the RCPI was banned. Subsequently, quite a few RCPI leaders joined the CPI. In fact, all over the state the RCPI gradually petered out. No doubt, the process was accelerated by the retirement of Pannalal Dasgupta, who ultimately took to nonviolent Gandhian path. CPI had, of course, got Tarunsen Deka elected to the state assembly in 1957. In many of its stronghold, RCPI had boycotted the elections of 1952 and though active till about 1957, it became irrelevant in state politics.

Though agriculture was the main stay of Assam in those days, as it was even today, even then the undivided district of Lakhimpur had the pride of place of being the highest revenue earning district in whole India mainly because of its tea, coal, timber and petroleum products. In fact, the Digboi Oil Refinery of the district, now in Tinsukia district, was the only oil refinery in India and the second one in whole of Asia. To be very precise, Assam was first to produce tea and oil in India. Even then, Assam remained far from being industrialized in the real sense of the term. The entire exercise in these field of economic activities, was colonial rule-oriented. Which is why, the benefits of the industrial revolution remained beyond the reach of the common Assamese; he remained either an agriculturist or a daily wage earner. Because of factors already mentioned above, Assam's per capita income was 10% higher than the national per capita income in 1950. But after 40 years in 1990, Assam's per capita income fell almost 20% below the national average for reasons which might again discern a colonial attitude on the part of the Union Government. Geographical isolation apart, such colonial treatment certainly did engender a sense of deprivation and this sense of deprivation roused a sense of alienation from the mainstream Indian community life. This alienation had subsequently degenerated into secessionism—a phenomenon which was still plaguing the socio-economic scenario of Assam.

Despite her tremendous potentials, undivided Assam did not have any hydro-electric project until the Umtru Project, came up in mid 50s of the last century at a time when big projects like Bhakra Nangal, Damodar Valley projects, etc., were changing the face of India. Certainly, it boils down to one conclusion: The weak leadership of the entire North-East failed to make its presence felt in New Delhi. Gradually an impression gained ground that New Delhi would never understand the voice of unarmed protests—let alone non-violent movements, demonstrations, satyagraha and the likes.

Even then, Nalbari was not a deficit area. It could feed itself. The Marwari community, which had benefited the most from the agricultural turnover of the area, did not fail to identify themselves with the indigenous people. Though not quite Jyotiprasad Agarwala & Co, they did try to integrate themselves into the local society for more than a century and these efforts were bearing fruits lately. Nalbari can today boast of quite a few litteratures, educationists and social activists from amongst the Marwari community. Besides, they have contributed immensely in building up quite a few institutions at Nalbari. And this applies to entire Assam as well. However, back to the economic front.

With the passage of time and in the absence of any modern ideas and technique of sustainable progress, the semi-feudal system of the agricultural sector was certainly not conductive to matching the challenges of time vis-a-vis the growth of population and enhanced rate of fragmentation of holdings. On the other hand, the habit of resting content with raising only one crop during the year, did not help matters either. As such, the sector betrayed symptoms of downhill journey in the early days of Independence and the pace of such degradation was accelerated by exploiting the vast stores of natural resources in a colonial manner. One with clear insight could foresee that such a state of affairs was sure to create complications in the future. To plug the gaping holes in the canvas of Assam's economic development, what is most significant, is to identify the reasons thereof. As such following observations may be eye opening factors.

2

What Ails Assam's Economy

It has been my strong conviction that fixation of wrong priorities has been the bane of planning for Assam's development. This has amounted to seeking right answers to wrong questions. The result has been that the aspirations for economic development have not been matched by efforts for removing the constraints thereof. Assam's geographical isolation being one of the main factors in stagnating her development, the first priority should have been the development of infrastructure, the chief sector being the communication network with emphasis on both land and inland water transport which until recently received scantiest attention.

The Brahmaputra, the lifeline of Assam, has degenerated into the "sorrow of Assam" after the great earthquake of 1950. Since then, the problem of flood and erosion has assumed unbelievably gigantic proportions and all corrective measures taken in this context have been mostly on ad-hoc basis and no serious concern has so far been in evidence for a permanent solution of these problems. Most of the centers for agricultural and industrial productions are situated in the flood-prone areas excepting the well-drained high ground of the tea estates. About 29 lakh hectares of Assam's land mass are flood-prone and protective measures are confined to frequently vulnerable embankments, better known for their corruption breeding performances rather than protective achievements. The absence of properly organized adequate irrigation system has aggravated the situation as cropping in planned manner round the year becomes impossible. In other words, the state suffers from too much water during the monsoon and too little during the dry season.

Adverse fallouts from an exclusively mercantile, if not colonial as well as those of an "enclave economy" sustained by the huge labour forces and thousands of employees of the tertiary sector manning more than 800 tea gardens, coal fields and oil field, have been also retarding the upward strides of Assam's economy. The outflow of primary goods and the inflow of consumer goods and essential commodities with no tangible steps taken to arrest this trend, if not reverse the process, are hardly conductive to capital formation at the indigenous level. This apart, agriculture in its present status, is suffering from very low productivity. Besides, over dependence on agriculture and that too with outdated technique and uncertain prospects, has shut the door for development of entrepreneurship elsewhere. In a technologically advanced country like the USA, it is not necessary for more than 2% of its population to engage in agriculture and still be in a position to export millions of tons of food grains whereas in Assam, about 70% of her population engaged in agriculture contribute only 57% roughly to Assam's SDP which does not suffice to feed Assam alone for the year. With the advent of high-tech culture and sweeping economic changes at the national level, the entire economic environment is changing; but in Assam, the local entrepreneurship is yet to rise to the occasion. Total lack of initiative and adequate exposure, infrastructural disincentives, non-development of a healthy work culture, red-tapism etc., have been major factors retarding the growth of entrepreneurship.

Demographic aggression/displacement coupled with environmental degradation has also resulted in gross shrinkage of productive potentials. The tremendous rate of growth of population since 1951 onwards for reasons other than natural has also resulted in very heavy pressure on land and other available resources, thereby negating all the benefits that were likely to accrue from so many years of planned development. In fact, the unprecedented scale of infiltration from Bangladesh has been upsetting most of the calculations of the planners. Misuse and wastage of resources and plan money have also retarded the growth of the economy. The total failure of the PSUs of the state has been not only a disincentive in colossal wastage and misuse of public funds but frequent resort to deficit financing and gradually increasing negligence of the most essential services is an unmistakable symptom of a sick economy.

Effective monitoring is a sine qua non for the modern management system. Unfortunately in Assam, monitoring is yet to receive the priority it deserves. In fact, inconvenient and inefficient officers are shunted off to the monitoring cell.

The social-ethnic and political unrest have also lately proved to be a major handicap in accelerating the pace of development and in creating a proper climate for fresh investment. The resultant hostile atmosphere has caused heavy drainage of economic resources diverted to security, law & order and anti-insurgency measures.

Summing up and broadly speaking, Assam's economy today is typified by the following salient features:

a It is predominantly a rural economy with the process of urbanization moving at a very slow pace.

b Industrial development being in a very backward state, employment opportunities in the secondary sector is very limited.

c Both per capita income and productivity are amongst the lowest in the country.

d Assam suffers from inadequacies of infrastructural facilities.

e Assam's is a predominantly mercantile economy further accentuated by the enclave economy of the major production centers while the villagers are having only a subsistence economy.

f Its overdependence on agriculture.

g Large-scale unchecked infiltration of alien citizens has retarded the growth of the economy as it has led to socio political unrest.

h Assam's immense natural and water resources are yet to be harnessed to her advantage.

i Her geographical isolation and the communication bottleneck make it imperative to develop alternate line of communication.

j She has perennial flood problem. Both short term and long term measures are necessary to control the same.

k According to Sivaraman Committee, the entrepreneurship in Assam is dormant and planned effort is required for its emergence.

l Infrastructural inadequacies have prevented the growth of a modern technological base.

These certainly cannot be the last words on the matter; but further planning is required to take these factors into consideration so that the benefits of planning reach the common man.

As I look back today in 2014, the regional imbalance has surfaced throughout the country. Even in the 50s of the last century, I could feel this during my long stint in Allahabad University. Those days, the journey to and from Allahabad by train, there being no other means of travel, seemed to be a never ending process. Only the facility of meter gauge railway line, which the British had set up for exporting tea and raw materials, was available and the journey used to take four days in the sweltering temperature of Bihar and UP.

Serious implications of such malady afflicting an integral part of the country, resulting in the aforesaid regional imbalance, had dawned upon the Planning Commission very late and it was only when preparing the 7th Plan (1985-90), the Commission observed that, "the problem of regional disparities in development has to be tackled at different levels. Part of the solution lies in the development of agriculture in the less developed regions. However, it is a much wider problem and its resolution requires a close re-examination of the mechanism for channeling the flow of finance, policies on industrial location, the distribution of investments in irrigation and infrastructure and a host of other matters. It is essential that the regional dimension of development is dealt with as an integral part of the 7th Plan."

No doubt, these were pious hopes; but the ground realities were even in 2011, at the end of the 11th Plan, far from being beneficial to the common man, although the upper middle class had been reaping a rich harvest. This applies not only to Nalbari area but to whole of Assam.

Nalbari in those days was a caste-ridden society, suffering from very many superstitions and prejudices, not excluding untouchability. Even irrational ritualistic compulsion used to restrain social interaction. I am reminded of a person named Ramlal— a sweeper by profession—a profession looked down upon but indispensible in the context of Nalbari's contemporary sanitary system. Ramlal's situation in life had caused an irreparable wound in my heart which I could not overcome till today. Ramlal was untouchable (though a Harijan in Gandhian vocabulary) because he used to carry a drum of night soil on his head before the sunrise to the dumping ground for the benefit of the citizens of Nalbari. The modern sanitary system was then nonexistent in the villages; the thickly forested backyard or any little open space with some cover or a river bank or any water bodies afforded sufficient space for one to relieve oneself in the primitive manner. But in a so-called town like Nalbari, a shade used to be set up as service latrine with a tin pot below for the droppings which fell to the lot of Ramlal and his co-workers to remove early in the morning. This inhuman practice gave me a rude shock and militated against my sense of dignity in my childhood. My entire inner self revolted against this practice when one day I saw Ramlal performing this act. And because Ramlal rendered this service, that made him an untouchable and he did not belong to the society! I do not know what has happened to this community today.

My father, a great humanist himself, did appreciate my concern for Ramlal and not remaining content with reading out Tagore's "He Mor Durbhaga Desh", he caused the construction of a pit latrine within about a fortnight, which must have been first of the kind in Nalbari area. In any case, the system of service latrine was replaced by pit latrines without, however, the society bothering the least for devising alternative means of livelihood for Ramlals! Now, of course, the pit latrines are also on its way out, yielding place to modern sanitary latrines. This remarkable revolution commenced its journey by mid 50s of the last century and today even in the remotest villages, one would find the vogue of this sanitary system which is kept clean by the inmates of the households, a job taken over from Ramlal & Co.

Though the pace of urbanization was slow in Nalbari area, as compared to Upper Assam, very many superstitious practices are noticed to be on their way out in the wake of urbanization. Upper Assam's was, however, a different story because of the impact created by extensive tea plantations, dominated mostly by Christian planters of the upper middle class. Even in some of the gardens, the labour class imbibed some virtues from their European masters. No doubt, the advent of Christianity had a discernible impact, resulting in a sort of discipline in community life.

On the other hand, Nalbari can boast of a very rich cultural heritage particularly in the fields of performing arts and studies of Sanskrit literature, grammar and allied matters. Towards the end of the 19th century, a system of opera, mainly based on Bengali dramas translated into Assamese, was introduced in Nalbari area and it prospered until the advent of cinema. The opera was popularly known as "Yatra Party". It was a sort of open air performance not associated with the stage mechanism of modern days. This opera system did exercise tremendous impact in moulding the character of the common man in Nalbari area of those days. The opera system may be called the forefather of today's very popular system of itinerant theatre troupe (Bhramyaman Theatre)—a very much improved and modern version of the opera system with various electrical and mechanical devices lending gorgeous colour to the whole exercise. However, what is more significant, is the permanent impact left behind by the "Yatra Parties". The dramas were mostly historio-political and mythological based on various episodes of the Puranas, the epics and historical events of India. In most of the dramas, there used to be a character with the nomenclature of "Vivek" (Conscience) who used to suddenly appear unheralded in the scene which was witnessing a very unjust, if not inhuman, aspect of contemporary times. Not afraid of the all-powerful king or the one exercising supreme power over human life and property the Vivek used to descend in his saffron robe to pontificate in hymnal mode about the ruination awaiting the perpetrations of such injustice, regardless of who was the perpetrator—the king or the emperor. And his warnings used to materialize. Not the result but the dauntless conduct of the Vivek left an indelible impact on the human mind which was discernible even today. Besides, Nalbari in the past was never near the seat of power which generated humility and submissiveness—a trait remaining alien to the people of Nalbari.

The "Ojha Pali" is another facet of rural Nalbari's legacy. Mainly, various episodes of the Puranas and the two epics are depicted by a team of 5/6 persons in musical lores, movements of bodies and symbolic gestures of both the hands (Mudras). Another cousin of opera and "Oja Pali", is the Dhulia troupe, a combination of drum, drama and acrobatics. In this rural discipline, the enactment of a drama is accompanied by beating of the drums and rural acrobatic tricks; but unfortunately, it has lost its past glory, glamour and vogue, rendering it almost moribund. Not professional in true sense of the term, rural people and peasants used to perform in the Dhulia troupe. Obviously, this rural version of modern day circus, has been another victim of modernization, thereby divesting the rural canvas of performing arts of another colourful discipline as also seasonal employment of villagers in their off season. Of course in many other fields of cultural activities, Nalbari continues to hold its head high even in 2014. Though the Yatra Parties, Dhulia and Ojha Pali gained eminence in Lower Assam, the culture of Bhaona, another edition of open air theatre with classical moulding did not feature eminently in respect of public entertainment possibly, because Majuli, the seat of this performing art introduced by Mahapurush Sankardeva, was far away from Nalbari. Likewise, Yatra Party was not widely in vogue in Upper Assam.

The curse of dowry system had never plagued the matrimonial negotiations in Nalbari area, for that matter, in whole of Assam. But, of late a predominantly parallel economy of black money, has gradually been making inroads into the otherwise healthy matrimonial practices. Even the rural sector is falling victim to such anti social practices, particularly in the wake of the globalised economy.

So far the environment was concerned, Nalbari was heaven on earth, sandwiched between two tributary rivers, namely Pagladia and Burhadia, Nalbari was skirted by rich forests particularly on the northern side, which extended right up to the foothills of Bhutan. But, now wanton destruction of forests and unabated encroachment upon forest land, have totally altered the scenario and biospheric degradation has been the logical result. However, a campaign of awareness and aforestation has been started by few Bodo youths lately and this augurs well for the future.

The account of my Nalbari days will remain incomplete unless I make a brief mention of late Balo Barman—Baloka for us, rather an insignificant illiterate commoner who thrived under the shelter of my father's patronage. He lived in the village of Balikorea, about a kilometer away from our residence. In course of time besides being a great domestic help, he became almost a member of our family. Our parents did all they could for promoting the welfare of Baloka's children. In fact, Baloka has figured in quite a few stories written by me. Apart from facilitating many of my angling trips, he and late Gopal Khura (father's cousin brother) used to thrill us, the children with very many ghost stories. Some of these stories are still alive in my fast-fading memory. According to their field of activities, these ghosts were named as Veera, Ghorapak, Kuber, etc. Some superstitious and enigmatic persons are even believed to have their own Veeras for helping them in many nefarious activities. Even in 2011, a very senior minister of Assam is suspected to have patronized a Veera and his miraculous escapes from more than one assassination attempts on his life are ascribed by the common man to the protection offered by his Veera.

So, that is Nalbari—a mixture of opposites, a mixrure of radical political activities, cultural refinement and superstitious Veera culture! May be some of these beliefs and practices had their origin in Tantrik discipline of worship. Anyway, it is high time I refrain from writing a treatise on ghosts and allied matters. Only memories of my association with Baloka and Gopal khura led to mentioning these trivialities. However, what ultimately transpires, is absence of scientific modern outlook and ignorance pervading different strata of the society. I must mention that in due course, both Baloka and Gopal khura turned out to be successful heads of their respective families. My mother did not lag behind either. The beneficiaries of her philanthropic activities were mostly destitute widows, irrespective of their caste and quite a few orphans, some of whom grew up to be self dependent in due course.

Meanwhile, Assam had to face two unforeseen catastrophes: Bharata Ratna Gopinath Bordoloi suddenly expired on 5 August 1950, leaving behind a host of complex problems and the other crisis suddenly befell Assam in the shape of the devastating earthquake of 15 August 1950. The adverse fallouts of this earthquake are yet to be fully neutralized.

To round up the Nalbari chapter, I cannot but mention and appreciate that there have never been any communal problem in Nalbari area between Hindus and Muslims despite the fact that a few Muslim families did adhere to Jinnah's programme. But ultimately they all ended up by joining the Congress in the wake of the Independence. The supporters of Bangladeshi infiltrators are yet to destroy this communal harmony.

Nalbari has since grown into a big town and become the district headquarters of the district of Nalbari carved out from the undivided Kamrup district. Unfortunately, Nalbari has been allowed to grow in a most unplanned manner with very many unforeseen problems surfacing to utter discomfort of the citizens, the most disgusting and troublesome being the water logging of the entire town during the rainy season. Following few steps may prove quite beneficial:

a Arrangement for draining out the rain water to Pagladia and Burhadia.

b The extensive water bodies between the eastern and western boundaries of the district, may be developed like the lake district of England with ropeways for the use of the tourists.

c To develop a satellite township in a flood-free area. To start with, the present site for Bhaskarverma University may be considered as the nucleus for such a project.

d However, these may not be the last words on the matter

3

Allahabad Days

So on to my Allahabad days. In those days, it was very difficult to get admission into the universities of Allahabad, Delhi and Madras, etc., only because, by the time results of respective examinations were out in Assam, the last date of admission into undergraduate and post-graduate courses of these universities used to be over. The result of my Intermediate in Arts (IA) examination was also not likely to be out in next few weeks whereas the last date of admission into Allahabad University was going to expire in about 6/7 days. So, with courage, I took faith into my hands and rushed off to Allahabad by train under the umbrella of my parent's blessings without, however, realising that I would never return to Nalbari again on permanent basis. And this was the turning point in my academic career. It took three nights and four days to reach the meter gauge railway station at Allahabad, there being no broad gauge (BG) line to Assam. The long tedious journey in humid climate was enough to dampen my enthusiasm. However, the first test of my endurance was in respect of food served for both lunch and dinner at the hotel I had put up for 3/4 days near the university.

Firstly, the non-vegetarian food which I was accustomed to was a rarity. Secondly, the food was very hot with lot of red chilly powder put in and above all, rice, my staple food, was served on special request only, that too, not cooked in a manner I was used to. "Chapati" (Indian bread) was served. In fact, the cook did not know how to cook rice. Of course, I adjusted to the sudden change of my diet within about a month and settled down in hostel life.

Prior to this, the main problem was to get admission which was straightway refused for non-availability of my IA result. I became desparate and one fine morning, gatecrashed into the residence of the Vice Chancellor, Prof AC Banerjee, an internationally reputed wrangler, who ignored the protestations of the gate-keeper and made me comfortable in his drawing room of Victorian style. Instead of chiding, to my great relief, not only he asked me to be seated but also offered me a cup of tea which cooled down the agitated state of my mind, if not stabilized my heart beats which after such dare-devil gatecrashing, I might have missed once or twice. Having heard of my woes and my determination to get admitted, he asked me about my father. On learning that my father was also an educationist, he appeared to me to be the Mahadeva, ever ready to sanction boons to his devotees and asked me the next question; "Are you sure you will get a first division?"

Pat came the reply from me : "Sir, not only a first division but I am sure to get a meritorious scholarship also (I did get) and if not, my admission may be cancelled after the result of my IA examination does not substantiate my claim."

The VC burst into a hearty laugh and looked at me with a mischievous smile. I kept my fingers crossed, but not for long. Prof Banerjee announced: "Go and see Govil, the registrar of the university, and he will admit you. In case of any problem come and see me."

So that was that.

Problems I did have, though not of my own creation. I had already settled down and some Assamese students were going around, running from pillar to post, for their admission. On my suggestion, two of them, accompanied by me, met Prof Banerjee who again complied with our request. Of these two, Mukut Sarma had in later life become a cabinet minister of Assam and Nagen Barua, an MLA, though from different parties. Both of them are no more in this world.

After about a month of commencement of the academic session a test was held facultywise and I was selected from the faculty of Arts for attending the "'Counsel and Guidance Class" once a week. As it transpired to me, the purpose of such a scheme was to extend a helping hand to a select few so that they could get proper guidance for developing their latent talents and aptitudes to the fullest extent. The selection for this class brought me for the first time in direct contact with legendary Prof AB Lal, the then Head of the Dept. of Political Science who subsequently went on to occupy the VC's chairs of as many as three universities, including that of Allahabad University. My association with this great scholar and educationist, lasted until his demise. Both he and Ms Lal, who was also a teacher in Allahabad University, looked upon me very kindly and bestowed all their blessings very liberally on humble self. Prof Lal was a man of erudite presence, grave but very conscious of the welfare of his students. His teachings of Plato and Aristotle are still reverberating in my ears. Above all, I learnt from him how to live and not to waste the life of limited span, although I wonder how far I could live upto his expectations with so many crises befalling me in later life. Anyway, more about it later on.

Soon came the summer vacation of short duration. Though feeling very homesick as I had been away from home, particularly my mother for the first time, I decided not to go home for few days only and instead, visited Agra, Mathura, Brindaban, Benaras etc., and never had to regret the decision. In fact, these visits roused in me an intense desire to know more about ancient and medieval India. Thus my scholarship money was very well spent; but what surprised me most, was the lack of knowledge about Assam on the part of even educated persons of this part of the country. At the Taj Mahal, two young girls came forward and introduced themselves as Miss Visweswari and Miss Ranga both hailing from the South and medical students in New Delhi. Both of them expressed a feeling of distress while taking our lunch together. It transpired that they also knew nothing about Assam. They had also come to see the Taj Mahal. The rickshaw driver had charged rather low rent much to their delight and taken them to a hotel where they could not sleep the whole night because of loud shoutings and obscene utterances. Ultimately, they came to know that the hotel was in the red light area. They practically begged me to do something about it. I told them frankly that the only way out was to change the hotel and ultimately they landed up in the hotel I was putting up. It transpired that they were financially much better off than me. The rickshaw driver turned out to be the villain of the piece. Both of them became very friendly and close to me. They used to correspond with me for a very long time and possibly after they got married, the line of communication snapped. But the memories of their association lingers on for reasons more than one. During my visit to Banaras, I met late Prafulla Goswami from Nalbari, who was doing his MA and LLB. In due course, he became a prominent lawyer. Besides, we came very close to each other. In fact, he acted as the "best man" in my marriage ceremony solemnized in December, 1959.

So, back to Allahabad. Prof Lal had certainly noticed that I was more interested in football, volleyball and badminton than my studies and that I was not left with much time for serious studies. Instead of chiding me in so many words, he was shrewd enough to eke out for me a very heavy schedule of studies in the "Counsel & Guidance" class, not necessarily confined to text books only but extending over a wide range of academic exercise, thereby drastically curtailing the hours I used to devote to the games. Sure enough, none of his students including me, could even think in terms of ignoring his instructions. Thus very tactfully, he compelled me to sublimate my urge to shine as a player.

Being throughout a student of Arts and Mathematics not being my strong point, I did not have even rudimentary knowledge of various disciplines of science. Prof Lal ensured that I should overcome this glaring deficiency and prescribed to me a book captioned "Essential Knowledge for All" which enriched my general knowledge beyond my own imagination. This helped me to score very high marks (about 90%) in the General Knowledge paper of the IPS examination held in later part of 1957.

In our BA class, we had as our teachers two very great poets, namely, Firaque Gorakhpuri and late Prof Haribans Rai Bachan, the father of the famous matinee idol Amitabh Bachan. Firaque Gorakhpuri was also in charge of my English tutorial classes. These tutorial classes, besides being very educative, used to be very interesting too. Interesting because Firaque had a very rich flair for describing very many interesting anecdotes nor was he reluctant to tell us boastfully the details of his so many encounters with famous personalities both within the university and without. In fact, instead of being a tutorial class in the real sense of the term, it used to turn out into a verbose monologue by Firaque about his past, only interrupted sometimes by our inquisitiveness, thereby goading him all the more to reflect on a wide range of topics. Though monologue, it never used to be boring and not less interesting than his lecturing on Shakespeare, Marlow, Shaw, Wilde, Byron, Wordsworth, etc.

Still fresh in my memory are two such narrations—one pertaining to Dr Amarnath Jha and the other to Pt Jawaharlal Nehru. First about Dr Jha: Dr Jha and Firaque were classmates with the latter excelling in academic exercises, a phenomenon not proving to be conducive to a friendly tie between the two. But the situation eased out for Dr Jha when Firaque left the university without completing his post graduation to become the private secretary of Mahatma Gandhi in the wake of the Non-Cooperation Movement. Thus Firaque lost an academic year or two; possibly he would have lost more if he could survive Mahatma's allergy to certain aberrant habits. His absence certainly facilitated Dr Jha's entry into the teaching fraternity of Allahabad University earlier than Firaque. After Firaque joined the same department with flying colours, the teacher's common room of the department, was converted by these two greats, into a veritable debating club, mainly deliberating upon the literary achievements of famous authors. Firaque's mischievous nature used to surface very frequently in these debating brawls in the shape of his taunting remarks aimed at irritating, if not belittling, Dr Jha. The glaring example, as narrated by Firaque himself, in his contorted alcoholic tongue is as follows : Once irritated by some remarks made by Firaque, Dr Jha announced that he had completed reading Shakespeare 16 times and then quarried of Firaque how many times the latter had read Shakespeare. Pat came the taunting reply from Firaque with his ever present mischievous smile, "It is now clear that you did not understand it for 15 times; but I had read only once." So that is that. The denouement may be surmised by the reader.

Now about Pt Nehru: Firaque was very faddy about speaking and writing correct English. True, we immensely benefitted from this fad of his; but it also gave us ample opportunities for attracting his boastful observations. On such an occasion, he boasted that there were only two persons in India who could write correct English: Obviously one was himself and the other Pt. Nehru. He, however, qualified his statement by adding that even Nehru had committed a mistake while using the expression 'family members' which should have been 'members of family'. He further added that the nomenclature, "Allahabad University" was wrong English; it should be "University of Allahabad". Needless to mention that none of us dared to question him how then it could be Oxford or Cambridge University. Before downing the shutter on Firaque affairs, to those, humble self not excluded, whom Firaque initiated into the mysterious world of booze, he invariably used to recite that

"Na pina haram hai
Na pilana haram hai
Magar, pike hosh me rahna
Haram hai."

(It is not a sin to drink nor to offer drinks; but to remain in one's senses after drinks is a sin.) No doubt, all poet's soirees used to be divested of all glamour in the absence of Firaque!

Gradually, Allahabad days were coming to a close. From the very beginning, I was intent upon appearing in All India Competitive Examinations and Allahabad presented the best ambience for preparing the mind for such a tough job. During our time, one could appear in the IPS examination at the age of 20 whereas for appearing in the IAS, etc., examination, one had to be 21. As such, I appeared in the IPS examination in 1957 almost immediately after joining the MA (Previous) class and came out successful in my very first attempt, although this was instrumental in my not appearing in the IAS examination later on. However, no regrets! In fact, I passed my MA

(Final) examination after the results of the IPS examination was out. My classmates, hostel mates and my teachers were very happy and they all inspired and encouraged me to join the IPS. My father was also retiring from service in another few months, which practically meant that I would have to take over the responsibility of educating my three younger brothers and the youngest sister.

I must mention that I did not make any particular preparation for this competitive test; my BA course sufficed to help me succeed. Of course, I had regularly read two national newspapers and two magazines which proved very helpful. My long stay in Allahabad imparted a broader view of personal as well as national life. Certainly Allahabad was instrumental in cultivating my reading habit and also a competitive spirit. The reading habit has convinced me that books are the best companion even in a period of distress and loneliness. I had also opportunities to see the rural life of UP and compare the same with that of Assam. The villagers and the landless peasants of UP were much more hard working than their counterparts in Assam. The soil was very dry and hard as compared to Assam's. In those days, the average peasant in Assam used to remain content by raising only one crop during the year whereas his counterpart in UP used to work hard round the year for ensuring that two ends met. As I noticed, it would not be an exaggeration to say that the happy go lucky commoner of Assam did not know in those days what real hard work meant. In fact, this mindset has created lot of problems for him now as it is not easy to change one's work culture. In the present context, this poor work culture has facilitated outsiders, including illegal migrants to dominate various sectors, particularly the economic sector, of community life. No doubt, the situation is changing fast and the awareness for rising to the occasion is gradually surfacing, although at a slow pace.

Allahabad further afforded opportunities for rubbing shoulders with contemporary intellectuals both within the university and without. It was here in Allahabad that I came to know prominent personalities like late VP Singh, late Chandrasekhar, Raj Narain, Dr Murlimanohar Joshi and brilliant students like Gopikrishna Arora, Otima Mukherjee, SK Singh, Rajamani, etc. Because of persuasion by my class mates, late Justice AK Banerjee, I also took to writing articles in *Amrit Bazar Patrika* and these articles were also published in Amrit *Patrika* after translation into Hindi. This proved to be a source of unexpected additional fund and fun. In any case, the atmosphere and circumstances compelled quite a few of us to keep abreast of current affairs and to read the latest books by reputed authors. I must admit this was the legacy of the "Counsel & Guidance Class".

As I was commencing a new chapter of my life after leaving Allahabad, following points remained uppermost in my mind; The "Ramlal phenomenon" narrated above, left a very deep, sad and demoralizing wound in my inner self. The lot of this community was not better off in UP either. In later years, while at Nalbari, I used to visit and help him within my limitation until late 60s of the last century. Poor man is no more; but his legacy haunts me till today. I even failed subsequently to trace his family.

The backwardness and superstitious environment, then prevailing in Nalbari area, determined, to a great extent, the attitude of the young generation. Thank God, I did not fall a victim to such a mindset.

From my Nalbari days to the end of my Allahabad days, the political scenario of the country as well as at the international level witnessed remarkable changes. India became an Independent Republic with Pt Nehru at the helm of affairs. Unfortunately, Assam was a far cry from Nehru's "modern temple of progress" and his promised "socialistic pattern of society". Assam continued to languish in post-colonial hangover even long after Nehru was gone. Five year plans were introduced with private sector juxtaposing each other, thereby causing the emergence of a kind of mixed economy which, however, failed to reach out to the common man.

Sandwiched between the Western and the Soviet blocks, Nehru promoted his policy of non-alignment, reaching its peak at the Bandung Conference; but the hollowness of his foreign policy was exposed by the Chinese aggression of 1962, compelling him to knock at the door of the USA without, however, abandoning his bias in favour of the USSR. The friendly relation with the USSR, it must be said to Nehru's credit, did pay rich dividend in due course as our relation with USA, unlike today, was not easy and in this respect, the Chinese aggression opened up a new dimension to the entire matter. True, the setback in Sino-Soviet relation also, of late, facilitated the augmentation of India's defense preparedness in collaboration with both the USSR and the USA. On the other hand, Nehru's Kashmir policy, as considered with the help of hindsight, was another Himalayan blunder of his otherwise chequered political career. Needless to mention that the Kashmir tangle is hanging fire even after seven decades. In any case, Nehru's dream of projecting himself as the messiah of peace in the strife torn international platform, was shattered by the Chinese invasion with the "Hindi Chini Bhai Bhai" slogan, once renting the Indian sky, foundering in the steep hills of NEFA (now Arunachal). One remarkable achievement of India within a very short period of her entry into the comity of independent nations, was to see late Mrs Vijaya Lakshmi Pandit elected as the President of the UNO. In another front, India achieved a very remarkable success inasmuch as more than 500 (to be precise 568) princely native states were integrated into the main national stream. The entire credit for this Himalayan piece of achievement goes without a shade of doubt to the then union home minister late Sardar Vallabhbhai Patel; else, even Hyderabad might have turned into another Kashmir. In fact, but for Nehru's intervention, it was quite likely that Sardar Patel would have nipped the Kashmir problem in its bud. Anyway, that is history now.

Though, the Parliament was studded with brilliant selfless patriots and scholars, a viable opposition capable of offering an alternative to Congress rule was yet to emerge. However, Pt. Nehru's greatest achievement was to create a vision of modern India which, even today, was proving to be the main driving force for progress although the vehicle for such progress had undergone sea-changes.

At the international level, these were the years of the "Cold war" with NATO and Warsaw Pact at each other's throat. The Stalinist approach to the national problems of the member states of the Warsaw Pact did not lead to form an integrated camp. Which is why Stalin's army had to march into Hungary and steamroll the nationalist sector. Nor can one forget that Marshall Tito did not come forward to fall in line. For, Marshall Tito was a leader by his own right, not interested in conniving at Stalin's campaign for expanding the net of

Soviet imperialism in Eastern Europe. The long and short of the whole situation was that the beginning of the plan itself had borne the seeds of downfall and the Hungarian crisis had simply highlighted the inner contradiction Stalin's enterprise had given rise to. Even in Poland, one of the strongholds of the Stalinist regime, the Polish Communist Party's claim to be representing the Polish proletariat, was being overshadowd by the emergence of the independent Trade Union, namely, Solidarity which was gaining ground very rapidly. However, the game of one upmanship went on unabated. The focal point had, of course, shifted, by the time I left Allahabad, to technology for predominance over the Space. However, in the post war era, Israel emerged as a strong factor to be reckoned with in international politics with strong backing from the free world. Besides, in the wake of Egypt nationalizing the Suez Canal in mid-fifties it became a constant source of tension with potentials for another world war. In the long run, Egypt's assertion of her right over the Suez Canal, irrespective of the ultimate result, made the Palestinian problem more knotty and explosive. The balance of power was certainly facing severe strain and the relation between the East and the West betrayed symptoms of degrading into uneasy terms. To cut a long story short, one may easily conclude that Israel and the sources of crude oil are going to determine the Anglo-American approach to the entire Middle-East as would be proved subsequently.

While concluding this chapter, I cannot help reproducing, in my own words, how Prof AB Lal visualized the future and his prophesy materialized in due course.

Prof Lal was very emphatic that the Stalinist regime of Soviet Russia was a transitory phase in the course of the development of human civilization and that it would not survive the century. He was sure that individual liberty and nationalistic aspirations could not be kept supressed for an indefinite period, particularly after the individual had come to understand and value his position in the existing set up and that the Soviet system would ultimately crumble on these two counts alone. He often used to quote Sri Aurobindo that, "Nationalism is an Avatar and cannot be Slain". His most prophetic opinion was that 'The third world war was started the day the 2nd world war ended."

Of course, he did not mean conventional warfare. What he meant was that it would be economic warfare against international colonial exploitation and that the days of colonial imperialism were numbered and its place would be taken by cut throat economic rivalries which would afford opportunities even to the exploited nations to assert their own presence. Physical and political domination would be on their way out, yielding places to economic domination. In the same context, he was very optimistic about the future of India. That with the spread of education coupled with development of science and technology, India would be on the top section of the developed nations, was his favorite theme. He was one with Pt. Nehru in this conviction.

How prophetic was his vision!

True, I came to love Allahabad but its dry and drab atmosphere reminded me daily of evergreen Assam and her people.

4

IPS Days

My police career commenced on 24 October 1958, the day I joined the Central Police Academy for my IPS training at Mt. Abu. Mt. Abu is a small hill station in the Aravalli range. Situated in the southern tip of Rajasthan, it is in the Sirohi district of the state. The small town is 1,220 meters above the sea level. Even then, it is dominated by the pre-eminence of the desert climate. During the winter, the average temperature may be four degree centigrade. Abu is famous for its Dilwara Jain Temple, a complex carved out of white marble between 11th and 13th century. The surrounding areas of this small hill station used to be full of wild life, but it was only in 1960 that Mt Abu Wild Life Sanctuary was established within 290-square-km area carved out of Abu Parbat.

In the police academy, besides the IPS recruits, cadets of the Intelligence Bureau also used to be trained and some of these cadets were very brilliant. Now, of course, the academy has been shifted to Hyderabad. The Mt Abu institution is now training the directly recruited cadets of the IB and the IPS recruits are trained at Hyderabad.

My memories of Mt Abu days are not very pleasant, in fact, some of these are quite forgettable. But during this period, I cultivated lifelong friendship with some of my batch mates. Quite a few of them are no more in this world.

This Central Police Training College was headed by the Commandant of IGP's rank, assisted by the Deputy Commandant of DIGP's rank. It did not take me long to realize that the head of the college went out of his way to prove that he was superior to all of us in every respect, which certainly he was not. On close analysis, I was convinced that his exhibitionism was the result of his deep set inferiority complex. In any case, I failed to develop any liking for him. Sure enough, the dislike was mutual. Having been for a long time under close guardianship of Prof. Lal and intimate with some of the brilliant products of the University, I could immediately discern the contrast and the reason thereof. Besides, his academic background was nothing much to write home about. He missed no opportunity to flaunt that he was an IP (not IPS) officer of British tradition, conveniently concealing that he was nominated from the state police service to IP (Imperial Police) and not a direct recruit to the IP whereas we, the trainees under him were direct recruits to the IPS, a fact he possibly found difficult to reconcile with. On the other hand, he had nothing complimentary to tell us about some of the legendary and still serving IP officers, including great BN Mullick. Ultimately, the cat was out of the bag. He had very high political connection and that was that! As the head of the academy, he certainly failed to mete out even handed treatment to all the trainee officers and betrayed his likes and dislikes on several occasions. His favourites were the convent educated boys with a strong prejudice against the not so privileged, treated as under dogs in his scheme of things. Carrying on the British tradition of discrimination against the "ruled" by the "ruler", he was not the least interested in appreciating the social, economic and geographical diversities of the country. Needless to mention that such attitude has been mainly responsible for failing to impart a people-oriented look to the police in free India. At times, he treated us like primary school boys although we were all highly educated persons with brilliant academic records behind us, a fact he failed to appreciate.

As against this scenario, the deputy head of the college, its mainstay and a directly recruited IP officer, was a very suave, considerate and well-read person albeit a strict disciplinarian. I had occasion to meet him after many years when he was the chief of the Tamil Nadu police administration and he was all attention to my comforts and allied matters during my entire stay at Madras (now Chennai). It was because of him that I gradually developed an abiding interest in police matters. He was very humble and modest about his success in various fields of activities as opposed to the exhibitionist, boastful nature of the other person I had narrated above. An example of his humility and modesty would be in order. An inhouse competition of revolver/pistol shooting was arranged. This great IP officer outdid all of us by hitting the bull's eye with every shot. When we all lavishly praised his skill and congratulated him, he, instead of taking the credit, attributed his success to his revolver by simply remarking that 'yes, this weapon of mine is very reliable' as if he personally had no role to play in this tremendous performance. His vast knowledge of Assam's flora and fauna was simply amazing whereas the other person just above him had only contemptuous attitude towards the entire North-east. Maybe because of his academic deficiency he knew nothing about the socio-political and economic realities of the North-east. His only remark about the North-east was to caution the trainees against the risk of contacting hill diarrhea he suffered from while visiting Shillong. Incidentally, I was in Shillong for a number of years and I cannot recall any such occasion. In fact, I found that most of the bureaucrats holding high position and hailing from the 'Hindi belt' suffered from an impression that they were born to rule the country. A seminar was held in the college on national integration, participated by quite a few IGPs from UP, MP, Bihar, etc. I was also a participant. After few speeches, my turn came to voice my perspective on the matter; during the course of my speech, I observed that "India is a multi-racial, multi-ethnic, multi-lingual and multi-religious country and as such, the issues of racial, ethnic and lingual identities, etc., can be addressed only by a truly federal Constitution", thereby attracting the ire of a few Hindi-speaking senior officers attending the seminar. Be that as it may, I was interrupted by one Chaturvedi, the then IGP of undivided UP, who ticked me off by remarking that my individious observation smacked of narrow vision and rank provincialism, much to the delight of the commandant of the Academy. Obviously, Chaturvedi was not conversant with the meaning of a federal state in the true sense of the term. And today, such controversies are even threatening the integrity of the country! I have my own doubt how far the institution of the All India Services has been able to do away with such myopic vision coupled with ignorance of ground realities. In fact, the conceptual banalities promoted by Chaturvedi and his likes, are still bedevilling the community life of the country. Suddenly, I have remembered two statements made by Pt Nehru in the context of what I have discussed above: (1) "--- I am alarmed when I see not only in this country but in other great countries too how anxious people are to shape others according to their own image or likeness and to impose on them their particular way to living. We are welcome to our way of living, but why impose it on others? 2) I am not at all sure which the better way of living the tribal or our own. In some respects I am quite certain theirs is better. There is no point in trying to make of them a second rate copy of ourselves."

How fervently I wish that Chaturvedi and other Hindi belt chauvinists should understand what Nehru said.

I and Lalbahadur Sewa (since assassinated in Mizoram by Mizo rebels) were allotted Assam cadre. While at Dergaon Police Training College for another brief period of training after passing out from Mt. Abu, I was married to Deepika Sharma, a girl with a brilliant academic career (in fact better than mine) on 14 December 1959. I did have occasion for feeling that she sacrificed a brilliant career ahead of her for a married life. Our married lives have extended over more than half a century and our children, grandchildren, nephews, nieces, brothers and sisters were all agog with celebrating the completion of the half century. Thank God, my wife was discreet enough not to be too eloquent about her experience of 50 years.

From Dergaon, I was sent to Silchar for practical training in police works. The brief stay at Silchar was not only very refreshing but very educative also. Here, I met and befriended two legendary figures of contemporary Assam, namely Batubabu (Dasgupta) and Sateebabu (SatindraMohan Dev). Batubabu was the tennis champion of Assam consecutively for many years and playing with him in the local tennis club, I improved my tennis beyond my own expectation, so much so that in 1960, I reached the semi-final of All Assam Tennis Championship tournament in partnership with legendary Nurul Amin and lost the match only because of my failure to rise to the occasion. Nurul Amin, no doubt, suffered only for my unexpected poor performance.

On the other hand, those days one could not think or talk of Silchar without mentioning Sateebabu. Besides being the Chairman of Silchar Municipality Board consecutively for many years, he was the live wire of both the outdoor and indoor life of Silchar. This apart, he was a famous freedom fighter with a revolutionary background. Though, I was of his son's age, he took me under his wings and both me and my wife became like members of his family and the tradition was carried on by me and his eldest son, Sri Santosh Mohan Dev (Rana), who had in due course become a powerful Union Cabinet Minister. Sateebabu ultimately retired from public life after serving as a cabinet minister of Assam for many years and left this world on 27 July 1971. Both Sateebabu and Batubabu were totally free from any communal bias and prejudices. In fact, both of them had operated as a bridge of amity and understanding between the Brahmaputra and the Barak Valleys. Batubabu also left for his heavenly abode on 1 March 1998.

Our pleasant stay at Silchar was suddenly interrupted by communal riots in the Brahmaputra valley in the wake of the state language agitation. Great tension suddenly encompassed the civic life at Silchar. I was advised not to go out of my residence without being adequately armed despite the fact that I was quite popular with the Bengali-speaking people. It appears as if communal frenzy may turn friends into foes overnight. Tension had built up because many innocent Bengali-speaking persons were victimized in the Assam Valley. Consequently, dissenting voices were sounded in the Barak Valley as a strong organized opposition to the adoption of Assamese as the only official state language. Here was a classic case of compulsion destroying co-operation. An atmosphere of mutual suspicion was building up. This virus of mutual suspicion and hatred, one could feel, had even infected the government officers and employees. Communal feelings borne of lingual fanaticism had thus vitiated the entire atmosphere of Assam—much more aggravated by the failure of the district police authorities in some of the districts in respect of taking timely strict action against the communal rioters. The undivided districts of Kamrup and Nagaon had suffered the most, mainly on account of the failure of police officers concerned to take strict preventive measures, although Guwahati witnessed firing by Police on a crowd of students, resulting in the death of an innocent student, namely, Ranjit Barpujari who had since been hailed as the martyr of this language movement. The death of this innocent student of Cotton College added fuel to fire. Ultimately Pt Nehru, the then PM, had to come down to Guwahati and announced that,"If Assamese will not be the state language of Assam, will it be the state language in Madras?" Nehru, all said and done, was the darling of the crowd and possibly, this was the first time that Nehru voiced something soothing to the heart of the Assamese. Such an announcement from no less a person than Nehru, did certainly assuage the feelings of the agitating youths of the Brahmaputra valley. But I still believe that the passage of the state language act was premature. Late BP Chaliha, the CM, was also apprehensive that such agitational approach might release divisive forces and time proved him right. There should have been no such hurry as the Assamese language was gradually developing into the 'lingua franca' of the entire North-east whereas the passage of the act generated suspicion in the minds of different ethnic groups of Assam about the aggressive Assamese chauvinism. The age-old composite society of Asam has been split asunder today only because of the mutual distrust created by this Act. Else, Assam would not have been officially a trilingual state. Not that tribal languages should not be developed but there must be left some scope for accommodating a "lingua franca" which the Assamese language had forfeited because of its undue haste. Will ever be the damage done repaired?

However, for me, the matter did not end with the end of the language agitation as the rancorous atmosphere created by this agitation continued to rankle relations between officers speaking two different languages. Even officers belonging to All India Services, irrespective of their ranks, betrayed their prejudices, a phenomenon certainly not healthy for an impartial administration.

The government commissioned T A Subramaniam IPS, to enquire into the widespread rioting in North Kamrup and fix responsibility for each case. On the other hand, I was suddenly transferred to Nagaon and directed to conduct departmental proceeding against 13 officers in respect of maintaining law and order. Of these 13, three were Bengali-speaking officers. The IGP had personally instructed me to discharge this responsibility without fear or favour and any prejudicial leaning. So it was a test of my impartiality also. Both the additional SP and the Dy SP (HQ) had already been placed under suspension for their similar failures, thereby leaving only the SP and myself to look after the day-to-day police administration of the district. Meanwhile, the SP also went on leave in order to get married. As a result, though a very junior officer, I had to remain in-charge for those days. Incidentally, this SP was never put in charge of a district again—obviously for his lacklustre performance during the state language movement (He had, however, maneuvered to work up to a position of unconstitutional centre of power during the days of the infamous National Emergency of 1975 and made lives miserable for many innocent officers entirely out of prejudices borne of lingual fanaticism.) He did not also fail to cultivate permanent grudge and animus against me for reasons explained below.

As already related above, the IGP had personally briefed me to be absolutely impartial in conducting these 13 enquiries so that I could arrive at objective, factual findings reflecting the preparedness and willingness of the officers concerned in the backdrop of the ground realities. Ground realities in this context implied, by and large, communication facilities, availability of adequate forces and above all, initiatives displayed by the officers concerned in the given situation under scrutiny.

Here, little digression may light up a better perspective. That the advent of the British in the early part of the 19th century into Assam necessitated the import of Bengali bureaucrats and clerical staff, was not only imperative for the colonial set-up but also a logical conclusion of the fact that the British had entirely depended on Bengal which they occupied first and much earlier, for recruiting their administrative staff. Irrespective of who were responsible for introducing Bengali in the day-to-day administration and court proceedings in Assam, it was simply natural for the Assamese to smell a rat and suspect that a conspiracy had been hatched to obliterate the Assamese language, a language more ancient than the Bengali language and resplendent with very rich heritage. Though the wrong was righted in 1873 and the Assamese language restored to its rightful place, the bitterness already generated, did not augur well for friendly and brotherly relations between the two communities and its legacy certainly did not help to improve matters. Even then, there was no open conflict as such. The partition of Bengal followed by the amalgamation of Sylhet, an overwhelmingly a Muslim majority Bengali-speaking district, with Assam, did not augur well either for soothing the injured feelings of the Assamese. No doubt, this was another outcome of the British policy of "Divide and Rule" so that rebellious Bengali could be weakened as far as possible. On the other hand, the intelligentsia of Sylhet district could never reconcile themselves to being part and parcel of Assam's community life. They even went to the extent of ridiculing a proposal for setting up a university in the Brahmaputra valley. This mindset was discernible in the Assam secretariat even after Independence as the secretariat had a very strong active presence of clerical staff of Sylhet origin. The transfer of the Karimganj district of Sylhet to Assam as a result of the Radcliff Award, coupled with largescale immigration of Bengali Hindus from Sylhet certainly did not help in promoting integration, a phenomenon I could personally feel and experience even in the 90s of the last century. During days in the BJP, it came to my notice that a prominent leader of BJP from the Barak valley found it very difficult to welcome the entry of any prominent person from the Brahmaputra valley into BJP. But I must admit that the new generation seems to be shedding off such inhibition and allergic attitude.

Be that as it may, the open conflict between the two lingual communities came to the fore in the wake of the state language agitation as if an old sore had become alive again. This virus of communal feelings, I must admit, did infect the then SP of Nagaon district. On return from leave after his marriage, he enquired of me about the progress of the departmental proceedings. I informed him that all the proceedings were in final stages and it should be possible for me to submit the findings in all the cases within a week or so. Remaining silent for few moments, he asked me not to submit my findings in respect of three officers. I could immediately detect the motive behind as all the three officers belonged to his own lingual community! Having failed to comply with his request in contravention of IGP's direct instructions, I incurred his wrath forever and he was chasing me throughout my days in IPS to find an opportune moment for throwing me into deep trouble and he did succeed in doing so in later years. This one single incident had haunted me till the end of my days in police and besmirched my entire career with motives which I never cared for. As for instance, when I had to resort to extremely strict action against some Bengali marauders while dealing with a serious law-and-order situation at Hojai in 1972 arising out of the murder of an Assamese student leader, namely, Anil Bora, I was branded as an anti-Bengali officer and after few days, when I had to open fire on a marauding crowd of immigrant Muslims, I was branded as an anti-Muslim officer! Such was the thankless job while dealing with a serious law-and-order situation in the wake of the medium of Instruction Movement launched in 1972 by the All Assam Students Union demanding introduction of Assamese as medium of instruction at the university level. In fact, I was put in charge of maintaining law & order in the entire Nagaon district, although I was then serving as the AIGP at Shillong. But I must admit that the IGP and the Addl. IGP very much appreciated the timely action I took and brought the situation under control. But I do not feel least hesitant to record from personal experience that this particular SP turned out to be the real "Shakuni" of Assam police—particularly during the period of the National Emergency days of 1975. He surpassed all previous records of manipulation of police documents and uplifting quite a few officers of his own community, taking advantage of the pliable political bosses.

My all dreams of changing the system and being a part of this change, crashed against factors not within my control and my thinking process. Ground realities were beyond the sight of persons like the SP I had been trying to highlight so far.

5

A New Chapter Of Life & New Challenges

For the first time, I had the privilege of getting a government bungalow as my residence after I was transferred to Tura as the SP of Garo Hills district, then a district of undivided Assam. Prior to this, I had to do with hired accommodation with a heavy drain on my income. In fact, the junior officers were placed in more difficult situation with no official facilities for them on this count. The modernization scheme for Assam Police was introduced quite lately in the seventies of the last century; but the subordinate staff were yet to get the full benefit of the scheme.

I am constrained to observe at the end of the day that the fund earmarked for the modernization scheme was not properly utilized and at times, the cause of personal benefits for few officers gained the upper hand. I still strongly believe that it was futile to speak of such modernization without any change in the mindset of police personnel who still suffered from the hangover of colonial legacy. Even today (2014), I have no reason to believe that there has been perceptible change of this mindset.

In the wake of the Chinese aggression, I was transferred from anti-Naga insurgency duty in Haflong sector to Tura as the SP of the Garo Hills district, then within undivided Assam. It was during those days of anti-insurgency campaign that a huge batch of Naga rebels, numbering more than 200, crossed over to East Pakistan, thereby making a total mockery of Indo-Pak border management policy of central government. Though a hue and cry was raised against the inadequacy of security measures, nobody, including the journalists had reflected on the poor management of Indo-Pak border in the Cachar sector. Though matters have improved now to a great extent, the Press was rather insensitive in those days to the central government's apathetic attitude towards effective management of the international border in this sector—a very significant factor contributing to incessant flow of illegal migrants from East-Pakistan.

My days in Garo Hills were by and large uneventful excepting that towards the end, a serious problem did surface and I developed very intimate relation with Capt. Williamson Sangma with serious implications thereof:

First, Sangma affairs: Those were the days of the Hill State Movement for carving out a separate state for the hill tribes of Assam. Capt. Sangma was one of the prominent leaders of the movement. In fact, he went to be the first CM of the hill state now known as Meghalaya. To my utter surprise, Chief Minister B P Chaliha summoned me to Shillong almost immediately after I joined at Tura. On a particular evening I met him at Shillong in presence of the Addl. IGP B K Barua. The CM's advise in my own words was as follows: "Bhattacharjee, I am particularly requesting you to be very attentive to Capt. Sangma and ensure that he does not turn out to be another Phizo. You must get familiar with every nook and corner of the district and learn the Garo language for facilitating your job. You will also get necessary fund for this purpose which you can spend as you like, to keep him in good humour while also keeping full track of his activities."

I did learn the language and never betrayed the trust, although the late nights I spent with him, certainly did not please my wife. Possibly, because of his outgoing and endearing nature, even otherwise also it was on the card that I would have become very close to him. Once while on a flight together to Delhi after I had left Tura, and before Meghalaya was born, he told me in no unambiguous words that "Bhattacharjee, now that the State Language Act has been passed, it has become easier for us to achieve the target of getting a hill state." And that is that.

The Chinese aggression did not have any noticeable impact in this far-flung area, although students of the local college and the civil society were very enthusiastic about organizing relief measures for the unfortunate soldiers of the Indian army and I had to play an active role in coordinating such efforts.

Mostly, it was a period of fun and frolic backed up by ample scope for hunting and angling. Capt Sangma's intimate terms with me certainly invited ire of the Congress MLAs of the district, including a minister of state. As a result, torrential flow of complaints to Shillong, both written and anonymous, against me assumed the proportion of a deluge. The arrest of one D Sangma, the district secretary of Congress in a long pending case of defalcating government fund coupled with the court's refusal to grant him bail, certainly did not help in improving matters either. On my request, the case was handed over to the CID for completing the investigation. The minister of state and also an MLA were so much angered by such audacity (?) of the police that they lost all sense of proportion and in no less a platform than the legislative assembly, this MLA leveled a preposterous allegation against me that I had threatened him over telephone with murder! No doubt, this created a consternation in the House while Capt. Sangma broke into a loud laughter which did not go unnoticed. Clouds became cloudier. Pat came a number of wireless messages from higher authorities asking for my immediate explanation. True, I felt quite concerned; but considering the whole matter silently and intensely, I suddenly recalled that on the particular day of the alleged telephoning threat, I was at Shillong attending a conference of the DCs and the SPs while the same evening, I was attending a dinner party hosted by the CM. In reply to the WT messages, I simply requested the authorities concerned to go through my relevant tour diary as well as to consult the trunk call records of the Shillong telephone exchange.

Later on, I was told that CM Chaliha while listening to some senior officers about the whole farce, he simply waved away the entire matter with a mischievous smile. Ultimately, I came to know confidentially that one of the staff officers of the DC, by nature a crank, known for his flair for making practical jokes, had committed the mischief by taking advantage of my absence from Tura without, however, anticipating that the matter might take such serious turn. It must be mentioned that unlike now, any such allegation raised in the Assembly used to receive serious attention of the government. The poor MLA, simple as he was, did not loose the opportunity to malign me. Be that as it may, this officer's another prankish feat left me dumb founded. In those days, being transferred to Lushai Hills district (now Mizoram) was considered as a punishment which this officer richly deserved for remissness of duties. And possibly as a punitive measure, this officer was transferred to Lushai Hills. He was a very cunning man and treated the matter very calmly, albeit silently contemplating a befitting rebuff to the authorities. He drew a large amount of money as advance pay and advance TA admissible under the rule and retired quietly to his parental home at Guwahati, forgetting all about his transfer to Lushai Hills. Frequent reminders from Shillong, the then capital of Assam, did not receive any response from him. Then he struck upon a most novel idea. The amount drawn as advance pay and TA was getting exhausted. But his uncanny sense of humour was intact. Possibly he had already decided to quit the government job. After about six months or so, he is reported to have served a notice to the government asking it to show cause why he should not be placed under suspension. An unprecedented move indeed! Once placed under suspension, he would have been entitled to 75% of his basic salary, but somebody saw through the trick. Belonging to an influential and respectable family, he managed to get out of the impasse, resigned from his job and joined a leading academic institution in an important administrative post. He died in harness. All said and done, his was a noble soul, full of life and humour with malice to none. May his soul rest in peace.

As I drew close to the end of my days at Tura, a very serious situation befell the district administration. Though my Special Branch had predicted the possibility of such a development on the basis of intelligence reports, Shillong failed to appreciate the magnitude such a development could assume. A brief account of what really happened is given below.

Never thought that I would ever take to writing after I left the university. Never imagined that I would ever become an essayist or a fiction writer. Which is why. I never kept any notes on my days in the IPS and my visits to Australia, UK, Philipines, Hongkong, Thailand, etc. The train of circumstances led me to the world of letters. As such, whatever I dish out here to the reader, emanates from my fast fading memory. Not being confident about my memory, I have been constrained to leave out many interesting anecdotes and some details.

The jurisdiction of Dalu PS of Garo Hills district skirted an extensive area along the East Pakistan border. From the border of Dalu, an all-weather road leads to Mymensing. In fact, on quite a few occasions we had used this road for visiting Mymensing for attending joint conferences of DCs and SPs of bordering districts of both the countries. The memory of the taste of a huge deboned and baked "Hilsa" fish served at the lunch hosted by the DC Mymensing, still continues to be mouth-watering. In any case, we had developed good and reliable contacts across the border for collecting intelligence reports, albeit at a considerable cost and invariably the reports emanating from non-Muslim sources proved to be correct.

The year was 1963 -- not yet the time for harvesting. Information reached us that non-Muslim people of East Pakistan (Hindus, Buddhists and Christians) were being subjected to atrocities of various nature. The victims of such atrocities were reportedly preparing themselves to flee East Pakistan once the harvesting was over and by and large, their destination would be Garo Hills which had a very long border with East Pakistan. This particular report by all standards, was certainly out of the ordinary as it was both reliable and confirmed. Meanwhile, I was let to know that I was about to be transferred to Dhubri, the district HQs of undivided Goalpara district, then comprising of present day districts of Dhubri, Kokrajhar, Bongaigaon and Goalpara. In fact, I was elated as such a heavy responsibility was awaiting me. But the aforementioned development delayed the matter.

In the month of March, 1964, suddenly surfaced a torrential

flow of refugees from East Pakistan across the international border of Dalu and Purakhasia. Initially, they came in hundreds and thousands but within few days, it became a matter of lakhs! Almost half a million refugees were rummaging through the hills and dense forests for shelter. Because of the multiplicity of routes of influx, it was not possible to register the details about them. For a small district like Garo Hills, the situation assumed a very serious proportion, besides creating an unprecedented law-and-order problem. I did not command enough resources to prove equal to the task. However, SOS messages from me and the DC (late Munin Gogoi) resulted in immediate visits by late B K Barua, the then Addl. IGP, late S N Borkotoky, the then Commissioner, Hills Division, followed by late L B K Dey, the then DIGP (Range and Border). These senior officers sized up the situation immediately and appreciated the multiplicity of difficulties confronting me. They arranged to place additional forces at my disposal. Besides, an Addl. SP,10 Dy SPs and two probationary IPS officers were also rushed to Tura for helping me. Also an Addl. DM and 10 Extra Assistant Commissioners (EAC) were placed at the disposal of the district administration.

Infrastructural inadequacy presented the main problem for looking after almost half a million refugees. From Shillong also rushed another senior IAS officer, namely, late LS Ingty, for helping us in respect of arranging rations, transport, etc.

It did not take much time for New Delhi and the international foreign media to learn about this sudden holocaust with the result that the police parade ground became a landing ground for quite a few helicopter flights daily, a phenomenon witnessed at Tura for the first time ever. This created additional problems for me as huge crowds were attracted from the neighbouring villages and the town itself for seeing these monstorous birds carrying a dozen persons each in their stomach!

First came the CM Chaliha with the heads of all the relevant departments. Discussions, suggestion galore were forthcoming at rapid pace. However, I must mention one incident and consequences thereof. During these eventful days, so many interesting developments surfaced that it would not be easy matter to determine which to choose and which to leave. So, I shall confine myself only to two or three which I am tempted to share with the readers.

Accommodation for the refugees was the biggest problem with heavy rains yet to be encountered. The PWD submitted a scheme costing few crores of rupees (If I remember correctly more than 10 crores of rupees and those were not the days of plenty of money at the disposal of the state government), which irritated both the CM and the commissioner who having burst out in sheer disgust, tore down the scheme to pieces in presence of the CM, thereby causing untold discomfiture to those who were conspiring to trade in human miseries. (I have been wondering over the decades how these engineers, who are supposed to be brilliant products of our secondary education system, could become so greedy to loot the public exchequer!)

The Commissioner immediately commissioned me to erect few thousand temporary shades built of forest materials with the help of the VDP volunteers. After serious consideration, I agreed to shoulder the responsibility provided the district council authorities permitted us to extract building materials from the hills and the forests. Modi Marak, the Chief Executive Member (CEM) of the District Council of Garo Hills, was present in the meeting with Capt. Sangma. Both of them readily agreed to my proposal. The Village Defence Parties of the bordering areas were maintained perforce at a very active level. Eventually, it was possible to muster about 600/700 volunteers from about 75 VDPs and they raised within 4/5 days about 1,500 temporary sheds. The cost of tea and some occasional snacks served to them amounted to about Rs 80,000/- only which the Commissioner gladly made available. The PHE stepped in and solved the problem of water supply. In this unforeseen melee, it was a question of providing the leadership necessary for co-ordinating the roles of various government departments which late Satyen Barkataki, the Commissioner did provide wonderfully.

The appearance of the international media with their TV crew proved to be very embarrassing for the Pak government. If anything, at least to demonstrate before the international media, the EPR resorted to firing on occasions, ostensibly to prevent the exodus with the result that quite a few Christian refugees were shot dead. Six or seven dead bodies were sent to Tura without any information either to me or to the DC. The very sight of these dead bodies triggered off a communal attack against the small Muslim population of the town. Quite a few houses and shops were torched and looted. However, the police party kept ready at Tura PS round-the-clock stepped in and controlled the situation after arresting 14/15 of the marauders.

The district council authorities refused to settle half a million refugees within Garo Hills. In fact, such a step would have had an adverse impact on the demographic structure of the district which they were not ready to accept, albeit correctly. Of course, they agreed to settle 10/12 thousand Christian refugees within the district. After great deal of deliberations, CM Chaliha decided that refugees should be transferred to Matia near Goalpara and Bamunigaon near Boko of Kamrup district. LS Ingty was put in charge of the whole operation and I was asked to assist him in making necessary arrangements for facilitating the movement of such a huge body of human beings.

The entire district of Garo Hills prior to this holocaust could have boasted of having 20/25 trucks and 9/10 buses only. As such, I had to beget trucks and buses from outside the district and altogether I could collect little over 400 trucks and buses from the districts of Goalpara, Kamrup and Darrang with the help of the respective SPs. The motely crowd of over 400 drivers and their assistants created fresh problems for me because of their unruly and salacious conduct. Extra resources had to be marshalled for protecting the helpless female refugees against the outrageous conduct of the drivers. Thank God, with the help of a dedicated brand of officers, it was possible to prevent the formation of any organized racket in illegal human trafficking despite the opportunities offered by the abnormal situation. No doubt, the situation was controlled with heavy hands but it was controlled. It took us almost two months to transhift all the refugees excepting those retained in Garo Hills.

Yet another thrilling experience in the midst of these hectic schedules and oddities of various hues, was in store for me:

Let's get back to Tura. This chain of events suddenly befalling the district administration did, however, offer some rare opportunities for interacting with some prominent personalities of India and Assam. The list is rather long, but to mention a few, I, as a very junior IPS officer, had to confront with the Union Home Minister Gulzarilal Nanda, CM BP Chaliha, Union Relief & Rehabilitation Minister Meherchand Khanna and few others. But uppermost in my mind has remained the interaction with the Union Home Secretary V Viswanathan ICS (Welles Hengen in his book captioned "After Nehru, Who" had called him the "uncrowned king of India" obviously for his omnipresence in the country's administrative matter) and the legendary figure of Indian Police, BN Mallik IP, the then Director Intelligence Bureau (DIB) and a close associate of Pt Nehru.

After his visit to Dalu area with Chaliha, the Union Home Minister and the CM met the senior officers at the Tura Circuit House for reviewing the situation and the measures undertaken so far to deal with the situation. I was possibly the junior-most amongst the officers attending the meeting. This review, no doubt, proved very helpful to the district administration; but I was apprehending that the DIB would be grilling me, particularly in respect of advance transborder information. Having anticipated such a possibility, I had arranged to keep all the secret files and secret source reports concerned ready for placing, if need be, before the DIB and the union home secretary. The moment the issue of law & order came up for review, all eyes were upon me and the DIB lost no time in alleging that I had failed to anticipate such an upheaval and also to keep the government informed about the likelihood of such a development. My immediate reaction as I thought within myself that, "Thank God, I have kept the relevant files and the source reports readily available." Having gone through the file and the source reports, Mallik handed these over to Viswanathan. After few moments of total silence, Viswanathan looked at me with a mischievious smile and asked me: "Well Bhattacharyya, you have kept the papers ready; but how did you know that the DIB would put this question to you?"

"Sir", I replied, "had I been in his position, I would have asked the same question."

Viswanathan burst into a hearty laughter and remarked, "Don't worry, you will be one day in his position" and then went out of the room with Borkotoky to partake of what was not unknown to me. This remark had certainly skyrocketed me into a new height of self-confidence and energy without, however, translating his prediction into reality in the long run for reasons not within my control. True, I was selected thrice for deputation to the Intelligence Bureau but for one or the other reason, I simply could not go to New Delhi. Destiny had planned otherwise! With the narration of another interesting and unforeseen event, Tura chapter may well come to an end.

CM Chaliha was on his next round of tour for assessing personally how things were progressing. He left me and the DC behind at Dalu and proceeded to have his last round of discussion with Borkotoky who was camping at the Adougiri IB, a village almost centrally situated between Dalu and Tura but not entirely free from the clamours of the refugees hovering around nearby. At Adougiri, I found both the CM and the Commissioner closeted and lost in a serious discussion. On my arrival there, both of them heaved a sigh of relief as if they were waiting for me only. Chaliha was having a cup of tea while Borkotoky was itching for his usual evening rounds of whiskey and my arrival afforded the opportunity he was looking for leaving the sitting room.

Little later, both of them presented a new problem for me. Borkotoky had picked up in the course of his daily tour an abandoned or quite likely a lost female child about 7/8 years old. She did not understand either Assamese or Garo. She was found crying loudly under a tree on the main road. She was alone. Borkotoky brought her to the IB where he gave her some food and spoke about the child to Chaliha also. In fact as I arrived, both of them were discussing about the measures to be taken for this unfortunate child. A Hajong constable, who was accompanying me could immediately understand what she was crying for as she was a Hajong girl. The constable obtained all the details from her which were as follows:

During the melee created by the firing resorted to by the EPR at the border, this child got separated from the other members of her family and somebody placed her in a truck transporting refugees. The driver of the truck dropped her near a refugee camp. Not knowing what to do, she walked along the road and when tired, took shelter under a tree and started crying. Her loud crying attracted the attention of Borkotoky who brought her to the IB, gave her some food and then found himself perplexed about what to do with the child. Even CM Chaliha was perplexed as he remarked that it would be simply impossible to find her own people in this sea of suffering humanity. Even then enquiries were made in quite a few camps with no favourable result. Then I arrived at the scene. After realizing the pitiable condition of the child, Borkotoky, possibly in a jocular vein, asked me casually if I would like to take the girl with me until somebody came forward to claim her. Chaliha immediately picked up the thread where Borkotoky had left it and asked me—"Bhattacharjee, we cannot leave her in this Iurch. Why not take her under your wings and rear her up?"

It was really difficult for me to say "no" to these two eminent persons of Assam whom I adored and respected from the core of my heart.

Thus Rumur as she disclosed her name, practically became a member of my family. Of course, my wife took quite a number of days to clean her and make her presentable. But all her efforts for making her a literate girl proved to be futile. In due course, she grew up to be quite a presentable maiden. In fact, she has figured in one of my novels. Ultimately, when I was posted to Haflong she married a constable working under me out of her own choice, if not because of some unsuspected romance. Both Chaliha and Borkotoky were very happy to hear about it and sent their respective blessings as also some wedding gifts to Rumur.

This particular, unexpected melee created by the influx from East Pakistan, left behind a rich store of materials for use in respect of man management, study of human character and above all, developing the qualities of leadership. As Field Marshal Montgomery had defined leadership in his memoirs (page 80) as "The capacity and the will to rally men and women to a common purpose, and the character which inspires confidence." So it turned out to be during these critical days. No doubt, this holocaust taught me very many useful lessons.

Thus ended my Tura days and commenced my stint at Dhubri.

6

Dhubri Days

On looking back, I cannot but feel that I was thrown from the frying pan to the fire! My stay at Dhubri, extending to nearly four years, was by far the longest as SP. I now really wonder how could I survive there so long amidst a host of adverse circumstances. Survive, I did but at the heavy cost of cultivating permanent animus of those who had strongly agitated for inclusion of Assam in Pakistan as Muslim League activists during the Freedom Movement but lost no time in becoming turncoats overnight as Congressites after Independence. In fact, some of them had subsequently become ministers of Assam without, however, giving up their loyalty to Jinnha. Really politics makes strange bed fellows. I was transferred from Dhubri on 2/3 occasions because of political pressures but on demands of the indigenous people, such transfers were cancelled on all these occasions as Chaliha had seen through the game of these pro-Pakistan politicians. But I had to suffer very heavily after Chaliha's death. More about this later on. When ultimately I was relieved of this charge, it was practically on my own request to Chaliha. I had been feeling really tired of hectic days continuously undergone for so many years. I really needed little respite.

Dhubri was really a hot bed of communal politics, a legacy of the Muslim League politics. Various other factors encountered during these years did not help either for improving matters. Issues which figured prominently during my stay at Dhubri, were the following:

1. Implementation of the "Prevention of Infiltration from Pakistan" scheme. Anti infiltration measures.
2. The Indo-Pak war of 1965.
3. Anti-dacoity and anti-smuggling measures.
4. Post State Language Act backlash amongst the Bodo youths generating the movement for a separate Bodo state.
5. General law-and-order situation which was mostly explosive —particularly on communal issues.

As such my task was cut out after proper briefings. I left behind some of the mistakes committed while facing the problem of influx of refugees and concentrated on building up a reliable team of officers which I could do by motivating some of the energetic Inspectors and quite a few Officers-in-Charge (OC) of police stations, including few Muslim ones who were suspects in many eyes until the other day, but who never failed me. Be that as it may, my job was made easy by the Addl. SP, Hqs Siddhigopal Tripathy and the Dy SP Hqs, Niranjan Roy, both trained during the British days. Both are no more. Their devotion to duty and loyalty to me afforded me enough opportunities for extensive and frequent tours all over the district, thereby enriching my knowledge about the situations in all the PS *elekas* and the Revenue circles.

To narrate the details of all the above mentioned issues, will be an unending affair. Therefore, only some of the salient features influencing subsequent course of events will be dwelt upon.

The issue of unabated torrential influx from East Pakistan to Assam, since the partition of the country, was not only creating unrest all over the state but also these illegal migrants betrayed widespread criminial propensities with incidences of murder, dacoity, kidnapping, rape and the likes assuming ever rising trend. The central government paid no serious attention to this grave problem changing the demographic pattern of the state. Also the scope for extending the net of communal politics was widened with the infiltration of each illegal migrant. But the Chinese aggression of 1962, alerted New Delhi. During this sudden aggression, the flag of Pakistan was hoisted in some places in central Assam. Also "Pakistan Zindabad" slogans were heard in quite a few places. BN Mallik, the then DIB, took up the matter immediately with all the seriousness it deserved. Some of us were summoned to Delhi and after threadbare discussion, the Prevention of Infiltration from Pakistan (PIP) scheme was prepared. The scheme energized the districts concerned for launching an intensified drive against illegal migrants from East Pakistan. Additional staff and other resources like vehicles and engine boats etc., were sanctioned–all by the Central government. The scheme became operational from the later part of 1964. It was intended not only to detect Pak infiltrators but also to prevent fresh infiltration. As the SP, Dhubri, I had to shoulder the heaviest responsibility because the main routes of infiltration, both overground and riverine, lay across this district. I had to open (if I remember correctly) as many as 58 Watch Posts to be on the look out for fresh infiltrators. Also a large fleet of engine boats was put into service for constantly patrolling the riverine routes along the Brahmaputra.

Demographic imbalance was already evident. Also the illegal migrants were registering themselves as voters in the ERs with the help of unscrupulous politicians, government officers and employees. Encroachment upon forest and other categories of government land, was also facilitated by these self-seeking officers and employees of the Forest, the Revenue and the Police departments. All these had to be put to a full stop. Else, the indigenous people ran the risk of being reduced to a minority in their homeland. (A full chapter will be devoted to this problem later on.)

The drive against these illegal migrants was stepped up and thousands of them were deported to East Pakistan during my stay at Dhubri despite occasional resistance from the EPR and sporadic border skirmishes. Under the PIP scheme, a post of DIGP was also created and the DIG was supposed to supervise the entire operation although his services were utilized more for non-operational administrative matters. As a result, the focal point of bitterly vocal opposition and maligning became the SP concerned and I was no exception. Then most of the illegal migrants being Muslim, I had to incur the wrath of all the scheming Muslim political leaders of the district, who wrecked their vengeance later on when a pro-Pakistan Muslim CM had come to power for few months. More about it later on. It is worth-mentioning here that Dhubri was the hot bed of Muslim League activities, targeting inclusion of Assam in Pakistan and the legacy was simply dormant.

To cut a long story short, all the ex-Muslim Leaguers of the district lost no time in projecting the entire operation as anti-Muslim, thereby fomenting constant communal tension. Another strong factor which kept the communal tension alive, was the very strong support voiced by the Bengali Hindus in favour of detection and deportation of the Muslim infiltrators. Not that everybody in the society was involved in such wrangling. Only those entertaining ulterior motives and communal bias, were very active in maligning the entire operation as well as raising wild allegations against me personally.

The maligning campain against me personally was stretched so far that two prominent cabinet ministers, namely, Fakhruddin Ali Ahmed and Moinul Haque Choudhury came together to Dhubri in 1966 to take stock of the situation. Ali Ahmed appreciated my stand that I had done nothing outside the ambit of the relevant laws, rules and government instructions while Haque Choudhury preferred to provoke a personal confrontation with me by accusing me of communal prejudices and shouting at me in extremely objectionable language and that too, in presence of the DC and my subordinate officers. Obviously, this was too much to stomach and having lost my temper, shouted back at him in equally loud voice telling him in no uncertain terms that if he had any valid charge against me, he could certainly report to the authorities but could not misbehave with the SP of a district in the way he did. He possibly did not expect such a loud and strong retort from me. I had intentionally made it loud so that it could match with his outburst in presence of my subordinate staff. Ali Ahmed intervened and took me away to his room in the Circuit House. Surprisingly, Haque Choudhury did not make any complaint against me to the authorities, possibly and also reportedly because he did not want others in Shillong—particularly his cabinet colleagues to know that he had received a very strong rebuff from an

SP. But could he really prevent it? Two ministers after about a month appeared at my residence and congratulated me for this daredevil performance. However, I had reported the entire matter personally to the IGP, the chief secretary and the CM. It transpired subsequently that Mr Ali Ahmed did not approve of the unbecoming behaviour of his colleague. I was told that the CM simply had a mischievous smile and the days of Haque Choudhury in Shillong had already become numbered for reasons more than one. So the campaign for detection and deportation of illegal migrants continued in full swing. Needless to mention that the rate of fresh infiltration recorded a downward trend.

The Indo-Pak War of 1965 did not help matters either. My district did not have any army detachment to counter any thrust by the Pak army. Tension was at its highest and rumours were afloat that Pak army might march in and take over Dhubri. I had to remain extremely alert about the situation. Of course, in case of need, I could draw upon the BSF which was still under the state government. As such LMGs, mortars, GF rifles and some other resources available with the BSF for use in case of need, bolstered not only my morale but of the entire district force. Certainly, it was a very difficult task not confronted earlier by the district police; but I must record here that nobody working under and with me, betrayed any lack of courage and dedication. That made my job easier. The drive against illegal migrants mentioned above, had already created a general consciousness amongst the common people. As such, it was not difficult to activate few hundreds of VDPs including the inactive ones, to extend a helping hand. Mainly, the protection of roads and rail bridges was entrusted to the VDPs against possible sabotages and they did it admirably.

Intelligence reports presented a gloomy scenario in that some pro-Pakistan activists were planning to welcome the Pak army in case of its arrival at Dhubri. As if we were not having enough of hectic time, I was suddenly awoken by a long ring of the telephone at about 2 am one night and at the other end, was the CM himself. Felt little embarrassed as the CM was still working and I was fast asleep.

The top secret message conveyed by the CM caused real consternation. Within moments, the same message was received from the State Control Room. According to the message, Pakistan may send across some demolition squads in some armoured motor boats of very high speed and demolish the Brahmaputra bridge at Saraighat. Secondly, some para-troopers may be dropped at the few landing strips available within the district.

Within less than 15 minutes of receipt of the message, all the officers concerned, including the DC and the BSF officers met at the District Control Room and took the following precautionary measures as suggested by the CM and other higher authorities:

1. Four huge Indian barges and two Pak steamers at Dhubri river port, were moved about 10 km downstream of Dhubri and located at places strategically convenient to cover all the possible approach routes by using LMGs, Mortars and GF rifles. All other engine boats and two steel motor boats available with the River Police, were pressed into service for round-the-clock patrolling along the riverine routes. Jibeswar Gogoi, the senior and very efficient River Police Inspector was put in charge of the operation under my direct supervision. Few JCOs of the BSF, were also inducted for assisting Gogoi.
2. There were four possible known landing strips in the district, one each in Dhubri and Kokrajhar subdivision and two in Goalpara subdivision. All these possible landing strips were put out of commission after few hours of hard labour. Also four squads of snipers were somehow organized and positioned strategically.
3. Another important message was received in the morning from Shillong. In the wake of the Chinese aggression of 1962, the DC of Tezpur, then headquarters (HQs) of undivided Darrang district, had deserted his post and fled to Calcutta as it was apprehended that Tezpur might fall to the Chinese any moment. The desertion by the DC amounted to pressing the panic button. (The DC was, of course, subsequently dismissed from service.) Wild rumours spread the panic and created utter confusion among the people. Also unprecedented administrative problems surfaced with full vehemence. Keeping this unforeseen catastrophe in mind, Shillong advised

me and the DC that under no circumstances senior officers of all the major departments could leave the district and above all, arrangements had to be made for setting up a secret HQs in case Dhubri really fell to Pakistan. This responsibility also had to be shouldered by me and of course, all arrangements were made accordingly, albeit secretly and the common man never knew about it. The morals of the people could be kept as high as ever.

4. However, I had to do another unpleasant job in this context, of course, on orders from Shillong. All pro-Pak and anti-national persons must be put under preventive detention under the Defence of India (DI) Rules as per the provisions of the Defence of India Act. I also took this opportunity to round up the notorious international smugglers under the D I Rules as they were all potential source of vital information for Pakistan. Though most of the political detenues were pro-Pakistan Muslim, mostly ex-Muslim Leaguers, the second category comprised of smugglers from all the communities, albeit dominated by Marwaris and Bengali Hindus. Warrants of detention were issued against two MLAs also. One of them went underground. We came to know that he had taken shelter at Shillong at the residence of one particular officer of very high position. We had definite information that all these anti-national politicians with fundamentalist agenda were preparing for the reception of the Pak army if Dhubri fell to them. Some of the detenues and their friends are still entertaining a feeling of animus towards me, although I personally had nothing against them. Needless to mention that I had to depend on intelligence reports and past records. This animus, mostly originating from my Dhubri days, had a very adverse bearing on my future days in the police. More about it later on. But I must observe that such draconian laws imparts an undemocratic character to a democratic state, although such measures become inevitable in the larger interests of the nation. But when these are used for wrecking personal vendetta as well as to perpetuate political hegemony, the state is stripped of its democratic fibres. This is what

> Indira Gandhi did to suppress political opposition and put down some democratic movements and she was ousted from power in the general elections of 1977. Though she recaptured power in 1980, her image had already taken a severe beating. Her all-out efforts to put down the historic Assam Movement, by means fair or foul, constitute another glaring example of undemocratic functioning of a democratic state.

With the passage of the State Language Act, 1960, the tribal people in general and the Bodos in particular had smelt a rat and become suspicious of chauvinistic attitude of the Assamese speaking people. They were apprehensive that the Assamese intended to perpetuate his dominance over all other ethnic groups of the state. During my visits to Kokrajhar, then a subdivisional HQs of Goalpara district, I used to meet the prominent persons of both old and young generations. They all had supported in one voice our extensive drive against the illegal migrants from East Pakistan. But they were certainly very sensitive on the question of language. They also felt very much discriminated against on many fronts. During his visit to Kokrajhar in January 1968, the matter was placed in its full perspective before CM Chaliha who very much appreciated my concern for the undercurrent of discontent and frustration engulfing the young generation.

He discussed the matter threadbare with me till about 3 am after partaking of a community dinner on 13 January 1968 and asked me to come up to Shillong with a comprehensive note on the matter discussed between us. My suggestions were to undertake a threefold approach on political, administrative and cultural levels. Cultural, because Bishnu Rava and Bhupen Hazarika, two famous artists of the country, were then MLAs and both of them could be taken into confidence and requested to usher in an atmosphere of mutual confidence and cultural integration. But destiny interfered before the project could take off the ground, although I had scripted the aforesaid note and handed it over to the CM.

Unfortunately, Chaliha was taken seriously ill and the downhill sliding of Assamese-Bodo relation continued. In fact it took serious turn during the tenure of Sarat Sinha ministry. In course of time, the movement for separate Bodoland surfaced with full vehemence amongst a section of more militant Bodo youths taking to arms for creating an independent Bodoland. Even now (2014) the situation continues to be in a state of flux. Ironically enough, the State Language Act which engendered the fear of domination by the Assamese chauvinist, is yet to be implemented whereas before the passage of the Act, the Assamese language had enjoyed the privilege of being the unofficial lingua franca of the entire North-east, let alone Assam. As if, all these problems were not enough for us to spending sleepless nights, added was the high incidence of cases of armed dacoities. Quite a few gangs of dacoits comprising of immigrant Pakistani Muslims and Bodo desperadoes were operating in the district and making my life miserable. While the Muslim gangs operated mainly in the areas under the Mankachar and South Salmara PSs as also in the riverine routes of the Brahmaputra, the Bodo dacoits operated between Alipurduar of North Bengal and North Lakhimpur on the north bank of the Brahmaputra. So far there had been no organized drive against these anti-social elements mainly because of paucity of resources. At times, as many as 4/5 cases of dacoity were reported daily. Obviously, it was only logical that such frequency of dacoity resulted in a hullabaloo in the state assembly whereupon it became easier for me to ask for additional resources. Once such additional resources as requisitioned by me, were made available, a really merciless operation under the code name “Op Rangapani” was launched and as a result, between 1966 & 1968 the annual incidences of dacoity came down to 3/5 cases. Quite a few dacoits were also shot down while conducting “Op Rangapani”. This was possible because of active assistance received from the villagers and the respective VDPs. There was only one main well organized and well-equipped Bodo gang comprising of nearly 100 members and operating in a vast area. If any member of the gang was seriously injured in any encounter, they used to chop off his head and take it away so that identification became impossible! It was possible to send up 72 of these Bodo dacoits for trial under section 400 IPC (Gang case) for habitually committing a series of dacoities over a long period. One Karmalal Bodo, the leader of the gang turned approver with two of his other colleagues. Altogether 52 of these seventy two dacoits were convicted and sentenced to long term of imprisonment. Of course, I took necessary steps for rehabilitating the three approvers so that they could lead a normal life in the society.

The general law-and-order situation was kept under control with strictest possible arrangements. Even then, the undercurrent of communal tension and a number of political agitations did pollute the apparently peaceful atmosphere from time to time. There were so many incidents worth mentioning but I would confine myself, to only one incident:

Late BK Barua, who served as IGP, Assam for a number of years after his long stint at the IB, used to emphasize on one particular point regularly in respect of performance by senior police officers, particularly in the context of maintaining law and order: The police officer in charge of maintaining law & order must be able to anticipate how a particular situation may develop in its subsequent stages. This particular lesson had really impressed me and I had accordingly planned my line of action in a particular given situation. On 26 January 1968, there was widespread rioting and large-scale destruction of private properties in Guwahati. The victims were non-Assamese businessmen. Fancy Bazar, the main hub of commercial activities in the North-east, was the main target of this senseless mayhem, resulting in widespread lawlessness. Shillong immediately alerted all the districts about the possible fallouts of the Guwahati situation. I had personally anticipated that hooligans instigated by communal vested interests might infiltrate from Kamrup district into my district and create communal troubles in the pockets of immigrant Muslims and Bengali refugees. As such, without loss of any time, two gates manned by armed police, were set up at the district boundary—one in the north bank at Manikpur and the other near Dhupdhara in the south bank of the Brahmaputra. Though nothing was reported from the Manikpur end, two truckloads of rowdies armed with lethal weapons, were detained and arrested at Dhupdhara. It transpired that their targets were the Bengali refugee camp at Matia. Thus a major crisis was averted and the district administration picked up 'kudos' from Shillong. (I strongly believe that the latest round of widespread violence in BTAD area, (July-August, 2012) could have been averted to a great extent if precautionary and preventive measures were taken in advance after the first symptoms were taken serious note of.)

7

The Days of Turmoil

Soon after, I left Dhubri on transfer to great relief of my wife. But this long tenure as SP in two districts had brought me face to face with some hard realities of our young democracy. I could feel that the social development in Assam after Independence, did not keep pace with whatever little economic growth was shaping the future. Beneficiaries were, by and large, from the upper and upper middle class. The people were not involved in the developmental activities nor did anybody seem to have felt the need thereof. This particularly applies to the officers, with rare exception, imported from outside Assam on the basis of results of competitive examination for All India Services like IAS, IPS, etc. Such failures have, at times, compelled me to wonder whether the purpose of instituting these statutory services had served the purposes intended to serve. I knew some such officers who looked down on the people of Assam as of inferior stock. There were another category of officers who, for their participation in the Freedom Movement had faced punitive measures and were subsequently appointed to administrative jobs after Independence, without, however, any administrative acumen and experience. As a result, they could make hardly any qualitative difference in improving matters in both higher and lower levels. At the time of Independence, Assam was left with quite a few ICS and IP officers with the result that the administration continued to be bureaucratic rather than democratic. No doubt, there were exceptions. The colonial hangover was yet to subside and a people oriented administration to emerge. Even the initial appointees to the IAS and the IPS pretended to be the legitimate inheritors of the so called "Steel Frame" left behind by the British and totally failed to identify themselves with the cause of Assam. Obviously, we were passing through a transitory period. Crippling incompetence was evident all over—mostly because of lack of commitment to the cause of the state. Politicians who could not either get a berth in the state ministry or qualify for a seat in the Assembly, were conspicuous by their scheming for getting their pound of flesh. Still worse, as Toyenbee observed during his visit to India, the most exploited and deprived were the peasants of India for last 3,000 years! Still I felt that we, as a nation, were entering into a new phase of what might be termed as another edition of 'renaissance'.

Meanwhile, I was selected for deputation to the IB. Subsequently, I came to know that BN Mallik very much wanted me to be an IB official. When I met him at Bhopal in an All India Police Meet after his retirement, his first question to me was "Bhattacharyya, have you still managed not to be in the IB?" Unfortunately, I was deprived of all the three opportunities for being an IB officer. On the first two occasions, I could not leave Assam because my children were studying in Assamese medium school and it would have been impossible to maintain two establishments on my part. Then, on my return from Australia after attending a course of 'Management' I was selected for the third time for deputation to the IB. But that was not to be. This time, the state government could not release me as Assam was confronted with a serious law-and-order situation on account of an agitation launched by All Assam Students Union (AASU) for introduction of Assamese as the medium of instruction at all levels, including the university level and the movement degenerated into serious communal clashes in the wake of the kidnapping followed by the murder of a prominent AASU leader, namely Anil Bora of Nagaon district. The state government was really short of experienced senior officers for tackling the situation. Looking back, I feel that I should have managed to go to the IB on any of these occasions. If I could have done so, the course of the rest of my police career would have been certainly somethig else.

In fact, (you may call me a fatalist) at every step of life's journey, I have felt unseen hands of some unseen super power, if not an unseen extra-super computer, in determining the course of my life. Possibly this is where "Bhagavad Geeta" steps in to reflect on the activities of previous birth, if there is one! Also I feel all the more convinced about this unseen super power whenever I reflect upon Napoleon's life.

I was deputed from Shillong when I was working as one of the senior staff officer of the IGP, to Nagaon district, the worst affected district in the aforementioned communal trouble. However, I could bring the situation under control with some desperate action and active help from the then Addl. IGP, Atwar Rahman.

Prior to this 'Medium of Instructions Movement', an epoch making event was recorded in the history of the Indian sub continent. Pakistan was partitioned and the emergence of Bangladesh as a sovereign independent country became a reality. In the wake of the freedom movement launched under the leadership of Sheikh Mujibur Rahman, Pak army resorted to a reign of terror with the result that more than a million refugees took shelter in Assam. At this time, I was holding charges of as many as three offices, viz., AIGP (TAPTW), the command of the 5 APBN and in addition to these two, I was also asked to raise the Armed Police Training Centre. It was mainly because of the last that I was entrusted with raising and training up two companies of Bangladesh's Mukti Bahini from amongst about 2,500 Bangladeshi refugees sheltered in a makeshift camp under my charge at a secret place, away from the public gaze. Altogether 234 able-bodied refugees were put through a crash course of Close Quarter Battle (CQB) and handling of small arms and grenades. On completion of training, they were handed over to Brig. M L Barua, then in charge of BSF in the southern sector of the North-east. The whole business was shrouded in such topmost secrecy that nobody came to know about such a training camp. On completing the training of these "'Mukti Bahini" jawans I was given another oral order to keep myself ready to move to Bangladesh at short notice so that I could take charge of a civil division there for the purpose of re-establishing civil administration which was rendered non-existent by the Pak army. In fact, there was no semblance of any administration at all. This had certainly roused a shrewd suspicion in my mind that Mrs. Gandhi was possibly thinking in terms of integrating Bangladesh into India as was done in case of Sikkim. But somehow or other, it did not come through possibly because of international complications such a step might have created. That apart, Mujibur Rahman, must not have wanted to go down in history as another Quisling. So at his insistence the Indian army withdrew after three months of liberation of Bangladesh.

Unfortunately, lakhs of refugees who took shelter in Assam did not go back to Bangladesh and now they are claiming Indian citizenship, thereby imparting extra wind to the sail of the fundamentalist lobby.

The hope for a stable Bangladesh soon receded to the background after the assassination of Mujibur Rahman and as in Pakistan, the control of the strings of power passed into the hands of the army. Fundamentalist forces resurfaced with the help of Pakistan's ISI and started creating problems for India. Internal strifes have been the hallmark of Bangladesh since Mujib's violent death. However, with the surfacing of liberal and secular forces, Bangladesh will certainly be ready to turn a new page of history.

In 1972, I was deputed to the South Australian Police Academy for training in "Management". Senior Police officers from 33 countries participated in this training programme.

This tour to Australia was not only very educative but was also an eye-opener for me in respect of very many other matters pertaining to national character of quite a few countries. Many of the officers from African countries were holders of Bar-at-Law degree. The lone Iranian officer was the most richly attired officer with gold plate covering the hood of his peak-cap. Even then, the tunic worn by IPS officers with its brilliantly polished sam brown leather cross-belt, earned me the applause of all concerned and that made me very proud indeed.

Unlike in our country, in Australia the Policeman is considered to be the real friend of the people despite the fact that he is very strict in enforcing the law of the land; but his behaviour is very pleasing and there is hardly any public resistance against strict enforcement of the law. The average citizen feels fully assured that he is certainly under the protective umbrella of the Police. An incident that took place in my presence was a real eye-opener. We were given holiday for a week and after visiting Brisbane and Melbourne, I went to Sydney to spend few days with Tushar Bhattacharyya and his wife Rekha. Though no relation of mine, they were known to my family for many years.

This holiday was combined with training for three days in traffic control, motor driving under trying circumstances and controlling the red light areas at the Sydney Police HQs. So virtually, I had a nine-day sojourn in Sydney excluding the both ways journey time by air. The training period of three days was not only very exhilarating but also educative in respect of uses of modern gadgets in all the three aforesaid fields. Conducted visits to the red light areas, both by day and night, were what I would like to describe as an eye opener—particularly in respect of cleanliness, display of medical certificate and the personal hand-book of each inhabitant of the area giving an account of her past, present and future plans. What surprised me most was that some of these girls had taken up this profession as a passing phase in their lives so that they might earn enough for settling down subsequently in married lives and that too, with the knowledge of their respective boy friends. The impression I carried back was that sex was being rationalised, devoid of any emotional degradation and social stigma!

Anyway back to Tushar and Rekha: On a week-end day Tushar and Rekha took me out to the Sydney Lion Park where the lions moved about freely and the visitors could see the lions in close quarters from inside their cars with all the window glasses fully raised but taking photographs was no problem.

On our return journey, our car was chased and signalled by two policemen to stop. Tushar was driving. Both the officers came forward, saluted us and apologised for causing inconvenience to us and then pointed out that Tushar had violated the speed limit prescribed for the weekend days because of large number of visitors to the lion park. Tushar was handed over a printed form duly filled up which stated that Tushar had been fined 100 Australian dollars (which then amounted to Rs. 850/- in India) for over-speeding. Handing over the order they once more apologised and after saluting left us. I felt very sorry for Tushar because he had taken me out on a pleasure trip. But his wife, Rekha consoled me not to worry much as Tushar was used to getting penalised frequently for overspeeding and she herself for slow driving. Thus Rekha made very light of the entire episode. On looking askance remorsefully at Tushar, he explained to me that the police here had power to fine upto $200; but they hardly imposed the maximum fine to avoid the offender going to court because the payment of a fine of 100 dollars or less would be much less than the cost involved in going on appeal to the court. Besides, the court is more likely to uphold the police order mainly because of two reasons: Firstly, the credibility of the police is very high unlike in our case and secondly, the reliability of the technical gadgets used in detecting such breach of law, is beyond any shade of doubt. Still more significant is that the entire amount thus collected is credited to the Police Welfare Fund. Which is why police patrols are very enterprising in detecting such violation of the law. Instead of going to the court on appeal, the offender prefers to deposit the fined amount to the government treasury within 21 days of receiving the notice as specified. A very striking feature of criminal administration of Australia is that false or mistaken accusation in any crime leading to court proceedings, is practically non-existent. Because, if a person accused of committing a crime is sent up for trial in the court and found innocent by the court, then the entire defence expenses have to be defrayed from the Police budget. Such steps have prevented the police from being instrumental in wrecking political and personal vengeance, a trait so prominently evidenced in India—paricularly during the black days of the infamous Emergency of 1975. The trend is very much active even today. Recounting all about the days I spent in Australia, would amount to digressing from the main theme of this treatise. As such, I shall close up the Australian affairs after narrating two unforeseen encounters with an all-time great and an eminent politician.

During a visit to the Botanical Garden of Adelaide, a co-visitor had pointed out to me a villa of striking attraction, little away from the main road and told me that it was the residence of legendary cricketer

Sir Donald Bradman. So, on one of the weekend days, contrary to all civil norms of a formal call, I practically gate-crashed into this villa and insisted on seeing the great cricketer. On learning that I was from India, the great man came out to receive me with the hint of a smile. After I introduced myself and explained to him that my only intention was to see him in flesh and blood, he shook hands with me and offered me a chair. Actually, once I had seen him, I did not want to take much of his time but he insisted on my taking a cup of tea. He was full of praise for Vijay Hazare, Lala Amarnath and Assam tea. I apologised for disturbing him without prior appointment as I took leave of him; but he did not betray any sign of displeasure. Rather, I felt, he was quite warm. As I came out, then only I realised that he had spent almost 35 minutes with me instead of five I wanted.

The other incident was an eye opener and equally interesting for me. On way back to Adelaide from Sydney in a 727 Boeing Jet, a well-dressed gentleman sat next to me at the window seat. As I was trying to look down through the window, he gracefully offered his seat to me in exchange for mine. As the flight cruised ahead, this gentleman took more than casual interest in me and ascertained all the details about my presence in Australia and visit to Adelaide. Having learnt that I was camped at Fort Larges, he enquired of me as to how did I propose to go to Fort Larges from the airport. I told him that I had sent a message to the Police HQs for sending a car but I was not sure if the message had been received. In case my message was not received, I would have to travel by train whereupon he offered to get me dropped in case there was no Police vehicle. A fool that I was, even then it did not occur to me to find out who he was.

Anyway, on arrival at the airport, the gentleman himself collected his two suit cases and put in the luggage berth of a large, shining Holden car. My car was also waiting. The driver constable gave a smart salute to the gentleman first and then another to me. He shook hands with me once again and gave me his card after requesting me to feel free to let him know in case of any problem faced during the rest of my stay in Australia.

After his departure, the driver constable sent to pick me up, enquired of me how did I know this gentleman. Then only, it dawned on me to look at the card he had given me and the card revealed to my utter surprise that he was Donald, DUNSTAN, the Premier (in our case, the Chief Minister) of South Australia. I was simply stunned and realised what a big fool I had been ! No Pilot car, no Escort car and not even a PSO for the Premier ! The rest is for the reader to conclude.

What impressed me most in Australia was the concern of the common man for conservation of the country's eco-system as well as everybody's concern for cleanliness of their respective cities. He was very alert about foreign tourists likely to pollute the environment.

On return from Australia, I was straightaway inducted into the staff of the IGP as the AIGP (Administration). This assignment also did not prove to be a bed of roses because of the frequency of political interference, particularly in respect of awarding departmental contracts running into crores of rupees as well as transfers and postings of officers. The old guards of the political front had been eased out earlier by political manouvering or even by death, along with the rich heritage left behind by them. The new guards were certainly not committed to what Bharat Ratna Gopinath Bordoloi, Bishnuram Medhi, Bimala Prasad Chaliha and Mahendra Mohan Choudhury had dedicated their lives to. Most of the new guards pursued a policy of self-aggrandisement while not ignoring to promote sectarian politics. The composite society of Assam was split up in all conceivable manners with the resultant social tension assuming a serious proportion. They simply did not bother about the future. As if that was not enough, came the nightmarish days of the Emergency of 1975. The state administration was reduced to a tool in the hands of few individuals never known for their commitment to the welfare of the state. The CM even had the audacity to plead for a committed judiciary! Personal loyalty and not professional efficiency, was the yardstick for picking up few bureaucrats entrusted with manufacturing so-called 'intelligence reports', thereby totally ignoring intelligence collection agencies.

The sectarian fragmentation of Assam politics dealt a heavy blow to the intelligence infrastructure and the ruling clique devised their own system of intelligence. Prescribed rules and procedures were thrown to the wind. A clique of officers intent upon self-aggrandisement and going on a spree of personal vendetta, had been surrounding the CM all the time and the CM, as in New Delhi, lost sight of ground realities and as a result, fell a victim to the cacophony of adulation of this clique of officers so much so that the CM even tried to promote his poetic potentials by penning some poems in praise of the Emergency—a result of the shrewd machination of the clique of officers. The soldiers of "Democracy" were removed from the scene—mostly by detention without trial. Fundamental rights were suspended as if our young democracy had reached the "cul-de-sac." With the freedom of the Press curtailed under a system of full censorship imposed, it became impossible to ventilate public grievance as well as instances of gross injustice. Channels of communication, thus, degraded to the narrowest possible extent, democracy became a farce in the hands of few self-seeking politicians and bureaucrats. All the opposition leaders excepting those who went underground, and even the inconvenient partymen were sent to jail without trial on grounds of national security. Even, Deveshwar Sharma, an octogenerian veteran Congress leader and freedom fighter, was not spared. He was also detained under the Maintenance of Internal Security Act (MISA) only because he was opposed to Indira Gandhi's and Sarat Sinha's autocratic and unconstitutional way of functioning. I really wonder even to this day how far national security was ensured by the detention of an octogenerian freedom fighter as many other thinking persons may like to consider! Besides, taking advantage of the Emergency, particularly suspension of fundamental right to take recourse to the court, Sarat Sinha's administration had dismissed many officers and employees from service without any trial and proceedings, thereby virtually creating a reign of terror at the instance of the same clique of officers mentioned above. In fact, some of these officers became expert manufacturers of dossiers of inconvenient officers. Officers, who had served the government for years on end, became overnight a threat to national security whereas officers with pro-Pakistan bias went scot free. For all practical purposes, it was an organised chaos that afflicted the entire fabric of the administration while, at the same time, ensuring the rise of unconstitutional centres of power both in New Delhi and most of the state capitals. The agony of terror, intensified by the total censorship of the Press, gripped the length and breadth of the country. The entire people were growing restive under an unforeseen pressure for new freedom-- freedom of being one's own self which would surface in due course. Particularly, the detention of leaders like Jay Prakash Narain (JP), Morarji Desai, etc., certainly did not endear Indira to the people. Then, the atrocities perpetrated at the instance of Sanjay Gandhi in the name of enforcing the birth control measures, also alienated the good will of large section of people. Indira did not get the correct feedback. Because the government policy itself had ensured that the channels of communication dried up to the narrowest possible extent. Out of sheer fear of falling from grace, the intelligence agencies chose to feed reports which would please the authorities in power. This is how the downhill journey of the administration in general and the police in particular commenced.

As I look back, the process of prostituting the administration has spread like cancer and I wonder how many more Anna Hazare will be required to stem the rot. To be very precise, corruption writ large over every aspect of the administration, has today surfaced as the main catastrophic bane of India's national life. It would be only a myopic perspective to assess the quality of national life by the economic growth which is yet to benefit the common man. By deliberating within myself again and again, I wonder why Indira, once a darling of the people, did this? Her father was certainly a democratic man to the core of his heart; but he certainly failed to inculcate democratic spirit in Indira while rearing her up to assume the mantle of leading a country of millions drenched in poverty and feudal mindset. She was never a democrat at heart and never realised that compulsion destroyed the path of co-operation. Allahabad High Court's judgement of setting aside her election to the Lok Sabha, turned her desperate and she resorted to all sorts of unconstitutional measures in defiance of the said judgement in order to sustain herself in power. True, she came back to power in 1980 but not with the same glamour she was earlier credited with. Above all, her divisive policies certainly gave rise to the legacy of divisive politics all over the country. It can hardly be gain said that Bhindranwale and All Assam Minority Students Union (AAMSU) were her creations.

However, volumes have already been written on the radioactive fallouts of the Emergency. As such, instead of dwelling upon the same all over again, let me confine to the predicament I had to face during and after the Emergency which had far reaching impact on my career in the police. Besides, I am sure, that the narration of some of the incidents will also go a long way in exposing the real character of the state government under the stewardship of Sarat Sinha:

Not remaining content with making my life miserable, a conspiracy was hatched to detain my old father under the MISA on the alleged ground of my father being a RSS activist! Having come to know about it, I met the CM and requested him to point out one single instance of anti-national activity on the part of my old father and if he could do so, then to depute me to arrest him. The CM preferred to remain silent and the matter ended there.

Sinha was certainly a very vindictive person; but at the same time, he was a past master in projecting the image of an honest and upright man which he was not. He tried his best to prove that he was a true Gandhian while not neglecting to promote material prosperity of his close ones. My refusal to accommodate his unjust and politically motivated requests during my Dhubri days, coupled with my proximity to Bimala Prasad Chaliha was, as it turned out, all the time at the back of his mind. So with little prodding from my adversaries, both from the political and bureaucratic areas, it rather became easy for a CM to make my life all the more miserable and he did not fail. Let me recount some of the happenings in this context.

The prescribed age-old procedure for transferring gazetted police officers has been that the IGP submits proposal for such transfer to the government. The government either accepts the proposal or turns it down. Generally, prior discussions are held with the government before submitting the proposal and the question of turning down did not arise.

Suddendly, one fine morning I was transferred from the post of AIGP (A) as SSP, CID without receiving any proposal from the IGP. The then IGP, LBK Dey put his foot down and treated the matter as a personal affront to his authority. The order was not given effect to.

The CM wanted a paricular contract under the Assam Police Housing Corporation to be given to an architect's firm owned by his son in violation of prescribed norms, which would have caused loss to the public exchequer. When this was pointed out to him, he presented a glum expression and did not proceed further with the matter; but he could not forget it as his subsequent action proved.

Then came the black days of the Emergency which afforded an opportunity for highhandedness to replace all set norms of administration as also for some officers in the secretariat to exercise unfettered authority. Thus was derailed the largest democracy of the world.

LBK Dey was suddenly removed from the post of the IGP, although he was confirmed in the post, IGP of Assam, by a regular gazette notification. I was then commanding the 5th AP Bn and the Armed Police Training Centre, besides being the senior-most selection grade SP in the state and marking time for promotion to the rank of DIGP. So what? They had a score to settle while my promotion could wait! I was suddenly transfered to a very small district as SP. Possibly, the calculation was that I would refuse to move and then, it would be too easy to dismiss me summarily from service for disobedience of order. I could see through their trap; besides, my consideration was also something different: If Menons from Kerala, Subramanians from Tamil Nadu and Gills from the Punjab, etc., could come to Assam, I could certainly go to Lakhimpur. So, I moved to Lakhimpur, leaving behind my wife and the school-going children at Guwahati, and thus compelling myself to maintain two establishments.

At Lakhimpur, I became very popular with the public in general and the young generation in particular, mainly because of certain measures I took for making the police more active, my sporting activities as well as for bringing the administration near the public. Much to the disappointment of Dispur, even the Congress activists were lavishly praising me. So, without relenting, Dispur was on the lookout for creating fresh problems for me. In Lakhimpur district also, quite a few persons were detained under the MISA on grounds of national security before I arrivesd at the scene. All these cases of detention without trial had to be periodically reviewed by the SP and his recommendation submitted to the detaining authority (in this case, the District Magistrate).

On the very first occasion of such review, I found that three college teachers were also under detention on grounds of national security. These three cases intrigued me and I decided to examine the full details of all the three cases. I was convinced that all of them were very simple persons with no potentials for causing any threat to national security. They were neither noteworthy public activists nor did they have any relation with any underground organisation. It transpired that two of them were known for their leftist leanings and their use of leftist vocabulary in their utterances. The other one subscribed to the rightist school of thought and remained busy with organising celebrations of socio-religious functions. As such, after scrutinising each case very minutely, I recommended for their release forthwith. The DM had accordingly released them. The matter, however, did not end there. The then state minister for home paid a sudden visit to North Lakhimpur. He told me in no uncertain terms that the government was unhappy with the release of these three detenues. Resorting to a rhetorical reply, I posed before the home minister—"Sir, what is the use of maintaining here a DC and a SP with such fat salaries if three unarmed teachers could threaten the security of the nation?" The minister burst into a loud and hearty laughter and considered that further pursuance of the matter was of no consequence; but Dispur did not! My detractors added one more point in my so-called dossier they had been manufacturing. So ultimately, without the knowledge of the IGP, Dispur sent to the Ministry of Home Affairs (MHA) a proposal for my summary dismissal from service on grounds of corrupt practices! I almost immediately came to know about it from my friends in the MHA. I was rather so far, impervious to all these intrigues and did not know what to do about it except depending on my past service records. Not receiving any response to the proposal, the CM sent a personal reminder to Brahmananda Reddy, the then Union HM. Still no response! Hence the second reminder sent by the CM to Reddy. I could no more remain silent and considering all the aspects of the matter, I informed my father all about it. He felt very disturbed and humiliated because of the allegation of corrupt practices—an allegation inconceivable for him and my family. My father had already crossed 75, but defying the constraints of old age, he rushed to Delhi and laid bare all the details of the heinous conspiracy before FA Ahmed, the President of India, who was shocked to learn about such development in his home state. He knew me from my childhood and was also aware of my service records.

Later on, Dinesh Goswami, then a Congress MP and a close friend of mine, told me that the President immediately sent for Om Mehta, then the union minister of state for home and directed him not to dispose of any such proposal sent from Assam without consulting him. I was also informed that subsequently Bipin Pal Das, the then union deputy minister of foreign affairs was associated with such consultation by the President and in the process, Bipin Pal Das rescued quite a few officers from such humiliation and utter ruination. As such, these conspirators had to wait for few more years to settle the score.

The Emergency had turned the heads of number of politicians and Lakhimpur was no exception. Some criminals of the district, particularly one Kasem Ali of Laluk, were fully exploiting the patronage received from one of the favourite deputy minister of the CM. This minister hailing from this district was throwing his weight about and trying to demonstrate that he was the supreme power in running the administration of this district. Kasem was a notorious dacoit of the district prospering under the patronage of this minister. Obviously, the Sub Inspector (SI) of the local police outpost was favourably disposed to Kasem so that he did not have to incur the displeasure of this Minister who had also assured him of his protection for favour shown to Kasem. On the other hand, public complaints were pouring in against Kasem. Laluk OP was under the jurisdiction of North Lakhimpur PS. So the OC of North Lakhimpur PS was directed to raid the house of Kasem, and arrest him. Not only he was arrested but huge quantity of looted goods were also recovered from his house and three illegal migrants from Bangladesh working as agricultural labour were also arrested from his house. That is to say, he was harbouring foreign nationals coming without valid travel documents—a serious crime under the Foreigners Act, 1946. Despite all the political pressure, Kasem Ali was sent up for trial in the court while the I/C of Laluk OP was transferred out of Laluk. So, the wrath was directed against me with a threat to transfer me within 24 hours. On the other hand, the image of the district police became brighter in public esteem.

Those who tried to get me dismissed summarily, did not refrain from causing pinpricks of sorts by creating some other problems. One particular incident is still vivid in my memory.

The state government had banned inter-district movement of paddy and rice, apparently to prevent artificial scarcity. This called for setting up few check-gates. Because of shortage of police force, these gates had to be manned by Home Guards. The contingent of HGs placed at the disposal of the police department, was under the control of the DIGP, Border who was responsible for obtaining the necessary monthly sanction from the finance department for drawing the wages of the HGs. The HGs deployed under me had not received their wages for more than three months, mainly because of the apathetic attitude betrayed by the DIGP, whose only purpose seemed to be causing embarrassment to me, if not dismissal from the service.

Meanwhile, the boys were practically starving. The concomitant spurt in cases of robbery in areas where the aforesaid check-gates were set up, roused my suspicion. After careful investigation of these cases of robbery, it transpired that some of the HGs manning the check-gates were involved in these cases along with some professional criminals. All the arrested HGs frankly confessed that they had no other way out than what they did. Even the grocers had refused to sell anything to them any more on credit. Already they owed substantial amount to the shopkeepers. Their credibility was totally lost.

I immediately got in touch with the DIGP, Border and the Dy Secretary, home department and I was assured that the problem would be solved within a week; but even after two weeks, nothing materialised despite my repeated telephonic requests! Meanwhile, another HG was apprehended by members of the public while trying to forcibly take away some foodstuff from a shop. This time, I lost my patience and having seen through the ugly game being played by these two officers, I dashed off a "Crash" WT message to the following functionaries : PPS to the CM/Chief Secretary/IGP/Home Secretary/ Finance Secretary/Commandant General of Home Guards and DIGP, Border. Mincing no matter, I described the real situation and proposed to disembody the entire squad of HGs placed at my disposal unless their wages were released within 48 hours. It was also pointed out that in such an eventuality, all the check-gates would have to be closed down.

The mesage was sent about 10 am. By 11 am, I received two frantic telephone calls—one from the DIGP(B) and the other from the Dy Secy, Home, with a request not to disembody the HGs and further informing me that action was being taken to release their dues. The Letter of Credit for drawing their dues was received by about 1 pm instead of the '48 hours' time limit set by me! Such was the nature of welfare being promoted during the much-hyped Emergency!

The discomfiture caused by such frequent pinpricks may only be imagined rather than described in black and white. Anyway, the Lakhimpur chapter was now coming to an end. The short stay there for little over a year was, however, quite enjoyable. It was made all the more pleasant for having the privilege of hosting late Dr. Bhupen Hazarika on quite a few occasions, the one being for well over a month when he was filming a Hindi feature film for Arunachal government at the instance of President F A Ahmed. This time, Ms. Kalpana Lazmi was also my guest for over a week. Those were the days of real fun and frolick as it was bound to be so in company of Bhupenda whom I used to address as "Daju". I was also glamourised as I was given by Bhupenda to play a major role in the aforesaid film (*Mera Dharam Mera Ma*). Thus, the days of distress were transformed into days of real fun, albeit much to the disappointment of my detractors marking time for more opportune moment to cause my ruination.

The capital of Assam was transferred from Shillong to Guwahati in 1974 in hot haste. CM Sarat Sinha was dwarfed by the shrewd, dexterous leadership of Capt WA Sangma, the first CM of Meghalaya. Sinha was allowed no elbow room to bargain for any concession as in the case of Chandigarh, the capital of both, Punjab and Haryana. The Secretariat of Assam government had to be accommodated in couple of warehouses at Dispur, the present site of Assam's permanent capital.

Late Dharmananda Das, the Chief Secretary, Late LBK Dey, the IGP and humble self, were the first batch of officers to be seated in the new secretariat. With assistance from Dharmananda Das and active help from the Punjab Governor, late Mahendramohan Choudhury who sent 200 rose plants from Chandigarh, I had the rare privilege of raising the first-ever rose garden at Dispur.

The stay at North Lakhimpur had presented many opportunities for angling in river Subansiri and river Semen. In fact, near the Semen, to be precise at Semenchapori, I had to set up a Border Outpost for preventing encroachment by Arunachal. This provided ample opportunities for angling in uncharted waters with the result that catches of various size ranging from 1 kg to more than 10 kg in weight were plenty to the delight of my company which included Tarun Choudhury and late Kanak Bordoloi, the famous footballer. Even games were plenty in the nearby jungles of the foothills. But when I revisited the area in 2004, the area was converted into a small township and both the banks of the river and the river bed were being mined commercially for collecting boulders, thereby totally divesting the area of its rich natural heritage. Jungles had disappeared and huge trucks of Second World War vintage were crisscrossing the river for collection of boulders. Assam government did not seem to be intent on preventing encroachment by Arunachal and Arunachal on its part betrayed total lack of concern for conserving the eco-system. Somebody's faces were brightened at the cost of darkening the face of Mother Earth ! However, the trips upstream of Subansiri in motor boat owned by Peter Castle, the Superintendent of the Dwijoo Valley Tea Company, were more thrilling. (The Lower Subansiri Hydel Dam, a highly controversial project, is being presently constructed in this area). Peter Castle had rescued hundreds of marooned villagers during the devastating flood caused by the earthquake of 15 August, 1950. One of Peter's prize possession is a personal letter written to him by PM Pt Nehru in recognition of the great service rendered by him. After this earthquake, the topography of the entire Assam valley had undergone very adverse changes with most of the river beds including the Brahmaputra becoming shallower. This particular phenomenon has contributed most to extending the flood-prone areas as also the frequency of flood with no scientific solution of the problem as yet in sight. Rather largescale deforestation, both in the plains and the hills, has further aggravated the situation with large number of people being uprooted every year from their habitats.

Meanwhile tons of water had flown down the Subansiri and the ambience was one of conflict on the issue of constructing the hydel project at Gerukamukh over the Subansiri by the the NHPC. The Krisak Mukti Sangram Samiti (KMSS) headed by Akhil Gogoi has declared an all-out war against this project on the issue of environmental disasters likely to follow the raising of a dam of high altitude at an earthquake prone area across the Subansiri. The raging debate over constructing a dam in a seismologically sensitive area, has so far yielded no conclusive findings, although CM Tarun Gogoi has announced his uncompromising determination for going ahead with the implementation of the project in defiance of the issues raised against the project. To an amateur like me without even an iota of technical knowledge, it seems that the crux of the debate centres round:

1. the safety of the dam vis a vis an earthquake like that of 1950;
2. while refraining from any observation on the technical aspect of the issue, one is inclined to believe that the issue of adverse downstream impacts offers valid reasons for largescale apprehensions.

Such apprehensions have emanated from the devastations caused by the release of huge volume of water from the Kureshi dam in Bhutan, the Kopili dam in Central Assam and the Ranganadi dam in Arunachal. Many villages in Lower Assam, Central Assam and Upper Assam are standing face to face with total extinction as a result of these unforeseen crises. Nor the government has come forward to explain what preventive measures have been contemplated to prevent further damages so that public apprehensions may be allayed—let alone the commencement of the process for preventive measures. After consulting some technical experts close to me, I am inclined to believe that the reduction of the height of these dams coupled with flood control measures would have reduced the possibility of recurrence of disasters of aforementioned nature; but sheer greed for generating more energy by the entrepreneurs bent upon pocketing highest possible earning/profit, had prevented them from considering such corrective measures. Briefly speaking, a multi-purpose project instead of generating hydel power only could have possibly soothed the injured feelings of the people. Besides, engineers may be experts for construction of dams; but certainly they are not experts on socio-environmental impacts on the downstream, likely to result from such projects. Still worse, it transpires from some of the Press reports that the NHPC did not lag behind in respect of hoodwinking the public on some vital issues either. I am worried that the authorities and the agitationists have failed to adopt a rational approach to such a sensitive issue and the issue of drawing political mileage has been rather uppermost. Anyway, this controversy centering round the Subansiri dam has surfaced after I left North Lakhimpur 36 years back.

Not because of the threat of the above-mentioned deputy minister but because of my personal request, home minister Hiteswar Saikia was kind enough to transfer me to Guwahati—of course to a non-cadre post. The post, however, carried a special pay of Rs. 300/-. In other words, I was kicked upstairs and once more placed under the inspiring leadership of Lala Dey who was then heading the Directorate of HGs and Civil Defence.

Suddenly, democratic rule had become an anathema. The adverse fallouts of the Emergency were discernible everywhere in the administration. CM Sarat Sinha was highly intoxicated with the heady brew of unlimited, also unprecedented, powers the Emergency gave him. The worship of 'personality cult' had become the order of the day. There was a rat race for cultivating the patronage of Indira Gandhi who behaved like the uncrowned Empress of India. In this race, Devakanta Barua, the then President of the AICC, broke all records by publicly announcing that "India is Indira and Indira is India"—albeit degenerating himself as a court jester in the esteem of the democratically oriented thinking section of the people throughout the length and breadth of the country. But then, Sarat Sinha also had to prove himself in this race. So he took the desperate step of inviting the AICC for holding its full session at Guwahati in 1976. In normal times, this would have amounted to: "Fools rush in where angles fear to tread"; but these were the Emergency days with no one venturing to question the misuse of government resources for a partisan purpose. Sarat Sinha misused the entire government machinery, including the services of officers, sepoys and Grade IV employees in order to demonstrate before Indira Gandhi his success in managing such a huge affair. The high-handed conduct of the Youth Congress activists was an evil to be reckoned with. Besides government vehicles, hundreds of other vehicles were requisitioned by the government for the use of those attending the session. Even then, Sinha claimed to be an honest politician as if misuse of the public exchequer was an honest deed. It was a total chaos. Everybody wanted the allotment of his vehicle first and nobody was ready to stand in the queue for his turn to come. In a word, it turned into a 'free for all' affair.

I was placed in charge of allotting the vehicles. Totally dismayed and discomfitted, I took resort to a cunning device: I pretended to telephone Sanjay Gandhi loudly (supposed to exercise supreme power those days) within the hearings of some of the rowdies, apparently appraising Sanjay of the chaos created at the motor vehicle depot. The device yielded the result and everything fell into proper place. The 'personality cult' was evident in its most naked form. One can well imagine the awe in which Sanjay was held in those days. It was rightly apprehended that the conduct of these rowdies, claiming to be Congress activists, was distinct portent to the shape of things taking place all over the country.

However, the session remained memorable for me on another count. A cultural show was held in the last evening of the three-day session. Dr. Bhupen Hazarika performed in the show and sang for about two hours and while rendering one of his own composition, he even cautioned Indira Gandhi against excesses and inaction as well. After the show was over, he accompanied me to my residence and listened till 3 am to his own voice played from the 78 rpm records in my stereogram. That evening, he was thinking loud and observed that he did not command the same voice as he did in the 50s and the 60s, although I, failing to appreciate the nuances, found it difficult to agree with him.

With the excesses of the Emergency in full swing, the session did more harm than good to the image of the Congress in the state as reflected in the general elections held in 1977 and 1978 for the Lok Sabha and the state assembly respectively.

Once again the Intelligence agencies failed Indira Gandhi. According to Intelligence reports, Indira would win handsdown if elections were held. The Emergency was lifted and elections held in 1977. Indira was thrown out of power and Morarji Desai of Janata Party became the Prime Minister. Likewise, Sarat Sinha was thrown out of power in 1978 and Golap Barbara of Janata Party became the CM of Assam. All these debacles were followed by a split in the Congress. Consequently, Sinha parted company with Indira. The Congress was split into Congress (I) and Congress (U). Sinha preferred to remain with Congress (U) and fought the Assembly elections of 1978 under its banner but failed miserably to recapture power. The results of the Assembly elections of 1978 were as shown below:

Party	Seats won
Janata	53
Congress (U)	26
Congress (I)	8
CPI (M)	11
PTCA	4
CPI	5
RCPI	4
SUCI	2
CPI (ML)	1
Independent	12
Total	126

Sinha found it very hard to reconcile to this state of affairs and started working overtime to destabilise the first non-Congress government of Assam. As such, the chair of the CM never proved to be a bed of roses for Barbara, who was leading a coalition government only. However, immediately after, I got my overdue promotion and was posted as DIGP, Border.

Barbara had appointed an Enquiry Committee to determine the misuse of government fund and other government resources for holding the AICC session. Sinha became alert and put himself on overdrive with the soul purpose of causing Barbara's ouster. Jogen Hazarika, the Speaker of the Assembly, was nursing the ambition of becoming the CM of Assam and despite being the Speaker, he failed to maintain a neutral position; rather got involved in narrow political manouvering in defiance of all democratic norms followed in respect of functioning of the Speaker. Hazarika and Sinha also manipulated the withdrawal of CPM's support to Barbara ministry. Barbara resigned and Hazarika was sworn in as the CM.

Dr. Ranjit Sabhapandit has listed, inter alia, the following factors (*Amar Asom*, 16/17 January, 2013) as the causes of the ouster of Barbara ministry:

Dr. Sabhapandit has pointed out three direct and three indirect factors contributing to the fall of the Barbara government. I entirely agree with his assessment, although I would like to add one more factor in due course. The direct factors mentioned by Dr Sabhapandit are as follows:

1. Barbara was intending to nationalise the plywood industry as it was responsible for large-scale deforestation of Assam's rich forests. This had sounded the alarm bell for the Birla group. For obvious reason, this group opposed Barbara's move and promoted the cause of Jogen Hazarika and his supporters with necessary assistance.
2. During Sinha's tenure, one Motilal Singh, hailing from Makum, had practically acquired monopoly rights over the business of country liquor; nobody else could expect to get a permit in this business. This man had tried to promote Jogen

Hazarika as the leader of the legislative party with his money power. On the other hand, Barbara, after assuming power, had evicted this liquor baron from almost all his liquor shops. So, this leaseholder went against Barbara and spent a huge amount of money to help dissidents like Hazarika, Gogoi, Mazumdar and the Jalan Group, thereby reinforcing the disidence within Barbara's Party.

3. Barbara's socialist programmes were causing worries to the owners of big mill and business houses. They were worried about losing their respective monopolies. So, they helped the dissident group so that Barbara could be ousted.

Indirect causes cited by Dr Sabhapandit are as follows:

1. Barbara was very worried about the grave implications of illegal migration and in the interest of Assam and the Assamese, he had contemplated some special measures. During its long tenure of rule, Congress had encouraged such infiltration for enriching its vote bank. In 1975 when the Emergency was in force, the Union government had issued instructions on 20 August 1975 to Assam government to take legal action against the alien citizens and deport them. But CM took no action on the matter. The students of Assam were also raising demands for the expulsion of the illegal migrants and Indira Gandhi had assured them of taking necessary action in this context. The Union government vide its letter no GOI MHA 14011/16/75-111 dt. 20 August 1975, had directed the Assam government to delete the names of the alien citizens from the ERs. Surprisingly, CM Sinha willingly remained silent about the issue. He had apprehended that 25 MLAs of the minority community, might turn against him if he took action as directed.

   Other ministers of his cabinet also preferred to remain silent. Sinha also directed that the elections to Lok Sabha of 1977, should be held on the basis of the ERs of 1971, thereby converting overnight lakhs of alien citizens into Indian voters. But Barbara, after coming to power, took resort to the Union government's instruction of 1975 and directed to delete the names of the alien voters from the ERs for holding the by-election to the Mangaldoi LS seat whereupon Congress (U), Congress (I) and the left Parties raised a hue and cry and created confusion in the minds of the people. Sarat Sinha went to Delhi and alleged that Indian citizens were being harassed by the Barbara government and demanded his dismissal. Thus, Barbara's position was made very shaky by the Opposition parties and the dissidents of his own party and Barbara had to ultimately resign.

2. Barbara had also appointed an 'Enquiry Committee' to determine the extent of misuse of government resources while holding the AICC session at Guwahati. The Committee concluded its enquiry within a month and half and in its findings, pointed out that Sinha was instrumental in misusing government fund to the tune of twenty lakh rupees. Sinha went all out to ensure the fall of Barbara government before the findings of the committee could be placed before the Assembly and in order to ensure this, Jogen Hazarika and the Janata dissidents were encouraged to hasten the fall of Barbara's government.
3. The anti-Assamese lobby of Bangladesh had also conspired to destabilise Barbara's government. The pro-Bangladeshi lobby exercising tremendous influence in Assam politics, had also joined the dissidents so that their ulterior communal motive could materialise.

In any case, I am inclined to believe that the ouster of Barbara was a part of a bigger game plan for promoting the causes of fundamentalist expansion as would be proved subsequently.

In the long run, it would transpire that irreparable damages had already been done. The decline in the credibility of the administration had become a constant source of irritation for the thinking section of the people. This crisis of confidence seems to have emanated from two factors. Firstly, healthy democratic traditions were yet to develop. The phenomenon of Lalbahadur Shastri's resignation had been a drop in the ocean. Lal Krishna Advani's alleged involvement in the demolition of the Babri Masjid, betrays a feudal mindset as if RSS is the only protector of Hinduism. Likewise, in Assam, the AASU activists consider themselves to possess the monopoly for loving Assam and her people as if nobody else is concerned with Assam's welfare. Such fascist outlook has put a heavy premium on national integration. Secondly, the sense of belonging to the cause of national welfare at large, is gradually receding to the background. In a welfare state, the dedication of the administration to the welfare of the people at large is a sine qua non which has been becoming conspicuous by its absence. The politicisation of every segment of the administration has not only given rise to vested interests but has also caused the surfacing of all the baneful effects on the morale of the people and in the process, both transparency and accountability of the administration have been put on very heavy premium. The concept of civil servant's political neutrality has been reduced to sheer mockery.

The presence and the absence of transparency and accountability in the administration are the distinctive features for determining the character of the administration. How far the operation of the RTI Act will deliver the goods, is a matter of anybody's guess. Because today in India, democracy is functioning as the umbrella whereunder neo-aristrocracy and unscrupulous politicians are prospering—both legally and illegally.

British India could not boast of any elected representative in the true sense. So, unlike in their own country, the British rule in India was neither responsible nor accountable to the people. Eye-wash measures taken from time to time in the wake of the Freedom Movement could not protect the interests of the people whereas despite being a monarchy, the Magna Carta and the Bill of Rights, had ensured over the centuries the accountability of the rulers in Great Britain as also a meaningful role of the Opposition which, in its turn, had resulted in rational control of state's resources and political powers. No government in great Britain could have afforded to misuse the public exchequer for holding its party session as Sarat Sinha had done. Accountability prevents abuse of power, thereby keeping open the way to better order of state affairs. Conversely, the absense of accountability in public affairs, opens the floodgate for irresponsible conduct, abuse of authority and financial irregularities as has been evident in our undemocratic democracy. Along with this emerges the predominance of black money resulting not only in an economic dichotomy but also in a dictatorial control of public resources with professional and social ethics degraded to non-entity. Gullible public servants become law unto themselves as if accountability and moral values are sheer anachronisim. Acquisition of creature comforts has obviously become order of the day in the land of Buddha, Gandhi, Swami Vivekananda, Sri Aurobindo etc. As if he had personally witnessed Indira's and Sarat Sinha's Emergency days, Sri Aurobindo wrote in "Ideal of Human Dignity" about the modern politicians as follows "--- what he does usually represent is all the average pettiness, selfishness, egoism, self-deception that is about him and these he represents well enough as well as a great deal of mental incompetence and moral conventionality, timidity and pretence. ------" Did he foresee the shape of things to come?

Rajmohan Gandhi, a grandson of both Mahatma Gandhi and C. Rajagopalachari, a close associate of Gandhiji, while writing "Rajaji A Life", a biography of Rajaji, has quoted from Rajaji's personal diary as follows; "We all ought to know that Swaraj will not at once or, I think even for a long time to come, be better government or greater happiness for the people. Elections and their corruptions, injustice, and the power and tyranny of wealth and inefficiency of administration will make a hell of life as soon as freedom is given to us. Men will look regretfully back to the old regime of comparative justice, and efficient, peaceful, more or less honest administration. The only thing gained will be that as a race we will be saved from dishonour and subordination." What a foresight and how prophetic !

The executive being the repository of public trust, it totally betrayed this trust and Assam Police was no exception. Indira's Emergency was a classic case of compulsion destroying co-operation. Hobbes's twin Fear was evident in all walks of life, be it timely running of trains or regular, timely attendance in government offices but it all turned out to be a temporary phase!

Looking back, I cannot but feel that these were the hallmarks of Indira's Emergency!

8

As DIGP Border

Dulal Barua was an indomitable student leader of yore. He became very famous and popular during the State Language Movement because of the aggressive role he played in the context of this movement. He was a very hilarious character. He had represented the Jorhat LA Constituency for many years. In the course of time, he became a very close friend of mine. He was the seniormost minister in Barbara cabinet. Though he held the PWD portfolio, he did not induldge in corrupt practices.

Dulal came to see me almost immediately after becoming a minister. He straightaway requested me to shoulder the responsibility of the Border Police Organisation so that the problem of transborder illegal migration threatening to wipe out the identity of the Assamese people, could be dealt with a strong hand. He also assured me that the government would support me strongly.

The organisation sanctioned and financed by the union government for implementing the PIP scheme, was converted into Border Police Organisation after the liberation of Bangladesh.

Vested interests had even tried to wind up the entire PIP scheme on the plea that there would be no more Pak threat from across the border. The very idea sent a shiver down our spine and many of us became really panicky. A team of officers led by Ghanakanta Medhi, the then DIGP, CID (Then there was no SB and no DIGP, SB. The Intelligence Branch was under the DIGP, CID.) waited upon CM Mahendramohan Choudhury and convinced him that the situation had, in fact, worsened now and that it was fraught with severely adverse consequences if the process of detecting illegal migrants from across the border was halted. After good deal of discussions, the CM agreed to retain the current arrangements and the organisastion's new nomenclature would be "The Border Police Organisation". My bete noire who was the originator of the plea for scrapping the PIP scheme altogether as also bent upon causing my utter ruination, came to know of the development and the role played by me while talking to the CM. But LBK Dey, the IGP had approved of our move.

I knew that Border Police had a huge police force and a large fleet of vehicles, etc. But these were being utilised for other police duties than the purpose for which the Border Police was being maintained. Even the fund sanctioned for Border Police was spent for building residences of senior police officers. I was very candid with Dulal and told him that if the following conditions were accepted, I would comply with his request.

1. Like the Special Branch, I must have the right to direct correspondence with the government, albeit not keeping the IGP in the dark.
2. All the men and materials sanctioned for the Border Police must be placed at my disposal.
3. I must have full liberty for re-shuffling the set-up. In other words, the power of transferring and posting the non-gazetted staff must rest with me.
4. Adequate fund must be made available for refurbishing the entire set-up which was certainly in a state of decay and fund earmarked for the Border Police must not be diverted to other segments of the police department.

Next morning, a meeting was held in the CM's chamber. Participants were CM Barbara, Dulal Barua, the CS (Paramasivam), the IGP (Pradip Das) and myself. They all agreed with my suggestions excepting that the transfers of SP and DySP would be proposed by the IGP only and that the IGP must get copies of all important correspondences made directly with the government.

Thus, I entered the final phase of my police career with a bang, only to be demolished with the fall of the Janata governments, both at New Delhi and Dispur. But the intervening period was full of events with significant socio--political impacts on the future of Assam. On the other hand, without any premonition in my mind, the final countdown for my total (?) ruination also began.

9

Demands For Three Ds

The first two of the three Ds connote detection and deportation of illegal migrants and the third one means the deletion of the names of these migrants from the Electoral Rolls (ERs). Thus the demand for a correct voters' list divested of the names of alien citizens became a major issue for many decades now.

It did not take me much time for revamping the Border Police. In the process of reshuffling, Inspector Makhan Hazarika was posted to Kharupetia. Few words about Makhan's association with me, may not be out of order.

When I was SDPO at Golaghat, Makhan was a probationary SI of Police at Dergaon PS within my jurisdiction. Both of us represented Golaghat football team in quite a few tournaments. Thus, I came to know him rather closely. But what impressed me most was his honesty and he remained the same Makhan Hazarika till the end. I also came to know about his active resistance to the temptation of bribery. Thus, he earned my respect too. Like many Police, Revenue and Forest officers, highly or lowly placed, he never facilitated the stay of any illegal migrants from Bangladesh or Nepal within his jurisdiction for monetary consideration. His such uncompromising loyalty to the cause of the Assamese people had landed two political heavyweights in serious possibilities of being politically extinct. One of them died prematurely and the other could never get elected again from the Legislative Assembly (LA) constituency concerned. They were late Ramesh Saharia, Education Minister for a short while, representing Paneri LA constituency and Syeda Anowara Taimur who had become the CM for about five months, courtesy Indira Gandhi, representing Dalgaon LA constituency, an extremely infiltration prone area where the indigenous people had already been reduced to minority. True, Assam was spared the indignity of Taimur Lung's invasion of unprecedented atrocities against medieval India; but Anowara spared no efforts for matching Taimur Lung's misdeeds when she became the CM for only few weeks. She started imitating the style of Indira Gandhi! She boasted of breaking the backbone of the legendary Assam movement way back in 1980-81, although the movement was yet to reach its peak subsequently.

In 1975 after the Emergency was enforced, the union government (home ministry) had sent the following instructions to Assam government as quoted by A B Vajpayee, the External Affairs Minister on the floor of the Parliament on 2 November 1978: "It has come to the notice of the Election Commission from time to time that large-scale inclusion of foreign nationals in the electoral rolls, specially in the north-eastern region, has been taking place."

"In August, 1975, the Ministry of Home Affairs instructed all the state governments that the state criminal department may be instructed to take immediate steps to check the electoral rolls, and if they discover the names of foreigners in the rolls, the fact may be brought to the notice of the concerned Electoral Registration Officers for getting such names deleted from the electoral rolls."

"The Election Commission has also issued instructions to the electoral officers of the states and union territories concerned that if it is found that a large number of foreigners have managed to get their names registered in the electoral rolls, recourse should be had to provisions of Section 22 of the Representation of the People Act of

1950 for getting the names of such persons deleted from the electoral rolls on the ground that they are not Indian citizens."

Instructions as mentioned by Vajpayee in his above quoted statement were issued by the MHA on 20 August 1975, when the National Emergency was in operation in full swing. The Assam government despite having fully supported the ongoing Emergency not only failed to take full advantage of the situation arising out of the proclamation of Emergency but also instead, totally hushed up the above mentioned circular issued by the MHA. The top Police official (in this case, the DIGP, Border) concerned found it more convenient to look the other way, lest he might incur the displeasure of his provincial Congress bosses. Of course, he was amply rewarded in due course. Nor did the MHA ever follow-up the matter, let alone ensuring the implementation of its own directives. Needless to mention that Assam lost a golden opportunity The Election Commission, as usually, preferred to be an onlooker only.

In fact, the total abdication by the Chief Election Commissioner (CEC) and his apathetic attitude to preparing a correct ERs over the years, were at the root of sustaining the six-year long Assam Movement. The Election Commission despite being a statutory autonomous body, was ever ready to take direction from the Union Government.

10

Assam Movement

Geographical isolation coupled with a sense of deprivation accumulated over the years, has ultimately led to a feeling of alienation. I wonder why the leading political leaders of pre-and post-Independent India could not visualise that such a state of accumulated grievances-- both real and imaginary—might create serious problems, particularly the new generation might not silently agree to such negligence for ever! A very defiant attitude on the part of the new generation was simply a logical conclusion in the background of socio-economic developments elsewhere in the country. An oft-repeated lamentation, if not a charge, that Assam never gets her dues without resorting to agitation whether it is a university, or an oil refinery or a bridge over the Brahmaputra or the extension of the broad gauge railway line, etc., had already started doing the rounds. The handicaps confronted by BP Chaliha in implementing the PIP scheme coupled with roles played by Golam Osmani and Zahirul Islam, two cabinet colleagues of Golap Barbora in respect of pulling down the first ever non-Congress government of Assam, were certainly not conducive to building up an atmosphere of mutual trust and understanding for addressing the burning problems of Assam dispassionately and Osmani's subsequent role in propping up a most communal government after independence in Assam, did not help matters either. In fact, these political manipulations did accelerate the appearance of Prafulla Kumar Mahanta and Bhrigu Kumar Phukan, two eminent student leaders of 70s and 80s, on the scene; but actually so many other factors had gone into the building up of the historic Assam Movement. Serious and meaningful attention to these factors was overdue which was, however, not forthcoming from Delhi. It is not considered necessary to go into the details of such neglect of Assam's cause in this discourse aimed at informing my countrymen how a whole people of the Indian mosaic are being reduced to a non-entity by hordes of Bangladeshi infiltrators without attracting the notice of the rest of the country. Having realised the danger looming large on the horizon, the indigenous people cutting across the line of caste, creed, language and religion, responded spontaneously to the appeals of the AASU leaders and came out to the streets with their three demands of 'detection, deportation and deletion'.

Tribals, non-tribals, Hindus, Muslims, Assamese, non-Assamese and the tea-labour community—all participated in the movement without hesitation and this was evident from the list of those who became martyrs for the cause of the movement. However, one doubts whether the AASU leaders had really understood the raison d'etre of the backing they received as their subsequent betrayal of the cause of the movement confirmed such doubts. The mass uprising attracted the attention of the world media, albeit much to the chagrin of Indira Gandhi, her Congress (I) camp followers and of course, the leftists.

The ignition point for imparting tremendous momentum to the movement was triggered off by the statutory need for holding a by-election to the Mangaldoi Lok Sabha constituency following the death of its MP Hiralal Patawari. Patawari died on 28 March 1979 and the Election Commission issued the notification for revising the ERs of the constituency on 27 April 1979. Objections and claims were invited by the Commission in the process of revising the ERs. On the strength of the MHA's above-quoted instructions, the Border Police Organisation swang into action to weed out the names of the foreigners from the ERs of the constituency after obtaining approval from the CM Barbara. The Chief Secretary RS Paramasivam stood solidly behind the entire operation. Of course, subsequently both Paramasivam and the DIGP, Border (who was the present scribe) had to suffer very heavily after the fall of the Barbara government for the patriotic manner they had displayed during the entire operation. Premkanta Mahanta was the senior staff officer of the DIGP, Border. His untiring efforts contributed volubly to the success of the operation. AASU activists also came out in thousands for filing objections against the foreigners whose names were included in the draft ERs. Nor did the members of the general public lag behind. The whole atmosphere was practically electrified.

Incidentally, though quite a few volumes have been written on the Assam movement, there have been lapses in respect of quoting the correct number of objections filed during this operation excepting that Sri Premkanta Mahanta who, having directly dealt with the matter, had subsequently written a postscript to the Assam movement and was careful in quoting correct data. His book, "*Rajbhaganar Para Kal Thokaloi*", written in Assamese not only gives a vivid account of how the movement originated but also the correct statistics. As the operation for identifying the alien voters picked up quick momentum, a hue and cry was raised by the Congress (I) leaders from Assam as well as from outside Assam and complaints were made to the CEC that many Indian citizens were being wrongly identified as foreign citizens. Tremendous pressure was brought to bear upon the CEC who ultimately succumbed to the pressure and called a halt to the operation. But before the operation was postponed, already 47658 objections were filed and the quasi-judicial process for disposing them of as per provisions of the ROP Act had commenced.

Of these 47,658 objections, 36,780 were sustained. That is to say, 77,17% of the objections were found to be correct. As such, the complaint of large-scale harassment to Indian citizens falls flat on the ground. Also one will do well to note that all the criminal cases sent up by the Police for trial in courts of law, do not end in conviction. Besides, the fact of the Police being misled and at times arresting innocent people during the course of investigating criminal cases, has also to be taken into account before bringing wild allegations. The margin for human error must invariably be admitted. The entire issue was given a communal colour and insinuations were made that Muslims were being harassed. On the other hand, it was never considered that 10,878 objections were rejected after proper hearing despite the fact that the AROs concerned could have upheld these 10,878 objections also if they had any malafide and communal intention.

Meanwhile, the Lok Sabha was dissolved on 23 August 1979, thereby entailing fresh elections to the Lok Sabha. Again commenced the statutory process of revising the ERs. Having witnessed the success of the operation in case of the Mangaldoi Lok Sabha Constituency, Chief Minister Barbara passed an order for extending the operation of identifying foreign voters in another 81 Assembly constituencies, thereby not only hastening the fall of his own ministry but also blowing up the hornet's nest once more.

It will be in fitness of things to scrutinise how did the AASU react to these fast developments:

In their original charter of demands formulated in the early seventies of the last century, AASU had focussed on the dangerous consequences of the torrential influx of people from outside Assam into the state and there was no specific mention about alien infiltration. Meanwhile, in March 1979, Prafulla Kumar Mahanta and Bhrigu Kumar Phukan were elected president and general secretary of AASU in its Sibsagar session. Late Lalit Rajkhowa, another contemporary AASU leader, was also elected as the adviser of AASU. Some officers of the Border Police Organisation persuaded these AASU leaders to take up the issue of the foreign voters and appealed to them to mobilise the AASU units spread all over the valley for filling objections against the Bangladeshi voters in the wake of the revision of ERs being done by the Election Commission. Their response was positive. The Purbanchaliya Loka Parishad and the Assam Jatiyatabadi Dal had already raised the demand for deletion of lakhs of foreigners' names from the ERs. In its executive committee meeting held on 23 May 1979, AASU criticised the government's weak-kneed policy vis-a-vis the alien infiltrators and the Congress (I)'s policy of appeasing the infiltrators for mere electoral gains. Further, in order to consolidate cross sections of the people in support of its resolution passed in the aforementioned executive committee meeting, AASU convened a joint meeting of the Axom Xahitya Xabha (AXX), Boro Xahitya Xabha (BXX), a few other non-political organisations and all the regional political outfits on 27 June and this is how the All Assam Gana Sangram Parishad (AAGSP) came to be formed as a common platform for the indigenous people of Assam to launch the legendary Assam movement.

Meanwhile, Chief Minister Barbara, not only called upon the youths of Assam to be on guard against the dangerous consequences of foreign infiltration but also appealed to the people of Assam to co-operate with the enumerators of ERs so that only the names of Indian citizens could be enrolled as voters. Barbara's appeal while touching the heart of the people, set in motion the conspiracy of the vested political interests for pulling down his government so that Barbara could not complete the mission of cleansing the ERs of alien voters. Barbara had to ultimately resign on 4 September 1979. After the fall of the Barbara ministry, as many as three short-lived ministries were sworn in but none survived the Assam movement. The Lok Sabha was already dissolved on 23 August 1979 with Charan Singh as the caretaker Prime Minister. While these political dramas were being enacted in quick succession, AASU was organising the people of Assam for the six-year long movement.

The AAGSP was formed on 27 August 1979 under the aegis of AASU and the following organisations joined the AAGSP as its members: AASU/AXX/Axom Yubak Samaj/Purbanchaliya Loka Parishad/ Axom Jatiyatabadi Dal/Assam Jatiyatabadi Yuva-Chhatra Parishad/ Plains Tribal Council of Assam/All Assam Tribal Sangha and Young Lawyers' Forum.

Though the following organisations did not formally become members of the AAGSP, they extended their full support to the demands of 'detection, deportation and deletion (deletion of names of foreigners from the ERs): The Banga Bhasiya Assamiya Samaj/ All Assam State Karmachari Parishad/All Assam College Teachers' Association/The Tea Garden Workers Union/The State Electricity Board Employees Association/All Assam Public Undertakings

Employees Federation/All Assam Bank Employees Parishad/All Assam Non-government Employees Parishad/Assam Unit of All India Sikh Students Federation/Assam Jagrata Mahila Parishad and a few other women organisations, etc. With enlisting the support of so many organisations, AASU succeeded in mobilising the people of the entire Assam valley to stand behind them for solving the vexed problem of unabated transborder infiltration. Meanwhile, the people of Assam valley boycotted the celebration of the Independence Day on 15 August 1979 in response to AASU's call for such a byocott. Prior to this, a 12-hour Assam bandh was successfully observed on 8 June 1979, again at the call of the AASU. Thus AASU was marching ahead from strength to strength: Gradually, the movement spread to the grass root level with all the students of all the colleges and schools of Assam valley responding to the call of the AASU executive committee. AASU had its units all over the valley in almost all the schools and colleges. Almost all the constituent units of the AAGSP also had their units all over Assam and as such, it became easier to form regional/ local units of the AAGSP, thereby further boosting the morale of the Assamese people in general and the student community in particular. Then followed a series of agitational programmes, the details of which might not interest readers. Suffice to mention that neither the successive state governments nor the Central Government tried to appreciate the agonies and apprehensions of the native people of Assam. Rather on the other hand, unprecedented repressive measures were unleashed on the people for suppressing the movement with Anwara Taimur's ministry topping the list in respect of committing inhuman atrocities, resulting in the recollection by the people, of the inhuman atrocities committed on Assam during the Burmese invasion in the first quarter of the 19th century.

However, the catalyst for generating a mass upsurge surfaced in the shape of the notification for elections to the Lok Sabha to be held by the end of 1979. The operation for identifying alien voters in 81 Assembly constituencies was in progress along with the process of filing objections against the Bangladeshi nationals who had managed to enroll themselves as voters. During this second phase of the operation, more than 5,83,000 objections were filed against suspected Bangladeshi nationals in addition to 47,658 objections already filed in the first phase of the operation. The vested interests depending for their political survival on the support of the Bangladeshi voters did not remain silent either. As already mentioned above, tremendous pressure was applied on the CEC to suspend the operation for identifying alien voters by the Congress (I), the Congress (U), the CPM and all other leftist parties. The CEC, succumbing to the pressure, made a complete volte-face and not only called a halt to deleting the names of alien voters from the ERs but also announced that Section 22 of the ROP Act which empowers the Election Registration Officers to delete the names of foreigners from the ERs on their own, would remain inoperative until the elections were over. On 18 Setptember 1979, the State Government issued its most controversial press-note no. 88 as already discussed elsewhere.

The CEC's aforesaid announcement as published in press note no. 88, generated sharp reactions from all sections of people and a "Student Movement" ultimately took the shape of a very large, unprecedented mass movement, surpassing even the "Quit India" Movement of 1942 in its intensity and expanse. Students came out of their schools and colleges, women their homes, government, semi-government and non-government employees their offices. They were all determined to prevent this unconstitutional election at any cost. Mass rallies were organised all over the valley, culminating in the huge all-Assam mass rally held at Guwahati on 6 October 1979 attended by people coming from all the districts of the valley, including Karbi Anglong and the NC Hills districts. The mass rally solidified the determination of the Assamese people irrespective of ethnicities, to prevent the elections. The rally was followed by many other agitational programmes, all of which were unusually successful. Still the Central Government and the Congress/Leftist leaders refused to accept the message conveyed by such developments. The government went ahead with making full preparations for holding the elections, thereby turning a blind eye to the gathering clouds. In the face of the defiant attitude of the government, the decision to boycott the elections and prevent the candidates from filing their nomination papers was spontaneous. As the zero hour approached for filing nomination papers, curfew was imposed in some of the district headquarters for enabling the intending candidates to file their nomination papers; but this too, did not succeed in the face of the unprecedented popular uprising excepting that Begum Abida Ahmed, the wife of late Fakhruddin Ali Ahmed, (a former President of India from Assam) succeeded in filing her nomination papers at Barpeta under heavy police escorts led by a senior DIGP. However, fate ordained otherwise: Her nomination papers were rejected by the Returning Officer on some technical ground! No election could be held in the Assam valley while elections were held in the Barak valley for electing two MPs from there. In the Barak valley also the indigenous people boycotted the election. The holding of the mid-term poll in the Barak valley, did not in any way devalue the Assam Movement because the movement did not have any significant impact on the Bengali-speaking people of this valley who constituted the majority. The Assamese people in their thousands violated the curfew orders and thus successfully prevented filing of nomination papers in the Brahmaputra valley and the first phase of the movement came to a successful end. To the credit of the movement leadership, the movement, by and large, remained non-violent despite provocations galore, both official and unofficial. A few sporadic instances of violence were, however, reported, mostly resulting from provocations.

The second phase of the movement commenced on 18 December 1979 with the adoption of the 'public pledge' in public meetings held all over the valley. The said pledge read as reproduced below:

"We pledge today to sacrifice our lives for the national cause of Assam and promise that we will continue to be active participants in the national movement started under the aegis of the AASU and we will save our motherland from the grips of the foreigners and from any other threats that may befall."

Despite the prevention of holding of the mid-term poll, the movement had so far failed to attract attention of the national press and the rest of the country. As such, the movement leadership embarked upon a programme of 'Oil Blockade', having realised that such a step would have an all-India impact, particularly in view of the fact that at that time Assam contributed more than 50% to India's oil production. All the oil installations of the state were blockaded on 27 December 1979 by thousands of men and women. The refineries at Bongaigaon and Barauni (Bihar) were starved of crude oil and both the refineries had to perforce stop production. Of course, the refineries at Digboi and Guwahati were allowed to function on the basis of a revised decision. Assam was even otherwise very unhappy with her 70% of crude oil being refined outside Assam, thereby depriving her of a huge amount of sales tax and employment opportunities. Which is why, the idea of an oil-blockade straightaway caught the imagination of the people. Nor did Assam receive oil-royalty at a fair rate. We, however, need not go into these details here. As calculated earlier, the oil-blockade started begetting front-page coverage for the movement, in the national press.

Meanwhile, anit-socials and the agents of the 'Infiltration Lobby' started communal riots in North Kamrup with many Hindu villages set on fire and numerous killings caused both by the rioters and the security forces. Rape, arson, physical torture, etc., had become the order of the day. On most of the occasions, the movement activists were the targets of both the law and order maintaining agencies and the militant immigrant Muslims. The climax of this chain of events came in the shape of the infamous "Duliajan Massacre". The oil installation at Duliajan was put under virtual siege by the movement forces since 27 December 1979. Having failed to hold the mid-term poll in the valley, the state administration, presently under the President's rule, was smarting under a vindictive attitude to wreak vengeance against the agitationists and was also eager to restore its sagging image before the "North Block". And in the process, Duliajan had to bear the brunt of rehabilitating Dispur in the court of New Delhi.

On 18 January 1980, more than 10,000 picketers were picketing at Duliajan. Such picketing had been continuing at Duliajan since 27 December 1979; but suddenly on the 23rd day of picketing, brute forces were let loose on the unarmed and peaceful picketers who were fired upon by the CRPF personnel without any provocation and warning whatsoever, resulting in the instantaneous death of four picketers and crippling injuries to scores of them. Dr Rabi Mitra was, on this particular day, in charge of the oil installation. The rowdy elements from amongst the picketters killed Dr Mitra after about an hour of the firing incident in a retaliatory step, which was however, later condemned by the movement leadership. It was evident that the situation in Assam was deteriorating day by day with no signs of abatement on any of the relevant fronts. In fact, non-violent leadership was under constant threat of being replaced by militant leadership. A militant section of AASU leadership had even betrayed the tendency of taking recourse to armed militancy during this period itself and the idea of receiving training in use of firearms and explosives was no more treated as a mere facet of adventurous (or misadventurous?) romanticism. It may not be out of place to mention here that the United Liberation Front of Assam (ULFA) was born, more out of frustration and disappointment caused by New Delhi's apathetic attitute to all the legitimate demands and dues of Assam in preference to partisan causes like patronising "Infiltration Lobby", piping out Assam's crude oil to Bihar and the likes. In fact, Delhi had prepared the ground for rise of militant insurgency as Lenin had most aptly once observed that "Society prepares the crime and the criminals commit it". For correct appraisal of the situation, it is absolutely neassary to clearly appreciate the distinction between secessionist militancy and democratically vocal reaction against deprivations and injustices perpetrated for decades on end.

Meanwhile, dramatic changes took place at Delhi and Indira Gandhi came back to power on 14 January 1980. Immediately after assuming power, she met the AASU leaders at New Delhi on 2 February 1980; but she, too, failed to rise above narrow partisan considerations. AASU's demands placed before her included, inter alia, the following salient features:

1. Detection & deportation of foreigners.
2. Deletion of foreigners' names from the ERs before any election is held in Assam.
3. Constitutional safeguards to the people of Assam.
4. Issuance of identity cards to all Indian citizens in Assam.
5. Rejection of all citizenship certificates issued by West Bengal and Tripura Governments for use in Assam and transferring the power of granting citizenship from the states to the Centre, etc.

AASU further demanded that for the purpose of identifying the foreign nationals/voters, the National Register of Citizens, 1951 and the ERs of 1952, must be used.

Indira Gandhi totally failed to appreciate the genuine apprehensions of the Assamese youths and did not agree to the use of the National Register of Citizens, 1951 (NRC) for the purpose of identification. Besides, she insisted upon 1971 to be the cut-off date for the purpose of identification, which the AASU delegation refused to accept. On the whole, the talks failed. Then Zail Singh, the then Union Home Minister, held another round of discussion with AASU at Guwahati on 22 February 1980, but that talk too failed to remove the impasse. Instead of solving the problem, Indira Gandhi went all-out to politicise it and evinced more interest in persuading the student leaders to lift the oil-blockade! In this background, the third round of discussion held on March 7 & 8, 1980 at New Delhi also failed. This time, the AASU and the AAGSP delegation had submitted a draft agreement incorporating all the salient points as mentioned above for acceptance by the Centre; but the latter preferred to reject it without assigning any reason thereof. As a result, the movement further intensified.

Having failed to persuade the movement leadership to cry a halt to the movement, Mrs Gandhi turned her attention this time to measures, which might weaken the movement. In other words, measures for sabotaging the cause of the movement as well as for blackmailing the movement leadership were resorted to:

Firstly, Subrato Mukherjee, the Youth Congress leader of West Bengal organised a week-long Assam Blocakade with the slogan-- "No oil, no food" as most of the essential food items were being imported for the entire North-east from other states of the country. Both, Jyoti Basu, the Chief Minister of West Bengal, and Indira Gandhi hereself defended the cause of the "Assam Blockade". Jyoti Basu even went to the extent of ridiculing the movement as a "picnic" while Indira Gandhi did not hesitate to brand it as communal and secessionist, thereby, of course, helping nobody's cause in the final analysis. Secondly, efforts were afoot, obviously at Indira Gandhi's behest, for imparting an "anti-Bengali" and "anti-Muslim" image to the movement. The result of this move was the emergence of the All Assam Minority Students' Union (AAMSU) mostly comprising Bengali-speaking Muslim and Hindu youths. The intention was clear. To drive a wedge between the Assamese and Bengali people of the State, thereby reviving bitter memories of the past. The All Assam Minority Students' Union (AAMSU) was formed in a meeting held on 29th & 30th March, 1980 at Jaleswar, a predominantly Bengali Muslim area known for harbouring Bangladeshi Muslim infiltrators and of late, reported to be organising armed Muslim militant outfits under the patronisation of local non-Assamese Muslim politicians. However, the AAMSU straightaway got into business by opposing the Assam movement and the policy of eviction from government land and forest reserves/VGRs/PGRs, etc.

Thirdly, with a view to bulldoze the movement, entire Assam excepting the district of N. C. Hills, was declared a "Disturbed Area" on 5 April 1980, thereby bringing the Assam Disturbed Area Act into operation. Also the Armed Forced (Special Powers) Act was made overactive as if the Assam movement was a secessionist movement! National leaders like AB Vajpayee, George Fernandes, Chandrashekhar, etc., condemned this action in no uncertain terms. The state government. employees also actively protested against the declaration by resorting to Satyagraha, while Indrajit Barua, a reputed civil engineer with a very strong public spirit, filed a writ petition in the High Court challenging the validity of the declaration. The High Court passed a stay order on 7 April 1980.

Having failed in all efforts at bamboozling, Indira Gandhi ultimately visited Guwahati on 12 April 1980 and this time she harped upon a humane approach to the problem and stuck to 1971 as the cut-off date for the purpose of detection while the movement leadership remained unyielding. Mrs Gandhi did refer to some international obligations, keeping in mind the clauses of Indira-Mujib Pact, which she had signed without ever taking the country's Parliament or the people into confidence. However, it must be admitted to her credit that in the late evening, the same day, she did have a little rethinking after having secret discussions with the high officials including the present scribe. The Governor LP Singh also participated in the discussion with a positive approach. It was decided to place a fresh proposal before the AASU executive committee, which was meeting the next day. The fresh proposal offered either 31 December 1966 or 1/1/1967, inter alia, as the cut-off date for the purpose of identification. This author as directed, met the AASU executive committee members the next day along with his staff officer Premkanta Mahanta at 10 am., but failed to convince the executive committee about the reasonableness of the new proposal and the benefits that would have accrued therefrom. They simply would not budge an inch from 1951 as the cut-off date. If accepted, 1967 as cut-off date would not have harmed Assam's cause because the PIP scheme was in full operation till 1969 and the success of this scheme hardly needs any elaboration. We failed to understand this adamant attitude at that time; but as the years rolled on and with the unfolding of the subsequent political scenario, it became crystal clear that the then AASU leaders had a deeper design in lengthening the Assam movement: It was obvious that with a settlement arived at, there would be fresh elections in Assam and if an agreement was made in 1980 or before these student leaders attained the age of 25, they would not be constitutionally qualified to contest in the elections. As such, the movement had to be continued until they were eligible to contest. In fact, as it transpired subsequently, the question of solving the foreign infiltration problem was never uppermost in their mind. They had led the entire people of Assam up the garden path and once they came to power, they dropped the issue like a hot potato on one or the other plea. There were other adverse fallouts also from the rejection of 1967 as cut-off date in 1980: Firstly, the catastrophic election of 1983 would not have taken place and secondly, the possibility of passing the controversial IMDT Act in 1983, would not have arisen. Above all, being what she was, Indira Gandhi would have honoured and implemented an agreement if it would have been arrived at in 1980 on the basis of her latest offer whereas the Assam Accord signed in 1985, is yet to be fully implemented, let alone solve the foreigners problem. The same set of student leaders made a turn of 180 degrees and accepted 1971 as the cut-off date while signing the Assam Accord on the night of 14 August 1985! For, they had by then attained the age of 25 to make themselves eligible for contesting in the elections. What followed next, is the historic letting down of an entire people! Still more mysterious, if not intriguing, is the fact that the AAGSP leaders or its executive committee were not taken into confidence while finalising the draft of the Accord. In fact, some of the AAGSP leaders refused to attend the Accord-signing ceremony and the party thrown by Rajiv Gandhi and instead, left for Guwahati by the first available flight.

What has just been highlighted, should suffice to explain why until August 1985, none of the talks held with New Delhi, particularly during Mrs. Gandhi's regime, did not succeed. On the other hand, because of such obduracy generated by absolute self-interests of handful of student leaders, the people of Assam had to undergo untold sufferings and inhuman atrocities for a long period of six years which witnessed all sorts of repressive measures including 'community punitive tax', detention without trial, physical torture, and more than 850 deaths resulting from Police firings besides a few thousand killings caused during the communal riots of 1983.

Having failed in her Guwahati mission, Indira Gandhi took the easy option cf a crackdown on the movement leaders and use of force to lift the oil-blockade. In the third week of April, 1980, many top leaders, including Bhrigu Kumar Phukan, Khanindra Chandra Barua (then in his late 70s), Nibaran Bora, Atul Bora, etc., were put under arrest. Prafulla Kumar Mahanta and Bharat Chandra Narah proved smarter by going underground along with a few others. Efforts were made to break the oil-blockade by use of brute force after clamping down curfew in Guwahati. Both the police and the Army were deployed to do the needful.

Now pause for a moment and see how much Indira's Administration (the State was under President's Rule) was divorced from the ground realities: The day was 20 April 1980. The army and the police had moved in the early morning and taken position as if they were about to launch a large-scale operation against some enemy units or some well-organised insurgent outfits whereas the picketters manning the more than 100-day old oil-blockade were all unarmed volunteers, both male and female, drawn from cross sections of the society. The news of the arrests made the previous night coupled with the promulgation of curfew orders, generated an explosive reaction from the common people already surcharged with intense emotional involvement with the movement. This aspect of the movement was not assessed and the multiple intelligence agencies available to Indira Gandhi, failed either to foresee or having anticipated it, failed to inform Mrs Gandhi and the state administration about the disastrous consequences of a move of the aforesaid nature as was proved by the fate of the curfew orders. There were no leaders as such, nor any organisation to channelise the popular reaction within such a short time. Therefore, one cannot but admit that whatever happened on that fateful morning of 20 April, was nothing but a spontaneous outburst from the common men and women in their lakhs! More than three lakh people collected at Narengi, the site of the oil installations and made a mockery of the curfew orders. The District Magistrate had no other alternative than to withdraw the curfew orders!

With the joining of HC Sarin as the Chief Adviser to the Governor, repressive measures were intensified instead of trying to understand the agonies of the Assamese people. Thousands were arrested and released. Some arrested leaders were transferred to the infamous Bhagalpur jail in Bihar. The government employees also responded to various agitational programmes announced from time to time by AASU and AAGSP and many of them faced punitive measures.

With the formation of the AAMSU, the "foreigners" lobby not only became more courageous but also got organised to start a counter-movement inspired by no less a person than Indira Gandhi herself. Even the state administration came forward to help them by withdrawing curfew orders in Barpeta. They took out mammoth rallies in the districts of Goalpara, Nagaon and Barpeta subdivision. In Barpeta sub-division alone, more than 3,00,000 processionists of foreign origin participated in as many as nine rallies held on 26 April 1980. As mentioned before, the shouting of a "Joy Bangla" slogan, the unfurling of the Bangladesh flag coupled with the display of Sheikh Mujibur Rahman's portrait, all with impunity, not only exposed the pro-Bangladeshi stance of Indira Gandhi for promoting the partisan interests of the Congress(I) but these also built up a strong undercurrent of communal tensions to be released at the opportune moment. These developments cannot be discounted while analysing the Nellie massacre. Towards the end of the month, Assamese Hindu villages were attacked, particularly in Nagaon district. Almost 1,200 Assamese people were rendered homeless after 300 houses were set on fire in that district. Many Assamese people were killed and hundreds injured. The organised violence continued almost for a week in Nagaon district. Altogether 39 persons were killed. At many places, the police had to open fire for quelling the communal disturbances. Most of the movement leaders were in jail while none of the Congress/Leftist leaders came forward to pacify the situation. Thus, throughout the year 1980, hartals, satyagrahas, arrests and detention without trial, police firing here and there, non-cooperation of the government employees, and police atrocities in various forms continued, thereby making the lives and properties of the people insecure, with the student community becoming the special target of the police atrocities. Virtually, entire Assam was converted into a battlefield! During all these harrowing days the Congress(I) was busy with devising means for installing its own government, although it had only eight legislators in the Assembly, presently under suspension. With the full blessings of Indira Gandhi horse-trading was started on a massive scale with a view to cause defections of MLAs and ultimately the Congress ministry was installed, not once but twice; but these ministries could not survive. Already we have referred to the terror unleashed during the Taimur regime. As a last resort, press censorship was also imposed but it also failed to defuse the situation. The only success (?) achieved during this period by the administration was to break the oil blockade with the help of the army while the military engineers stepped in to operate the oil pipelines. The flow of crude oil to Barauni Refinery was resumed in February, 1981; but the situation took a turn to the worse. A series of bomb blasts took place with the oil installation and the railway line being the main targets. Because of the repressive policies of the government, the movement gradually betrayed signs of losing its non-violent character which, once again, Indira Gandhi failed to realise.

Indira Gandhi became more determined to teach a lesson to the Assamese people. After a long period of lull, another drama of holding a tripartite discussion amongst the central government, the opposition parties and the AASU & AAGSP was enacted in the first week of January, 1983. Nothing transpired. Suddenly, the talks were abandoned by the Centre on 5 January 1983 and a unilateral announcement was made that elections would be held in Assam (the Assembly was in the meantime dissolved) on 14/15 and 20th February 1983. The issue of revising the ERs and deleting the names of foreigners was totally ignored, thereby throwing a direct challenge to the movement leadership. Some of the hot heads from amongst the AASU and AAGSP delegation indiscreetly announced that there would be a blood-bath if an election was forced upon Assam. On their way back to Guwahati from Delhi, all the movement leaders were arrested at Borjhar airport, thereby entailing a spate of loud protests from the entire Assam valley. A direct confrontation with the police and the CRPF personnel became imminent. Press censorship followed in quick succession. Another black chapter was added to the history of our infant democracy! Sinning Indira totally forgot the lessons of 1975! The Congress (I) activists were overjoyed with the announcement of the schedule of elections without least realising that they would forever be mortgaged to the "Bangladeshi Lobby" which would not hesitate for a moment to leave them high and dry once it could be sure of its own dominant role in calling the shots. (Exactly this is what happened on the eve of the 2001 general elections to the State Assembly.)

The announcement of the schedule of elections followed by the arrests of the top echelons of the movement leadership and that too in a most anti-conventional manner, blew up the hornest's nest once again, thereby giving a fresh lease of life to the already four year old Movement. The entire people of the valley excepting a handful of Congress(I) and Left parties' leaders, shouted their protests in one voice spontaneously and resolved to boycott and resist the imposed elections. The people of Assam received the message that the treachery perpetrated by the CEC indicated in no uncertain terms that the political future of Assam and her people was not secure in his hands and that they themselves must be more enterprising for securing their own future. The CEC was possibly asked to bend a little bit but he readily knelt down!

However, Assam was not alone while voicing her protests against the imposed election. The national leaders who tried their best to postpone this unwanted election included Atal Bihari Vajpayee and Jaswant Singh of the BJP, Raj Narain and Madhu Dandavate of Janata Dal, Shyamnandan Misra of the Lokdal, etc. Even leaders like Charan Singh and H N Bahuguna, never known for their anxieties for Assam's welfare, had appealed to Indira Gandhi for postponing the elections. Karpuri Thakur of Bihar had also lent his support to the boycott of this elections. All these honourable leaders of the Opposition, having realised that in the name of discharging constitutional obligations an electoral farce was going to take place. It would have far-reaching adverse consequences also, and they had petitioned Indira Gandhi even to amend the Constitution for postponing the election, whereas Assam's indigenous leaders like Sarat Sinha, Hiteswar Sakia, Dr Bhumidhar Barman, Hemen Das, Pramod Gogoi, all the time professing to stand by the distressed people, remained oblivious to the impending disaster and were also determined to participate in the elections. If popular demands are not responded to, how could one claim to be the leader of the people, is a question yet to be addressed by this brand of leaders. Incidentally, all these Leftist leaders have become close allies of AGP today with the latter having mastered the art of unholy compromises for the sake of sheer occupation of the seat of power! It took no time for the gathering dark clouds to burst open and as the Mehta Commission had pointed out, widespread violence was witnessed at places like Chenga, Sipajhar, Mangaldoi, Tangla, Dakshin Chuburi, Samaria, Puranigudam, Samuguri, Kampur, Jorhat, North Lakhimpur, Nagaon, Berhampur, Daplong, Laopani, Goreswar, neighbouring areas of Tezpur, Nalbari, etc. After three "Satyagrahis" were shot dead near Mangaldoi, police inspector Ghanakanta Handique known for his integrity and devotion to duty, was lynched to death by the irate mob, although he was not responsible for the killings of the three "Satyagrahis". Samaria Satra, a seat of Vaishnavite culture and worshipping, under Boko Police Station of Kamrup district, had the misfortune of being the target of a direct attack by the Bangladeshi miscreants from the neighbouring "Char" areas. Ms Ganga Kalita, a young girl in her late teens, had taken the lead in resisting the Bangladeshi attack but fell a victim to the marauding hordes.

That violence begets violence was proved once more and at many places the indigenous people also resorted to violent methods of confronting the situation. There was none to control them as most of the movement leaders were either in jail or had gone underground. On 15 February 1983, a Congress(I) candidate was done to death; but the most atrocious and inhuman happening had taken place at Sipajhar on 2 February 1983: Three young movement activists, namely, Prahlad Sharma, Chitra Barua and Tapan Barua while on a publicity campaign for boycotting the election, were apprehended by the CRPF personnel and thrown alive into fire! Needless to mention that all the three subsequently succumbed to their burn injuries at Gauhati Medical College Hospital (GMCH). It will be of interest to note that the conducts of the CRPF peronnel during this holocaust at different places all over Assam presented a contrast: While at places they behaved most inhumanly and ruthlessly in order to foil the move for boycotting the elections, at other places some contingents of the CRPF were reported to have connived with violence perpetrated against suspected Bangladeshi nationals! Those who fell victims to violence at Samaria and Gohpur were of indigenous Assamese origin while those who fell at Nellie and a few other interior places of Nagaon district, were of Bangladeshi origin. Indira Gandhi never bothered to pay attention to Samaria and Gohpur but lost no time to attract the attention of the media to the Nellie massacre, obviously with a view to pamper the Bangladeshi voters, thereby making her intentions very clear! One, however, must not lose sight of the fact that the Bangladeshi miscreants had started the clashes at most of the places. The violent clashes between the indigenous people and the miscreants of foreign origin had assumed such serious proportions, as at Samguri area alone, 30000 indigenous people had been rendered homeless. On one day alone (22 February 1983) 22 Assamese villages were totally destroyed in Nagaon district by setting these villages to fire. Some of the Bangladeshi miscreants were reported to have used khaki police uniforms also! It can hardly be overemphasised that the Bangladeshi miscreants had received support from the vested interests of certain political parties. In fact, it was in retaliation of the ghastly happenings of Samaria, Nagaon district, Mangaldoi sub-division, etc., that the Nellie massacre took place, an aspect so cunningly concealed by Indira Gandhi from the world media when she visited Nellie.

To sum up, the announcement of the schedule of elections without deleting the names of lakhs of foreign nationals from the ERs, witnessed the following developments: Firstly, the Movement leadership had to undertake many fresh agitational programmes directed towards resisting the forcibly-imposed election. This time even the indigenous people of the Barak valley had also responded to these programmes. Secondly, the administration had to take resort to unprecedented repressive measures and unconstitutional steps for frustrating the programme for boycotting the elections so that the whims of Indira Gandhi were satisfied and her partisan interests well secured. Thirdly, as already highlighted, Indira Gandhi's refusal to see the writing on the wall coupled with her efforts, foul or fair, for installing her own government at Dispur, had motivated the Bangladeshi lobby to come to direct violent clash with the indigenous people. Fourthly, these inhuman repressive measures perpetrated on an unprecedented scale, had brought in their trail many socio-political and administrative upheavals, certainly detrimental to the healthy functioning of the democratic process, the very life-blood of the traditional Indian society. There is no denial of the fact that the happenings of 1983, had certainly constituted the major factor for ULFA's determination to defy Delhi and emerge as a strong militant and secessionist outfit. The atrocities to which the native people were subjected, had already created widespread resentment amongst all classes of the state government employees excepting those handful few who were angling for carrying Indira's favours. The tension and widespread dissatisfaction thus generated amongst the government employees of the state, reached its climax on 16 February 1983 when, at Goalpara, the district headquarters of the westernmost district of Assam on the south bank of the Brahmaputra, some Assam Police Battalion personnel came to armed conflict with the personnel of the CRPF and the Rajasthan Armed Constabulary. Matters, however, did not end there in as much as the state government employees refused to do any election duties. Even the local printing presses refused to print the ERs, which, as such, had to be printed outside Assam. Above all, 8,800 government officers and employees had to be airlifted from Delhi to man the polling stations. Even after invoking the Essential Services Maintenance Act, the native government employees could not be coerced into co-operating with the electoral process.

Meanwhile, Indrajit Barua had filed another Writ Petition in the High Court praying for postponement of the election which, however, could not be carried to its judicial conclusion on the plea that the electoral process, once set in motion, could not be postponed. The local print media could not do much either because of the strict Press censorship, excepting that occasionally the editorial columns and spaces earmarked for any particular news relating to the election, used to be kept blank. Otherwise, until the censorship was imposed, the local press played a very vital role in spreading the message of the movement so much so that the circulation of *Daink Asam*, an Assamese daily published from Guwahati and edited by none other than Kirtinath Hazarika himself, had gone up to much more than 1,00,000 whereas the dailies published from Calcutta had spared no efforts for not only under-reporting the developing situation but also under-estimating the same.

However, amongst the agitational programmes, the "Janata Curfew" proved to be the most effective weapon in the hands of the Movement leadership. In fact, wherever Indira Gandhi was to go for her electionering campaign, "Janata Curfew" was declared and as a result, she had to keep her electioneering campaign confined to the infiltration-prone immigrant Muslim areas. This must be admitted by the future historians that not only the Movement leadership had exhibited tremendous organising ability in the face of serious odds in respect of motivating the indigenous people for boycotting the elections, but also the indigenous peoples of various ethnic groups and the state government employees rose to the occasion as one man for boycotting the elections.

The Asam Jatiyatabadi Dal and the Purbanchaliya Loka Parishad, the two leading regional political outfits had already announced their decisions to boycott the elections. Appeals were also made to the national political parties for boycotting the elections and only the BJP, the Lokdal and the Janata Dal responded positively to the appeal by refusing to participate in the election whereas the Congress(I), the Congress(S) and all the Left parties were overjoyed with finding a vacant battlefield. Even the women folk did not remain silent. On 3 February 1983, massive women rallies were held all over the valley for conveying their unequivocal message of resisting and then boycotting the entire electoral process. Still Indira remained unmoved! Rather, the entire valley was made to assume the look of a battlefield by inducting a huge number of additional forces of the CRPF and the BSF. It is also further worth mentioning that the majority of the indigenous Muslim population had also boycotted the election.

This apart, the list of those who became martyrs in this "Resistance Movement", boasted of names from the tribal and tea-labour communities as also from Bengali-speaking communities of the valley.

However, a Congress(I) ministry ultimately came to power with Late Hiteswar Saikia as the Chief Minister. While the repressive measures against the agitationists continued unabated, the most infamous act performed during the tenure of this ministry was the passage of the IMDT Act, 1983. The main architect of this anti-Assam Act was Abdul Muhim Mazumdar, a member of the aforesaid Saikia cabinet. Even then, he became a member of the AGP ministry and was working overtime to defend the continuation of this unconstitutional and discriminatory black law in defiance of the professed stance of the AGP government vis a vis this Act! A brief mention of the salient features of this Act is certainly called for in the context of our present discourse:

All over India excepting Assam, The Foreigners Act, 1946 was applicable. In terms of the Assam Accord, provisions of this Act for the purpose of detection, is applicable in Assam only in case of those infiltrators who came over between 1 January 1966 and 24 March 1971 and that too, only for determining their citizenship and not for the purpose of deporting them. If determined to be foreign nationals, they are to be disenfranchised for 10 years from the date of such determination and their voting right will be restored after expiry of this period of 10 years whereas the IMDT Act, 1983, will be applicable to the post-25 March 1971 stream of foreigners for the purpose of detection and deportation. The preamble of the IMDT Act admits that "--- a good number of the foreigners who migrated into India across the borders of the eastern and north-eastern regions of the country on and after the 25th day of March, 1971, have, by taking advantage of the circumstances of such migration and their ethnic similarities and other connections with the people of India and without having in their possession any lawful authority to do so, illegally remained in India--- etc, etc". The preamble further states that "the continuance of such foreigners in India is detrimental to the interests of the public of India". As such, there cannot be any controversy about the aims and objectives of the Act whereas the Act stipulates such unrealistic, unpractical and impossible conditions that any detection under this Act becomes practically impossible, let alone deportation. The following table will illustrate how difficult it has been to detect these infiltrators under this Act, thereby not only making a total mockery of its aims and objectives but also striking a sharp contrast to the results achieved under the Foreigners Act, 1946: (these figures indicate the status as on 31 May 1999)

1. Total number of enquiries made under the Act: 302554
2. Total number of enquiries completed: 300165
3. Total number of enquiries referred to Screening Committees: 296564
4. Total number of enquiries completed by Screening Committees: 293636
5. Total number of cases referred to the IM(DT)s by the Screening Committees: 31264
6. Total number of cases disposed of by the IM(DT)s: 15142
7. Total number of persons adjudged as illegal migrants: 9625
8. Total number of infiltrators deported: 1467
9. Total number of enquiries pending with Tribunals: 16122

(*Source: Government records*)

Out of 9,625 cases, expulsion orders could be served only on 5667 persons only; the rest were missing. And out of 5,667 persons, only 1,467 could be traced for actual physical deportation! What a fraud has been committed on the people, may be well judged from the figures quoted above. Out of 2,93,636 enquiries completed by the Investigating Agency, only 31,264 cases could be sent up for trial and only 9,625 cases were disposed of in favour of the state. Such sordid state of affairs is attributable to so many reasons; but any further dissection of this undemocratic and anti-national Act will be redundant as the Act has already been struck down by the Supreme Court as unconstitutional. Still Assam's Tarun Gogoi Government tried its best to bring back the operation of the Act by dubious means which again the Supreme Court rejected.

Anyway, back to the infamous elections of 1983: The total failure of the CEC in the context of the ROP Act, had aggravated the situation further. The EC itself had invited objections after the draft ERs were published for the elections of 1980. Lakhs of objections were filed in the prescribed form. The ROP Act does not empower the EC to keep any properly filed such objections pending and hold the elections. But the EC simply did not bother to take necessary action for disposing of these lakhs of objections before holding the elections in 1983. In fact, these objections are pending disposal even till date (2014). And most significantly, no member of Parliament had raised any question in this context, be it AGP or BJP members. Only reason I can assign to such silence, is that nobody was actually serious about the matter. Also I have reasons to suspect that the MPs from Assam, particularly those belonging to AGP and BJP who had supported the Assam Movement, were not competent enough to get themselves involved in such a highly intricate legal and political debate as also they might not have cared to go through the provisions of the ROP Act and the relevant rules framed thereunder.

However, I shall always claim the credit for questioning the constitutional validity of the IMDT Act by filing a writ petition in the Guwahati High Court, but my lawyer returned the brief after he was appointed as the Advocate General of Assam in 1996 by the AGP government. I failed to find another lawyer as some lawyers of the Guwahati Bar found some technical deficiency in my petition. On the other hand, I did not command necessary financial resources for hiring the services of lawyer from outside Assam. So, I decided to argue the case myself and devoted myself to preparing for the purpose. Meanwhile, Sarbananda Sonowal of AGP (now he is in BJP) filed a writ petition in the Supreme Court, challenging the constitutional validity of this Act and thus ended my efforts aimed at the same purpose. Be that as it may, the fact remains that I had certainly set the trend for legal action.

All said and done, the Assam movement had, to a large extent, neutralised the apprehensions and mistrust caused by the State Language Movement of 1960 and the Medium of Instructions Movement of 1972. As mentioned earlier, the movement gave rise to a sense of oneness amongst the people of Assam against a common enemy, cutting across ethnic, racial, linguistic, religious identities. But the short-sighted and self-seeking policies of the first AGP government of 1985, washed away all the positive fallouts of the Assam movement, thereby facilitating once more the rise of Assamese chauvinism on the one hand and ethnic dissents on the other. CM Prafulla Kumar Mahanta failed to rise above chauvinistic interests and preferred to be an Assamese CM only, totally ignoring the ethnic aspirations of so many tribal entities, particularly of the Bodos who had participated in the anti-foreigners movement very enthusiastically. The new generation of the Bodos was totally disillusioned with the discriminatory attitude of the AGP government. The Bodos became very vocal and active under the leadership of Upen Brahma, deified as Bodofa, with their demand for a separate Bodo state. Thus was paved the way to the rise of quite a few ethnic movements, not necessarily all non-violent in nature, for consolidating their separate identities in the shape of separate states, autonomous units and the likes. Quite a few rebellious armed outfits surfaced and the situation gradually became very explosive. Thus, the 'espirit de corps' generated by the Assam movement totally evaporated during the tenure of the first AGP ministry with politicians of different hues not failing to fish in troubled waters. And above all, the much vaunted Assam Accord proved to be a still-born baby! True, the people of Assam survived the atrocious regime of Anowara Taimur, but I have my own doubts as to how many decades will be necessary to neutralise, if at all neutralised, the adverse fallouts of Prafulla Kumar Mahanta's two regimes of 1985-90 and 1996-2001! Both the terms were clouded by very many scandals and the future of regional politics seemed to be doomed for an uncertain period.

11

Detention And Dismissal

Allegations of corrupt practices could not ensure my summary dismissal from service even during the Emergency days as already narrated. So my detractors mulled that much more serious allegations with strong political backing might do the trick!

Now, I must revert back to what happened to me after I failed to convince the AASU leadership to accept 1967 as the cut-off date for detecting illegal alien migrants. AASU kept on insisting on 1951 to be such cut-off date—an unrealistic proposition betraying total lack of insight into the socio-political, economic complexities and ground realities. To begin with, I am constrained to observe that those were the days when the Rule of Law was thrown to the winds and the supreme consideration emerged in the shape of political and financial mileage. The entire atmosphere was agog with political and agitational activities-- both peaceful and otherwise coupled with a race for pocketing unearned easy money as much as possible. On the other hand, like many others, I totally failed to understand why the AASU leadership was obstinate about 1951 as the cut-off date and instead, chose to linger the movement. The reason thereof became crystal clear when they accepted 1971 as the cut-off date while signing the Assam Accord. Their only intention was to linger the movement so that they could attain the age of 25 years—a statutory requirement for contesting any election either to the Assembly or the Parliament. Thus their pseudo-patriotism was unmasked in due course. How unfortunate were the people of Assam to have handed over power to such a gang of self-seeking youths!

Months of hectic activities took a heavy toll of my health and unfortunately, I suffered a heart attack on 25 April 1980 early in the morning. Dr Deba Sharma, head of the Medicine Department of the Gauhati Medical College, rushed to my residence and immediately shifted me to the ICU of GMCH. After necessary investigation, the experts of GMC detected malfunctioning of the left ventricle of my heart and admitted me as an indoor patient for how long only God knew.

Meanwhile, I was transferred to New Delhi as the DIGP of the Central Industrial Security Force. But it was not possible for me to move out of Assam with my current state of health. Besides, my children were in Assamese medium schools, thereby making it impossible for them to move out of Assam. On the other hand, it was not possible for me to maintain two establishments—one at Guwahati and the other at Delhi. Thus, I was placed between the devil and the deep sea. Such mental agonies certainly did not help to recover from my ailment.

Dr Manish Bhuyan, the leading cardiologist of Assam, and Dr Deba Sharma advised me to go to Vellore for further investigation and better treatment without loss of time. They not only advised me to consult Dr Cherian there but also wrote two personal letters to him for helping me. But the problem was shortage of funds. I did not have any savings to fall back upon. As an IPS officer, I was entitled to travelling allowance for the journey to Vellore as also the cost of treatment. But the home secretary not only refused to sanction any advance to me but also misbehaved with me by using very rude language. I really felt very hurt as an officer junior to me in service, behaved so rudely. I had not asked for any undue favour but possibly he did not want to displease somebody who was not keen on facilitating my treatment.

Even then, some of my colleagues were not totally divorced from humane feelings. B S Baber, also a DIGP and three years senior to me in service, came forward with a proposal to help me. He proposed to raise funds with contribution from few other IPS ofifcers and hand over the money to me for enabling me to go to Vellore. Instead of straightaway accepting the offer, I stipulated a condition that I was ready to accept his offer as a loan only and that I would pay back the loan in due course.

Meanwhile, having heard of my predicament, LBK Dey, the retired IGP of Assam, came down from Shillong to see me and he was very hurt to learn about the state of affairs. Magnanimous and very kind as he was, he offered me Rs. 8,000/- for facilitating my journey to Vellore for treatment. Realising that I was hesitating to accept his offer, he made it clear to me that he was simply giving me a loan and he would accept my repayment at my convenience. So, I accepted the offer. The gesture of Baber and Dey also helped me to realise that I was still not alone in this world! Both of them are no more.

The physicians of Christian Medical College of Vellore confirmed the findings of the doctors of the GMCH. Besides advising me to take full rest for four months and then come back after six months for fresh assessment of my heart condition, Dr Cherian simply added one more medicine to what was prescribed to me at the GMCH. HC Sarin, the Principal Adviser to the Governor (Assam was then under President's rule) had suspected that I had manipulated the medical report at Guwahati without realising that Dr Cherian was under no compulsion to ditto the reports of Dr Bhuyan and Dr Sarma. Further, when I was undergoing treatment, the Union Home Minister Zail Singh made a statement to the Press that a DIGP was directing the Assam movement from his sick-bed! However the SIB, the Union Government's Intelligence Agency, and the Special Branch of the state government had nothing to report against me as it subsequently transpired. The inhuman attitude betrayed by both Sarin and the state home secretary was causing total loss of my confidence in human character when Baber and Dey appeared on the scene as angels and revived my sagging morale. I realised that the society was not yet devoid of kindness, loyalty and fellow-feelings and that the 'milk of kindness' was still flowing! Which is why, life continues to be worth living.

I came back to Guwahati and started for all practical purposes, the life of a recluse as most of my friends were afraid of visiting me, lest they might incur the wrath of Sarin & Co! My wife was not only working hard to augment the yield of her mini dairy farm but also took to tutorial job for making both ends meet. Those were the days of real hardship. But still worse was to follow:

Because of my ailment, I had to go on long leave; but Dispur would not sanction my medical leave. On the top of all these, Sarin summoned me one day to his presence and threatened me with dire consequences unless I moved out immediately to Delhi on transfer. Sarin was credited with putting down (?) some rebellion in the South and he thought that he could do the same in Assam also without realising that the Assam movement was a non-violent one, that too on legitimate grounds. After a hot altercation with him, I told him in no uncertain terms that he was up against a wrong man for cowing him down with red eyes.

However, there were reasons behind my becoming a suspect in the eyes of few ICS/IAS officers imported from outside Assam during the President's rule promulgated on more than one occasion when the State Assembly was kept under animated suspension. Besides, few police officers belonging to a particular community did not lag behind in adding fuel to fire by frequently poisoning the ears of these imported officers who knew nothing about my past records as a Police Officer. As I look back, I am inclined to believe that two particular incidents, inter alia, were instrumental in creating such suspicion whereas from professional point of view, both the incidents should have been appreciated as glorious achievements for a police officer charged with maintenance of law and order in a very emotionally surcharged atmosphere. Brief accounts of both the incidents may be of some interest to the readers.

(1) It all happened in the context of elections to the Lok Sabha in 1980 which was opposed by the AASU. For, they wanted the elections to be held on the basis of corrected ERs divested of all the names of foreign citizens. The movement had meanwhile gathered enough momentum which the government either failed to assess or did not want to assess with a 'could not care less' attitude. A coterie of officers,

hand in gloves with few politicians, was determined to frustrate AASU and AAGSP's call for boycotting the elections to be held on the basis of an incorrect voters' list. Indira had become desperate to recapture the seat of power aided by her camp followers including some of the high ranking bureaucrats and ex-bureaucrats.

Briefly speaking, an item in the agenda for preventing the elections, was the announcement of "Janata Curfew" on the days of filing nomination papers as well as to resist any attempt to file nomination papers.

Defying the call of the AASU, the AAGSP and the Indian citizens of Assam, Abeda Ahmed, the wife of late Fakruddin Ali Ahmed, the ex-President of India, proceeded to Barpeta on the night of 9 December 1979, with very strong police escorts under the leadership of KPS Gill who was subsequently called the "Super Cop" of India for his sterling performances in controlling the secessionist militancy in the strife-torn Punjab. Prior to this, possibly on 8 or 9 December 1979, I was placed in charge of maintaining law & order within Guwahati city. I, however, did not know the reason of such sudden change. It transpired subsequently that the temporary change was only to make Gill's services available for escorting Abeda Ahmed safely for enabling her to file her nomination at Barpeta. Anyway, Abeda faced stiff resistance at quite a few places on her way to Barpeta; but groups of people's unorganised resistance was no match for Gill's huge police force, although very strong and uncompromising resistance was faced at Bhabanipur. Gill's police force swung into action for clearing the road to facilitate Abida's efforts for becoming an MP and then possibly a union minister. I have my own doubts whether her husband would have approved of her motive under the prevailing situation. True the road was cleared but at the cost of a precious young student leader's life. Abeda filed her nomination papers but as mentioned earlier, her nomination papers were rejected on some technical ground. Nowhere else, nomination papers could be filed in the Brahmaputra valley. Even a stalwart like Devakanta Barua was prevented at Nagaon by thousands of picketeers from filing his nomination papers. He was kept under 'gherao' at Nagaon Circuit House until the time for filing nomination was over. Khargeswar Talukdar's death in police action spread like wild fire and on the morning of December 10, the situation in Guwahati turned extremely explosive. Large-scale apprehensions coupled with panic gripped the entire city when the news of Khargeswar's dead body being taken to Guwahati in a convoy by forces not known for their care for public order, rather keen on promoting violence, reached the city. The chief secretary and the IGP summoned me at about 7 am on 10 December 1979 to the IGP's residence. (Paramasivam was meanwhile replaced by B S Sarao as the CS). Both of them were in a gloomy state of mind when I arrived there. I could well appreciate their anxities and apprehensions. To be very precise, instead of giving me an order, both of them, practically begged of me to ensure that the dead body could not reach Guwahati. Else, they apprehended that Guwahati would go up in flames which I fully agreed with.

Much time had already been lost and the convoy carrying the dead body was reported to have already crossed the Brahmaputra bridge. Obviously, no instruction was issued to the police stations the convoy had come across on the way to Guwahati for stopping the convoy. Nobody seemed to have felt concerned about the likely development. However, without much deliberations, I rushed to Jalukbari with only two PSOs of mine; but before I reached Jalukbari, the convoy had already crossed Jalukbari. I confronted the convoy just under the railway overbridge at the western end of Maligaon with few militant, angry student leaders leading the convoy. I could immediately assess that any application of force would simply aggravate the situation. Without taking much time to decide, I, disarming myself in full public view, handed over my revolver to my PSOs and directed them not to follow me at close quarters but to keep a close watch on the situation. I had also meanwhile deputed a shrewd police officer to the university campus with a request to some senior teachers of the university for rushing to the spot. The same instruction was given to the I/C of the Jalukbari Police OP and also to make necessary transport available to the professors.

Thus, I confronted the convoy all by myself without any police escort—a very risky business in an emotionally explosive situation, if not foolhardy. Then immediately, I engaged the leaders of the convoy in talks about the measures to be taken in respect of the dead body. My strategy was to cause as much delay as possible until the arrival of the senior teachers on the spot. The DC could not come as he as the Returning Officer, had to remain present in his office to receive nomination papers, if any. On the other hand, the student leaders were adamant about being allowed to take the dead body to AASU's central office in Guwahati. All my reasonings and entreaties seemed to be falling on deaf ears. Then, to my great relief, a team of senior professors of the university led by Prof. Hariprasanna Das, the Rector, appeared on the scene. They were impressed with my patient reasoning and very appreciative of my reluctance to use force. After good deal of deliberations, they all agreed to take the dead body to the campus of the university. I tactfully led the convoy to the campus of the university hospital which was soon thronging with hundreds of students and members of the public shouting all sorts of slogans. The key to the situation was one of holding one's patience and remaining calm. The question of legally obligatory post mortem examination cropped up; but the VC who had arrived at the scene was rather reluctant to allow the PM examination to be held in the university hospital. After long discussions and veiled threat (which better remains unelaborated), the PM examination was held there and Guwahati city was rescued from an imminent catastrophe.

Here was an instance of non-application of force saving the day for the government. But insinuations galore were made that it was because of my secret understanding with the student leaders which did the miracle!

(2) The other incident was yet of more significance in the context of non-application of force and instead resorting to the strategy of negotiations.

Santiranjan Dasgupta was a cabinet minister in Jogen Hazarika's short-lived ministry and known for his antipathy towards the Assam movement. On the other hand, the rowdy elements of AASU were fuming against the anti-movement politicians—particularly after Khargeswar's death in police action. And when Santiranjan Dasgupta was returning to Guwahati from Hojai, his home town, his car was stopped at Khanapara reportedly by few students of the Assam

Agricultural University (AAU) and Dasgupta was abducted and then taken to an unknown destination, followed by all sorts of rumours about his fate, thereby causing commotion all over the capital. Before I left for the spot, information reached me that he had been taken inside the university campus which, to its rear, had a vast thickly forested area. Meanwhile, the CM and the CS met me on my way to the AAU and advised me to recover Dasgupta alive. Obviously, it was a very difficult task and one had to be very cautious while dealing with the situation. As I arrived at the spot, a huge crowd of students and non-students had already gathered at the main gate of the AAU. These boys had developed in their mind a soft corner for me because of non-application of force against the students on 10 December 1979 which I could discern. Once more in full public view, I handed over my personal weapon to my escort and again approached the boys alone, directing my escort to remain at safe distance. The CM and the CS had seen the crowd on their way to the State Guest House for meeting the Governor, LP Singh. Which is why, both of them were very much concerned with the physical safety of Dasgupta. On the wireless set of my car, I came to know that DN Srivastava, the SP of Guwahati was proceeding to raid the rear area of the AAU. Obviously, I was very much alarmed as such a raid might not only complicate the situation but might also result in physical harm to the abducted minister. Srivastava had not taken any order from me; obviously there was a communication gap. Anyway, I asked him to withdraw immediately and return to the control room. Now ensued the marathon argument with the abductors for more than five hours or so. It was real test of my patience and theirs as well. Ultimately they gave in and I held out. They seemed to have developed cold feet after I pointed out to them that Dasgupta belonging to the Bengali community, any physical harm caused to him after his abduction, might send out a wrong message. This particular argument seemed to have cut ice, particularly because the agitationists were from the very beginning professing that their agitation was not against any community but only against the alien illegal migrants.

Minister Santiranjan Dasgupta was handed over to me in a most exhausted condition at about 4 pm. The minister's car was already put out of commission by letting out air from all the four wheels. So I requested him to get into my car; but his immediate reaction was a hostile attitude to me as if I was responsible for his predicament instead of being grateful to me for his safe recovery! Despite his reluctance to get into my car, I pushed him inside my car and speeded off to Dispur. No doubt, it was great relief for me, if not a great achievement for a police officer. I, personally handed him over to his agonizingly anxious family at his official residence and left for the CM's residence where the Cabinet was in session. With a smart salute, I informed the CM and his colleagues that Dasgupta had been recovered unharmed and restored to his family. All of them congratulated me warmly excepting a senior member of the Cabinet who enquired of me about the number of arrests I had made. I simply reacted with a scornful smile and replied that my first priority was to recover the minister alive as per CM's order and that arrests could be made subsequently also. Any arrest made at that moment, would have resulted in the situation aggravating beyond control. True, I had taken a great risk by walking unarmed and unescorted as I myself could have been abducted by the agitated leaders of the crowd. But my self-confidence had got better of such consideration, egging me on to take a calculated risk.

Taking leave of the CM, I left for my residence. Later in the late evening, CM Hazarika surprised us all by landing at my residence unannounced and once again profusely congratulated me. More significant was his expression of gratitude for preventing a major embarrassment to his government. Before leaving, he did little loud thinking by remarking that he would see to it that I was properly rewarded for this remarkable achievement without, however realising that the days of his ministry were also to come to an end shortly.

Anyway, I only did my duty not in expectation of any reward. Ensued another spell of President's rule in the state and the penultimate blow to my career was also drawing nigh very fast.

My confrontation with the AASU boys seemed to be unending as if they were dogging my every footstep. I was also holding the charge of the DIGP Southern Range. As such, I had to rush off to Silchar and camp there for ensuring necessary police arrangements there for holding the elections for two LS seats therefrom. AASU's agitation had no impact there; but suddenly AASU woke up and rushed off a convoy of Assamese students in two buses to Silchar in order to prevent elections there. A preposterous proposition indeed! So here too, it was no cakewalk. Elections were to be held on January 3 and 6, 1980 and the AASU boys left for Silchar on 1 January for preventing the elections as if it would be a cakewalk without the support of the people of Barak valley! They were not prevented anywhere during the long journey and I was informed at the last minute with instruction to prevent their entry into Silchar as it might trigger off another communal riot between Assamese and Bengali communities.

I wondered how they could be allowed to undertake the journey after their intention was known to Dispur. They could have been certainly prevented much before reaching the Barak valley instead of burdening me with such a serious problem just on the eve of the election. This sudden development created an impression that nobody in the Brahmaputra valley could command enough courage to confront the two buses of student leaders. Anyway, the convoy was stopped at Gumra near Katigara PS and keys of both the buses were taken away by the police officer I had deputed after proper briefing to prevent their entry into Silchar. Next day both the buses were on their way back to Guwahati.

However, problems were unending. As soon as the election of January 6 was over, widespread communal riots broke out between Hindus and Muslims. All efforts for snatching away ballot boxes could be foiled as we, having anticipated such trouble, had worked out a foolproof plan for combating any such emergent situation. Silchar/Hailakandi witnessed widespread troubles. The situation could be promptly brought under control with a heavy hand only because we had well anticipated the surfacing of such problem. Precautionary measures were put in place in full measures. In the process, I had to spend most of the time in the Police Control Room for 6/7 days continuously. I could not sleep even for 2/3 hours at a stretch. Thus started my health problem with my blood pressure shooting up. In fact, Dr S Barua, the principal of the Silchar Medical College, had advised me total rest which was not simply possible. My withdrawal from duty at this crucial hour, would have set a bad example before the officers and the force I was commanding. The blood pressure could not be controlled for quite sometime which ultimately resulted in my first heart attack as already mentioned above.

What did I get ultimately for having performed my duty in such a dedicated manner, has already been narrated above.

Anyway, Sarin's innings was bound to come to an end as the Constitution does not allow the President's rule to continue for more than a year. Earlier, or course, it was three years but during the Janata regime, it was reduced to one year. As such, it was constitutionally imperative to form a ministry before 12 December 1980.

Congress(I) had only eight MLAs in the Assembly. Nobody had even imagined that Congress (I) could form the government with its eight MLAs. But the long spell of President's rule had afforded enough opportunities for largescale horse trading—all the more facilitated by the split in the Janata legislature party. So that was that! Anowara Taimur, MLA of Congress(I), was invited to form the government despite not commanding a clear majority in the House. She had an axe to grind against me as hinted upon earlier. In essence a communally motivated politician, she was vindictive too. My detractors drove it home to her mind that the aforesaid operation in Dalgaon LA constituency was intended to destroy her politically. So they all ganged up not to miss this golden opportunity for manufacturing my dossier in the context of the Assam movement. Already a secessionist motive was imputed to the agitation against the alien nationals, thereby trying to create adverse opinion against the agitation in the rest of the country. Also the Union home minister had made a statement that a DIGP was conducting from his sick bed the agitation spearheaded by AASU. Thus it became easier for my detractors to frame me in some anti-national activities as they knew by now that the allegations of corrupt practice against me were not likely to hold water. In the context of corrupt practices, I am reminded of a very interesting incident which I am tempted to narrate.

Phani Roy with his Sylhet origin, recruited as a SI of Police had worked, by means fair or foul, his way up to the rank of a SP. He had even manipulated the record of his age for enabling himself to be nominated to the IPS; but he failed. Entirely on the basis of communal back up, he had become the most trusted lieutenant of Samar Das—the infamous 'Don' of the still more infamous Emergency days. Samar Das utilised him for preparing the brief for my dismissal during the Emergency as mentioned earlier. Also he was mainly responsible for preparing the dossiers of many other officers for their summary dismissal during the Emergency. Of course, they were reinstated during the Janata regime.

Sometime in later part of 1975 or early part of 1976, he landed up with his team at my residence for evaluating the amount of money I had spent in constructing my residential house, conveniently forgetting that I had taken two building advances from the government and had also withdrawn a hefty amount from my Providend Fund—both refundable and non-refundable. But what surprised me most was that he had commissioned the services of no less a person than Dr Nirmal Kumar Choudhury, not only a leading civil engineer of the state but also the principal of Assam Engineering College who subsequently went to become the VC of Guwahati University.

Anyway, back to where I had disgressed from.

On the early morning on 29 January 1981, I was awakened at about 3.30 am and served with an order for my detention under the National Security Act. My house was surrounded by about 100 CRPF personnel so that I could not escape! What a precautionary measure! But when I saw one Siba Sharma amongst the officers who had come to take me away, I did not take much time to understand what had taken place secretly. Inspector Siba Sharma was the secretary of the Junior Police Officers' Association. At that time, 2 or 3 anti-corruption enquiries were pending against Sharma with M I S Iyer, the DIGP, CID. These are matter of records unless the files concerned had already disappeared. Sarma one day suddenly appeared before me and requested me to prevail upon Iyer to drop these enquiries as he considered Iyer to be very close to me. I had, of course, flatly refused to make such an unjust request. So, now, he has reasons to feel triumphant. During the hearing of my habeas corpus petition in the High Court, it transpired that a false report was extracted from him in his aforesaid capacity of being the secretary that I had incited him from my sick bed to foment rebellion in the Assam Police force as if he could have done that! Such was the level to which Samar Das & Co had stooped down!

I was really intrigued to understand as to how I had become a threat to national security! I did not know whether to weep or laugh on receipt of the order for my detention. Few days back when my wife was attending the marriage ceremony of Iyer's daughter, Samar Das had announced within the hearing of my wife and a friend of mine that this time he was sure to succeed. The matter was reported to me and as such, I was not very much astonished with this development. Possibly mentally I was prepared to face some fresh crisis but certainly did not expect that I might be put under arrest. It seemed to me that the spineless Chief Secretary and the IGP had totally destroyed the administrative fibre and the neutrality of Assam's administration. According to the detention order, I was to be lodged in the Guwahati Jail. So I did not collect sufficient clothes and other essential commodities for daily use. When contacted over telephone, Baber informed me that neither he nor Pradip Das, the IGP, knew anything about my arrest. Even if they knew, they possibly could not have been able to stave off the crisis. I left behind my wife with her tearful eyes betraying total helplessness and my three children with their vacant looks, failing to understand what was happening to their father.

After spending 3/4 hours in Guwahati Jail, I was flown in a special aircraft to Ranchi, surrounded by 10/12 CRPF personnel. Of course, an army doctor accompanied me on the flight. After spending the night at the Ranchi Circuit House, in the morning I was taken by road to Hazaribagh central jail. The two DySPs of Assam Police who were escorting me could not check their tears while taking leave of me after handing me over to the jail authorities.

I was taken to the security ward and locked up in a small cell without any toilet facility and electric connection. It turned out to be a solitary confinement for all practical purposes. The campus of the security ward extended over 1,200 bighas of land, although it could not boast of any worth-mentioning security measures excepting the strong door of my cell made of iron rod with a very strong locking system of British days and another iron door at the entry point. In fact it was from this ward that some freedom fighters had escaped during the freedom movement. Of course, the thought of escape did not occur to me as I still entertained deep faith in the neutrality of the judiciary of independent India.

My mind got bogged down in all sorts of deliberations within myself. I could not figure out where did I make the mistake, if any. What were the grounds of my detention? Is it not because I was instrumental in detecting lakhs of alien voters in the ERs? I knew that I would never be in a position to avenge such gross injustice as my detractors, too, knew it very well. Which is why, my detractors could become so desperate. But God did avenge: Because Samar Das did not believe the Assamese doctors, he went to Vellore for a minor surgery and died a premature death. And Anowara Taimur could never win an election again excepting a Rajya Sabha seat with dubiously undemocratic means. Still more disgraceful for her was her ignominious exit from Congress(I) and joining a fundamentalist party, albeit a logical end to her traits.

One cannot but admit that a coterie of bureaucrats and police officers in powerful positions who deviated from the democratic and traditionally proven mode of administration, made a total mockery of our young democracy and reduced it to an all-time low of undemocratic functioning. It amounted to ignoring not only rule of law but also the rule of an organised society with the urge of dominating over fellow beings reaching an unprecedented pitch possibly a hangover from the Emergency days. Also communal consideration had its own toll of victims. This is what exactly happened during Taimur's short regime. But the damage was done to the long term interests of Assam as after what happened to me, no police officer would venture in future to be active in respect of detecting illegal alien migrants and that is what was actually intended to achieve by arresting me and strengthen the fundamentalist front.

If there is a hell, then it must be in the jails of Bihar. Hazaribagh central jail had in the past accommodated political prisoners like Rajendra Prasad, Rahul Sankritayan, Subhas Bose, etc. Even in free India during the Emergency, this jail was filled up with detenues of eminent position in public life. Even then, the living conditions and the administrative affairs of the jail have not improved by an iota. This was a different world. Prisoners here could never expect to get their dues, although the officers of the jail were getting richer by the day at the cost of the prisoners. Hazaribagh central jail holds out great attraction to the jail officials and I was told that most of the posts of the jail were practically put on auction! Nobody wants a transfer from this jail; even there are instances of forgoing promotion for the sake of staying in this jail for a longer period. It is alleged that there ensues a tug of war between the DC and the Commissioner for getting their own candidate appointed to the post of Superintendent of this jail.

At Hazaribagh jail, I used to brood over the happenings in Assam for last 15/16 months. After analysing various developments, I had developed a shrewd suspicion that Indira Gandhi was never let to know the ground realities and that the agitation did not suffer from any secessionist intention as vested interests were trying to depict. Else, a clever and versatile leader like Indira Gandhi would have made a correct appraisal of the situation in Assam instead of making a wrong assessment, although her partisan interests were topmost in her calculations. The submission of wrong intelligence reports with ulterior motive has been, on many occasions, responsible for derailing the administration and throwing overboard many political calculations. Nobody knew it better than Indira Gandhi. Even then, she was making the same mistake all over again.

Looking back, I am inclined to observe that the emergence of the Assam movement in its full vehemence may be ascribed to SL Sakhder, the Chief Election Commissioner. Setting aside the advice given by the governor, the chief secretary and the chief election officer of Assam, Sakhder issued an order that elections must be held in 1980 in Assam; but nobody could file nomination papers in the Brahmaputra valley as mentioned earlier. Even most of the opposition parties had also advised against holding the elections forcibly. The Janata Party, the Jana Sangha, (now BJP) and the Lokdal etc., refrained from participating in the elections. Surprisingly, the Janata Party failed to draw any political mileage from subsequent developments despite its anti-foreigners stance and the fact that Janata government of Assam had started the process of weeding out the names of alien voters from Assam's ERs.

Meanwhile, I was facing tremendous difficulties in the jail for even getting the semblance of two meals because Assam government had authorised the jail authorities to spend only Rs. 8/- per day on me whereas the jail authorities were spending Rs. 11/- on an ordinary prisoner and I was a class I security prisoner! The daily quota of rations given to me did not suffice for two meals although I did not eat much. So I resorted to cooking only one meal in the afternoon so that it could meet the need of the night also. Even then, I used to feel hungry late in the night and had to fill up my stomach with drinking water which, however, was not denied as yet! The quality of the ration was also very poor. Rice less than 100 grams, 'arrahar dal' of very poor quality about 30 grams, two potatoes, one onion, little mustard oil and a kg of coal used to make up the daily quota. Still worse, not even sufficient water was made available for taking bath.

It seemed to me as if time was hanging still inside my cell. The frightening all pervasive silence of the night seemed to have silenced my own consciousness. I did not know how to spend the time. However, during the day, I used to spend the time by reading *the Geeta*, *the Bible* and Tagore's *Sanchayita* which I brought along with me. Even adequate period of sleep was a rarity. Owls' occasional loud hootings during the night certainly did not help in easing out the atmosphere. Invariably, I used to remind myself of my most favourite stanza from Browning: "I have ever been a fighter, so let me fight one more—the last and the best--" The only hope which kept me optimistic about the future was that my younger brother, Anil Kumar Bhattacharyya, who was emerging as a brilliant lawyer, would certainly take necessary measures for filing my habeas corpus writ petition as I still possessed immense faith in our judiciary.

All said and done, this period of imprisonment afforded an opportunity for having an insight into a world so far unknown to me. The inhuman and corrupt practices indulged in by the jail officers and employees, unknown in a civilised society, really shocked my inner self. To be very precise, this is a lawless world. All political philosphers have agreed that a welfare state while enacting laws invariably hankers for social and moral sanction without which laws suffer from sanctity. But here I found that the moral compass was not powerful enough to register such moral sanction; it was a different world altogether.

Being locked up at 5 pm and nothing to eat during the night, I used to wake up at about 3 am and wait for the cell to be unlocked at 6 am. For more than a week I could neither take bath nor brush my teeth for want of necessary requirements. I was really stinking and only after the civil surgeon who came to see me, had directed the jail doctor, a piece of soap, a tube of toothpaste and a tooth brush were ultimately made available to me from the hospital.

On 2 February 1981, one SI of police who never had the courage to look at my eyes and now growing fat out of proportion on his ill-got money, brought the grounds of my detention and served on me. Subsequently, some of the jail officers told me that this SI had informed them that I had distributed arms/amunitions/explosives all over Assam and that the agitation had subsided more than 75% after my arrest. Thus instead of myself deporting illegal alien migrants, I was deported to outside Assam. Having gone through the grounds of my detention, I did not know whether to laugh or to weep. I wondered how could high ranking officers resort to so much lies and fabricate so many wild allegations! Thank God, I did not do so when I was myself a powerful officer. But during the Indo-Pak war of 1965, I had noticed that some Hindu police officers of Sylhet origin, had gone all out to fabricate allegations against some respectable and innocent Muslim persons of eminence. Now I really thank myself that I did not fall a prey to such machinations. The underlying truth is that the Hindu police ofifcers uprooted from Sylhet were invariably disposed inimically against the Bengali-speaking Muslims as if they were born sworn enemies. Even now, this state of affairs is very much in vogue—a constant factor against achieving Hindu-Muslim amity.

That white lies fall flat on the ground, would be proved by the following : One of the main allegations against me, inter alia, was that on 26 November 1980, I had held a secret meeting with some student leaders and leader of an extremist group at my residence for arranging to distribute bombs/arms/ammunitions, etc., amongst the students and I had also donated Rs. 300/- for manufacturing bombs!

Now, please hold on and look at the facts: I had gone to Vellore on 19 November 1980 and on 26 November 1980 I was undergoing treatment under Dr Cherian and Dr. Krishnaswami at the Christian Medical College, Vellore! Readers are at their liberty to draw their own conclusion.

Another preposterous allegation was that on 31 August 1980, when I was bed-ridden with heart ailment, I was reported to have gone to Jagiroad and secretly conferred with AASU leaders there whereas I did not even know if there was an AASU unit.

That I had tried to foment rebellion in Assam Police was the most serious one. This has been highlighted elsewhere.

In fact, none of the allegations were based on truth. Which is why I was constrained to put on record that Samar Das and his most trusted lieutenant Phani Roy had acquired the expertise for fabricating allegations to compile dossiers which could not be subjected to verification as per provisions of the NSA. Even the Supreme Court had no say in the matter. Now, please look at the self contradiction of the system: Confessions made before a Police officer during the investigation of any crime, is not admissible as evidence in a court of law whereas the contents of a dossier compiled by subordinate police officer in order to malign somebody, are not justiceable under the NS Act. Even the highest court of the land is not authorised to question the truth or otherwise of such dossiers! What else can be more undemocratic and arbitrary? This smacks of medieval feudal mindset and practices. Let us examine a hypothetical situation: If I had in the past punished some officers thereby incurring their displeasure, what would prevent them later on to team up with Samar Das and submit few false reports against me? But this what exactly happened while compiling my so-called dossier as it transpired during the inspection of relevant documents by my lawyers in the course of the hearing of my habeas corpus writ petition. False reports were extracted against me from Inspector Siba Sharma and Inspector Bakul Nath—obviously on pains of severe punishment unless they obliged as desired. I, however, must admit that after the period of my detention was over, Bakul Nath came to me and profusely apologised to me with tears in his eyes. The then DIGP Special Branch, who went on to become the

DGP of Assam, was also pressurised by Samar Das and another senior DIGP to fabricate some source reports against me but he declined to oblige. He himself had divulged this secret to me in 2012. No wonder that today he is acknowledged as one of the honest top intellectuals of Assam, besides being a Sahitya Akademi Award winning litterateur of the state. Such dossiers compiled on the basis of so-called source reports, are treated as so sacrosanct that the question of legal and constitutional validity is divested of any meaning whatsoever.

Needless to mention that this system is a great challenge to the Rule of Law. As I am scripting this on 23 February 2013, an observation made by Justice A K Misra, the Chief Justice of Kolkata High Court, is very relevant in this context: "—that it was an established principle that a bureaucrat, even when he is implementing an order issued to him by a superior, cannot evade responsibility for his action. Moreover, if such an order violates rule of law or the Constitution, the concerned officer is well within his rights to refuse to carry out the order. Indeed it is his duty to do so." (quoted from *Seven Sisters* Post, 23 February 2013).

Conversely, if unscrupulous officers conspiring to ignore/bypass the Rule of Law, superiors cannot evade responsibility for succumbing to such conspiracies. Obviously, when both the Devils are hands in glove, the Satan goes to his dinner! This is how the commoners are fast losing faith in the administration. The Rule of Law and constitutional principles are being sacrified at the altar of feudal mindset of the political bosses, although an IPS officer has to take an oath of his allegiance to the Constitution at the time of joining the service. What the ordinary citizen can expect from the administration when no less an officer than the union home secretary suppresses an order of the Union Home Minister and distort the same only for wrecking vengeance for communal consideration? Still we continue to bask in trumpeting that ours is the largest democracy in the world! Was it not because Burney, a Muslim union home secretary, felt no compunction while distorting the order of the union home minister in order to comply with the proposal for my summary dismissal from the IPS sent by a Muslim chief minister? These are some of the questions the so-called largest democracy had so far failed to address and instead, rewarded Burney with a governorship. Then where was the much vaunted accountablity of public servants? Is it applicable to only the lowly and helplessly placed government employees?

After my detention on grounds of national security, my dismissal from service was only a logical conclusion which Anowara Taimur and Samar Das were hell bent on achieving. The order of dismissal was served on me on 27 March 1981 in Ranchi jail only to be rescinded by the Supreme Court in 1995 after 13 years of legal battle; but the date of my retirement had already passed off and that was a trick played on me by delaying the submission of the union government's response to my petition so that I could not put on my uniform once again whereas they had lost no time in filing an appeal against the order of my reinstatement passed by the Central Administrative Tribunal.

Meanwhile, I was transferred to Ranchi for better medical attention which, however, did not prove to be adequate as there was no ICU unit. A room in Ranchi Medical College was converted into a prison cell guarded by about a platoon of Bihar armed police personnel. The Superintendent of Ranchi jail who served on me the order of my dismissal, was accompanied by a team of physicians for attending to any medical setback my health might suffer on receipt of the order. They were all very surprised to find that I treated the entire matter very calmly. They tried to console me and I had to put them off by simply telling them that under the circumstances, this was very much expected and that I was neither surprised nor shocked. The order of my dismissal was served at a time when my habeas corpus writ petition was being heard at the Guwahati High Court—obviously with the intention of prejudicing the opinion of the Hon'ble Court. Here the students of the medical college and the doctors were not only looking after my daily needs but they had also made some reading materials available.

While in Hazaribagh jail, many unfortunate prisoners, most of them having been deprived of any legal aid, used to come to me narrating their tale of woes and injustices they were compelled to confront for no fault of theirs. They sincerely hoped that I could give them necessary advice for redressing their grievances without ever realising that I was myself a helpless prisoner. Some of their tales brought tears to my eyes with no means of rescuing them at my disposal.

Hazaribagh district had a large population of *Adivasis*. As such, Hazaribagh jail, too, had a large number of Adivasi prisoners. Some of them were convicted prisoners and others were under-trial prisoners. Almost all of them were illiterate. Most of them were involved in cases of murder. I would like to place few cases before the readers so that they could realise how the poorer section of the society was being deprived of the prescribed legal procedure only because they are poor and ignorant of their dues.

Ranjit Kole, arrested in a case of dacoity, had been languishing in this jail for last 14 years as an under-trial prisoner. When sent to jail, he was only 15 years of age. Ranjit claimed that he was the victim of factional rivalries of his village. Because the case diaries of the case are missing, he had not been sent up for trial since 1966. I failed to understand why the provisions of the amended CrPC, had not been applied to his case. Nor the officers responsible for the stalemate, had been taken to task! Whether this would have been possible in case of a well-to-do person, must be addresed by the society in general and the jurists in particular, sooner or later.

Then, consider the case of Parameswar, the only bread earner of a very poor family. Employed in a tea stall in Calcutta at Rs. 50/- per month, he was bed-ridden for eight days with high fever and could not attend to his duties with the resultant vacancy filled up by somebody else. Not only he was a victim of the unorganised labour sector but also the benefits of any system of social security were not available to him. He was paid his dues of Rs. 62/- which he kept with a fellow villager who disappeared with his money. His hope of saving some money for his wife and the younger brother evaporated for ever and he was arrested in the train for travelling without ticket on his return journey home and booked under Section 109 CrPC as an anti-social element although he was not a criminal. Nor did he have any criminal record in the past. The police did not verify his antecedents. He could not pay Rs. 5/- as demanded by the two constables who arrested him. Still worse, he has not been sent up for trial for last five months. The question that cropped up in my mind, was that if all the unemployed youths were to be booked under Sec. 109 of CrPC, how could India's 1,219 jails accommodate them? Thus Parameswar was languishing in the jail for how long nobody knows!

The case of Karmee Devi is much more heart-rending and most inhuman. She is an under-trial prisoner. She claimed that she was not guilty of the crime she had been accused of. About a month back, she was sent to jail with her 1.5-year-old daughter and she was expecting another baby very soon. Still she was not granted bail by the Police who ignored her advanced state of pregnancy. Her husband did not have the requisite fund for filling a bail petition in the court.

Meanwhile, Karmee delivered a male child in the jail. Having come to know about it, her husband sold off some household articles and engaged a lawyer for getting Karmee released on bail. With the bail order, he came to the jail at 12 noon. Karmee and her husband did not know that the court order would not suffice for her release unless the warder of the jail gate was given his 'pound of flesh' amounting to Rs 5/-, as claimed to be the rule for all prisoners going out on bail. The amount of money thus collected for the whole month, was shared by all the employees of the jail with a share making upward journey as well. Karmee's husband was swept into the darkness of utter despair as he was not left with a penny after paying the lawyer's fee. He took recourse to the poor man's only resort—his tears; his tears failed to soften the attitude of the gate warder. All his entreaties fell on deaf ears. Even the source of his tears turned dry and he left the jail gate at 3 pm in quest for the amount of Rs. 5/-, the service tax for the warder. Karmee also kept on hoping that her husband would come back with the warder's fee. But he did not or could not come back in time. On the other hand, Karmee would have to be released under legal compulsion before the cells were locked up at 5 pm. So ultimately, shouting the choicest invectives available in the dictionary, the warder released Karmee under legal compulsion. Karmee came out with her two babies but could not find her husband, thus confronting an unforeseen situation. Next morning Karmee's husband came back and paid Rs. 5/- to the gate warder with the request to release Karmee. When informed that she was released the previous evening, Karmee's husband felt as if a bolt from the blue had struck him! Will he ever be able to trace his wife and the children? This question caused total loss of my mental peace and I wondered how many more Karmee Devis were suffering in this manner in our largest democracy! Even next day, I was fully absorbed in worries for Karmee, her husband and the two children. This amounted to nothing less than organised banditry committed upon helpless fellow citizens!

Having had nothing else to do, I was delving deep into the past life of quite a few prisoners. I found that most of the prisoners had been accused of offences related to property disputes, mainly land dispute and offences committed for taking revenges or family vendetta for one or the other reason—mostly resulting in murders.

Even among the prisoners, a sense of class distinction pervades the entire atmosphere. Those who are accused of committing murder or condemned to death penalty, belong to the highest class in the roll of honour (?). Immediately below them, are those accused of committing dacoity and those accused of offences like theft, affray rioting, etc, belong to the lowest class with nobody bothering for them excepting utilising their services as menial labour. Many of the heinous crimes could have been averted but could be committed because of inaction on the part of the Police. Corrupt practices in Assam Police were likely to pale into insignificance if compared to those of Bihar Police. Not that Assam Police is not gradually catching up!

Ravi Kesari, an Adivasi youth, who had been convicted to life imprisonment in a murder case, was a glaring example of police inaction resulting in the murder committed by Ravi for avenging the murder of his elder brother. After the murder of his brother he went to the police station for registering a case but he, even after running from pillar to post, miserably failed to get the case registered and prompt and proper investigation done. It transpired that he could not make any payment as per demand made at the PS. Ultimately, he lost his patience, took the law into his own hands and killed his brother's murderer. He had no regrets as he had restored the lost prestige of his family caused by the murder of his brother. He neither escaped after committing the murder nor denied the charge in the court. Rather, he boasted of vindicating the honour of his family!

The desert of inhuman practices in the jail with self-aggrandisement as the soul motivating force, was drying up all my hopes for any regeneration of India's officialdom. But possibly unexpected surprises impart some fragrance to the otherwise dry and drab ambience : Chief Warden Jamadar Nanda Singh, a giant of a man, more than six-feet tall with a robust physique, had been a terror for even a hardened criminal for last 24/25 years. Nobody had even the courage to look directly at his eyes. Dr Bhupen Hazarika, the legendary bard of Assam, in one of his famous number, had sung that- "life is a theatre of little smile and little tears"; but so far in the jail it had been all tears only all around. However, Jamadar Nanda Singh's visit to my cell with Chunu Gope, a life convict, presented an altogether different scenario. In fact, I was totally flabbergasted to see tears in Nanda Singh's eyes which he could not hold back despite his best efforts. It transpired that the society was not yet bereft of parental feelings: As I looked askance at him, he handed over to me a letter written in Hindi. When I could not read the hand-written letter, Koka Singh, another life convict, explained the whole matter to me. When Chunnu Gope had come to jail his only daughter, Munni, was only 3/4 years old and being very fond of her father, even now she had fond memories of her father. She had since grown up to be of marriageable age and all the villagers were insisting on Munni being married away; but she would not agree as she wanted her father to be present in her marriage ceremony for personally blessing her. So she wanted to wait till Chunnu was released from jail. For last 14 years Chunnu had not seen his daughter and on receipt of the letter, he broke down and sought Jamadar Nanda Singh's help for doing the needful so that he could attend the ceremony. The emotionally surcharged situation reminded me one of Harry Belafonte's famous number :

"I had to leave her a little girl

In Kingston town—"

Having witnessed the reverberation of a song from faraway Jamaica, I myself felt very much touched and before my moist eyes could betray me, I withdrew to inside my cell, lest I might not have to follow in the footsteps of Nanda Singh! After some time, Nanda Singh came back to my cell and requested me to prevail upon the jailor for facilitating the transfer of Chunnu to Jamshedpur where his family lived. Further Nanda Singh said that he himself would also try to get Chunnu removed to Jamshedpur jail. How much I wished that the "overlords" of the jail administration had as much human feelings as Nanda Singh!

A pair of sparrows had in an upper corner of my cell built up their nest after I had come to occupy the cell. They had practically become inmates of my present household. Long back, I had read a book captioned as 'The House Sparrow' written by Dennis Summers Smith, a British citizen. This pair of sparrow with their nest inside my cell reminded me of this book. Smith had in this book, described the well organised life style of the sparrow. Further Smith had very aptly pointed out that the deep interaction of human life with nature commenced first through the house sparrow. Though, we see number of sparrows daily, we hardly care to know about them. Their life style is no less organised than ours. The loyalty to each other in their marital lives, is something which may put many a human being to shame. The attraction to the animal world, if cultivated from childhood, goes a long way in founding a close relationship with the nature and in turn, such children can never behave in cruel manner later in life, as I have seen this happening in case of my own children.

A CPI MLA of Bihar assembly, had been sent to jail few days back as an accused person in some case. His name was Ramendra Kumar; his father Jogendra Sharma was also a CPI MP. Ramendra Kumar came to see me. Absolute surprises were in store for me : He told me that he had heard from the jail staff that I was the leader of the secessionist forces of Assam! It was crystal clear from his talk that widespread wrong impression had been created about the Assam movement outside Assam with his own party falling a victim to such wild rumour mongering along with other Left parties. To oppose the movement is one thing which they have every right to do but to call it a secessionist movement amounts to criminal insinuation. I had almost lost my temper. But when I asked him to point out a single instance of a man from Bihar or Rajasthan or Punjab being harassed on account of the movement, he had to remain silent. Also I pointed out to him that Guwahati alone had a few thousand Biharis and that many of them had actively supported the movement; in fact most of the drivers of rickshaws and pushcarts were Biharis whereas not a single rickshaw or a pushcart had been damaged on account of the movement. After I furnished him with full details about the movement, he seemed to have been convinced. But like many other Marxists, he, too, viewed the entire problem through Marxist glass!

It seems when problems come, they come in a crowd. On 13 February 1981, few hours after my cell was locked at 5 pm, I suffered another heart attack. There was nobody to respond to my cries for help nor was there any medicine for my use in an emergency. Excruciating pain on my left hand, made me cry in sheer agony. I had four sleeping tablets and swallowed them all with the hope that this would induce sleep. I must have fallen asleep within about 15/20 minutes and when I got up next morning well past 9 am, I was totally disoriented and could not make out where I was lying. However, the presence of Dr TK Das, the jail doctor, reminded me of what I had experienced during the night. Dr Das rushed to the civil surgeon and brought him to my cell. Dr Madhusudan Narain, the civil surgeon, found my blood pressure to be very high (180/125). He, immediately, advised the jail superintendent for taking an ECG and prescribed some medicine to be immediately made available to me. The jail doctor had no power to purchase medicines even in such cases of emergency. The jail superintendent simply did not respond to the CS's recommendation and kept the matter pending for four weeks until Ramendra Kumar, the CPI MLA, having been released on bail, requested the DC to take necessary action on the advice of the CS for my treatment. Subsequently, I was told that on hearing about my health condition, my wife, brothers and few prominent citizens of Guwahati had also pressurised the authorities for making arrangement for my necessary treatment. In this context what is more significant is the apathetic and inhuman attitude of the jail superintendent who on being asked to explain his such conduct by the DC, tried to shift the entire blame to Dr TK Das! One may well imagine what an illiterate, simple prisoner would have to encounter under similar circumstances! And that is my intention for informing the reading public.

However, my predicament was nearing an end—uncertain

though—with the visit of Prof. (Dr) C. N. Sahay from the Ranchi Medical College for examining my health condition and he found my blood pressure still very high at 180/110, besides detecting other malfunctioning of my heart which was of serious nature. Dr Sahay had come to examine me after 29 days of the recommendation made by the civil surgeon. All the delay was entirely due to the inhuman mentality of the superintendent. Dr Sahay had also expressed his extreme displeasure about the most unhealthy condition of the cell I was confined to. Dr Sahay assured me that he would submit his findings and recommendations in writing to the authorities. Even then, I was not given the medicine prescribed by Dr Sahay for two days and when given the medicine prescribed by Dr Sahay after two days, the main medicine for controlling blood pressure was not given.

The nightmarish memories of Hazaribagh jail used to haunt me for several years. Not remaining content with ensuring my detention followed by my dismissal from the IPS, Samar Das had resorted to ridiculing and taunting me also. There was a teacher in Hazaribagh St Xavier's School named Arup Sinha whom I had never met, let alone knowing him personally. He was reported to be very close to Samar Das, possibly on the Christian net. I had not even heard of him. It was reported to me that Samar Das had asked him to come to the jail and enquire of my welfare and how I was taking to jail life! I did not even know that there was a St. Xavier's School at Hazaribagh. Sinha tried to find out if I was ready to see him. Of course, I did not know whether Sinha knew the message Samar Das was trying to convey to me through him. Samar Das's anxiety to cause me as much loss of mental peace as possible, as I saw it, was nothing but a self-inflicted punishment perpetrated on himself!

Ramendra Kumar before going out of the jail on bail, had narrated to me a very interesting experience of his: Ramendra Kumar was a labour leader of many coal mines of Bihar. Each mine had about 4,000 to 5,000 labourers. At the time of payment of weekly wages the workers used to be deprived of a fraction of their wages which could be paid in coins only, on the plea of non-availability of coins. Such unpaid money amounted to several thousands of rupees per week and used to be pocketed by the disbursing officers of the respective mines. All efforts having failed for reimbursing such dues to the labourers.,Ramendra Kumar and his associates embarked upon a novel idea: They succeeded in getting such dues deposited in a labour welfare fund and the first month of starting the said fund, saw an amount of Rs. 7,000/- accumulated in the fund and the authorities realising the benefits such a fund could cultivate, agreed to deposit equal amount of money to the fund. Ramendra Kumar and his associates utilised this fund for building up a modern high school at a place called SYAL for the children of the labourers at a cost of rupees eight lakhs! The lesson from such an exercise one can draw, is that what is required is selfless commitment to address the grievances of the poor and the exploited people whereas crores of rupees are being looted in Assam by the politicians and the government officers in the name of implementing so many welfare schemes. In fact, lately many scandals of misappropriating public funds, have unmasked quite a few politicians and bureaucrats and some have been even sentenced to imprisonment of various terms.

Lenin had once observed that, "The society prepares the crime; the criminal commits it." In the jail I had rare opportunities of interacting with both desperate criminals and innocent prisoners as well. The more I do so, the more I am convinced that a sizeable percentage of criminals in India, are the creation of the police. On a close analysis, I find that such roles of the Police may be attributed to the following circumstances:

1. In order to please the superior officers and even the public, many officers of police stations resort to arresting innocent persons either out of sheer suspicion or for only evading the allegation of inaction. Once arrested in cases of heinous crimes, it becomes difficult to get away from the jail. As a result, such arrestees are deprived of their means of livelihood with their families confronting unforeseen crises. On the other hand, the association with hardened criminals, breeds criminal propensities in many of them. They gradually start harbouring hatred and revengeful attitude to the society and the authorities and on being released from the jail, they do not hesitate to commit crimes whereas if innocent persons are not arrested, many new criminals would not have surfaced.

Efforts for preventing this malpractice, have so far remained confined only to criticism of varrying degrees in the media.

2. Many of the criminals—both with criminal records and many others without such records and acquitted by the court as innocent seriously intend to lead a normal, stable life because they had developed hatred and aversion to the jail life. They try to live within the limits of law; but the police would not allow them. In police eyes, once arrested in some criminal case, they would continue to be suspects rightly or wrongly. They are arrested on the slightest pretext without considering the court's verdict in a previous case. Briefly speaking, they are subjected to all sorts of harassment by the police without ever considering that they were working hard to eke out a living—a serious phenomenon deserving serious consideration in the interests of the society; but he becomes a criminal in the eyes of the society also after being arrested repeatedly! Our society, social scientists, law makers and the jurists seem to have drawn a blank in this context. Unless the social commitment and accountability of the police functionaries are ensured, it will be simply impossible to eradicate such malpractices. I had already mentioned how in Australia, such propensity on the part of the police had been done away with. I am constrained to observe from personal experience that the Police personnel are hardly trained for defending the constitutional rights of the individual—let alone any motivation course. In fact, the residues of the colonial system are yet to be got rid of. In any case, the home truth is that officers entrusted with training the police personnel, are either found to be unacceptable to their senior officers or inconvenient by the political bosses, regardless of their aptitude and ability to function as trainers. A welfare oriented system should have ensured that the under-trial prisoners and those arrested on mere suspicion, should have no opportunity for interacting inside the jail with convicted criminals.

3. Lately, it has been seen that some politicians of the party in power try to utilise the police for wrecking vengeance against

persons considered inconvenient for them. In addition, some police officers themselves induldge in wrecking vengeance on personal grounds. The failure or refusal to grease the palm of police officers, also lead to some innocent persons being arrested. Such condemnable, anti-social conspiratorial propensity of some politicians and Police officers have been resulting in the arrests of innocent and non-criminal persons since the colonial days. The need of the hour is to free the entire Police set-up of the country from political pressure and motivate to function as a people-oriented service like in the UK, Australia and many other modern democracies. An example of how personal vendetta is likely to derail the police is cited below: In 1960, I was the ASP in Nagaon district. The younger brother of a political heavy weight of national prominence, had pressurised me to arrest one Benu Saikia, the lessee of a country liquor depot on false charges of having been involved in some anti-Bengali rioting case. Of course, I refused. So he found out an alternative for wrecking vengeance. He pressurised his powerful brother to declare Nagaon as a dry district so that Saikia's business was ruined although nothing was done to prevent large scale bootlegging. Possibly, one reason for cases of gross injustice remaining unnoticed and unaddressed, may be that the Law of Torts has neither developed healthily nor has it attracted the serious attention of our jurists and law-makers—let alone its wide application. But one can certainly hope that with the passage of time, new trends will surface.

4. In our society, the police is looked upon as an opponent-- not as a friend. This is so, mainly due to the maltreatment and severe torture experienced even by innocent citizens while in police custody. Even many feature films and tele-films are also responsible for portraying such a monstrous image of the Police. *Amar Asom* and *Dainik Agradoot*, two Assamese dailies on March 9, 2013, reported a latest example of such Police atrocities: One Hiranya Hira of Marigaon district, committed suicide when he could not bear up with Police atrocities. Prior to this, a senior CPI leader, Manoj Deka had

> also committed suicide for similar reason. But the police officers responsible for such inhuman act, were yet to be taken to task and the administration remained satisfied by simply announcing that an enquiry would be held by a magistrate into Hira's suicide only after Marigaon PS was gheraoed by hundreds of agitated members of the public.

On the other hand, quite a few police commissions, both at the national and state level, had submitted their recommendations long back; but all these reports are still gathering dust in the files. As for example, long back it was recommended that Guwahati should be placed under the administration of a police commissioner and we had been hearing this for more than three decades but nothing had transpired so far. Only when a serious law-and-order situation befalls Guwahati, Dispur goes on the air to assure the public that the city will be placed under a police commissioner very soon. Needless to mention that the system, of Police Commissionership entails a more co-ordinated and tighter control over the likelihood of the breakdown of law & order and frequent violation of traffic rules. This system has stood the test of time. Then why not? The simple answer is that vested interests would not allow it to materialise!

As days were passing into weeks and weeks into months, I was becoming more anxious to know about the fate of my writ petition filed in Guwahati High Court. But, meanwhile disturbing news were pouring in from Assam. The non-violent movement was being interrupted by sporadic violent incidents. What disturbed me the most was the news of Parthasarathi's murder. He fell a victim to a bomb explosion in his own office chamber at Jorhat. He was the SDO of Kokrajhar when I was SP at Dhubri. Undoubtedly, he was a very honest and efficient officer with a promising career ahead. When killed, he was the Commissioner of Upper Assam division. This was certainly a meaningless killing and Samar Das, who was now in charge of the SB and security matters, had totally failed to anticipate such happenings. This was a glaring instance of his non-imaginative functioning. I was sure he would go scot-free. In the past, Samar Das had lost his mental balance and turned violent. In fact, he had to be confined by force on more than one occasion. As such, it was a Himalayan blunder to entrust him with such heavy and serious responsibility as a bonus for his political manipulation.

On the other hand, those who conspired to cause Parthasarathi's elimination failed to understand that such killing of innocent officer could not advance the cause of the Movement even by an inch. The message of the Movement was already clear and loud—heard all over the entire country. Besides, lakhs of people could participate in the Movement because it was non-violent. So was the case with Gandhiji's Non-Cooperation Movement during the freedom struggle. Once violence gets the upper hand, it becomes impossible for the commoners to participate in any movement. Violence begets violence and now it would be easier for the administration to resort to draconian measures for putting down a genuinely non-violent movement and that was what the detractors of the anti-foreigners movement wanted. That the violent elements are surfacing, is the result of inept handling of the entire matter by the administration, can hardly be gainsaid. New-Delhi seems to have totally ignored the message of this mass uprising. It will be seen that such inept handling of the situation had led ULFA to become proactive with incidences of violence and lawlessness assuming an unprecedented rise.

It is said that, "no news is good news." But here in solitary confinement, neither 'no news' nor good or bad news could mean anything for me. In other words, I was dumbfounded to hear about the aforesaid murder and engulfed by a confused state of mind. Suddenly came to mind the forewords written by Jean Paul Sartre in a book (caption of the book I fail to recollect) written by Frantz Fanon. If I remember correctly, the book was a revolt against the status quo. However, I am at the moment concerned with the forewords. Succinctly reproduced, at times in my own words, it will mean the following : "-- I am willing to believe that at the beginning you did not realise what was happening. Later on, you doubted if such things could be true. But now you know, and still you are dead silent. The blinding sun of torture is at its peak and it is lighting up the entire nation (country?). Under the blinding merciless glare, there is not a laugh that does not ring false; not a face that is not made up to conceal fear and anger -- not a single action that does not betray your disgust and everybody's complicity------". There must have been much more but I do not remember at the moment. Sartre's and Fanon's words had caused extreme agitation in my mind. Which is why, these words came to my mind.

At such lonely hours, I was further reminded of the false and motivated news published in some of the newspapers against me when I was conducting the operation for detecting the names of alien citizens in the ERs. Some of these newspapers not only wrote against me but they did not spare even my old father. One sample of such journalism may be worth submitting to the readers: On November 14/15, 1979, *Dainik Basumati*, a Bengali daily published from Calcutta with government aid, had accused me of being an extreme chauvinist. I am reported to have personally deleted 50,000 names from the ERs of Mangaldoi LS constituency. It seemed the reporter did not know that a DIGP had no such power as to interfere in preparing the ERs. Still worse, the breasts of two Bengali girls were chopped off in my and Atwar Rahman, IGP's presence ! Rahman has been depicted as a very communally minded person. I have worked with him very closely and never traced an iota of communal feelings in him. Anyway, how can an educated reporter and a Daily could print such motivated reports? Obviously, the intention was to drive a wedge between the Assamese and the Bengalis. I am happy to announce that the Bengali society of Assam simply did not bother to place any importance on such falsities. But please note that the same Daily had played a very strong role during the Freedom Movement. How could they compromise with their rich legacy? The aforementioned report about the Bengali girls might or might not have been motivated by communal consideration but it was certain that the propensity to cater for sensational news regardless of its veracity or otherwise was the root cause. Still worse, Letters to the Editor in protest of such false and motivated news did not find the light of the day! On the other hand, senior journalists like B Verghese, Kuldeep Nayar, Rajmohan Gandhi, MV Kamath, Mark Tully of BBC did their best to present an objective picture of the situation. None of them had anything to report against me. Also two young female journalists (if I remember correctly, they were Ms Niroja Choudhuri and Rupa Saini) reporting for the journal *Himmat*, earned the gratitude of the

Assamese people by portraying the picture of the Assam Movement in correct perspectives. Rajmohan Gandhi was ahead of everybody else in voicing the feelings of the people of Assam when he wrote the following significant words: "--- The rest of India does not see us. If seen, we are not recognised, we are not remembered. And we are not heard. This has been the charge of the citizens of the North-east against the Indian majority." (*The Wounds of Indifference* by Rajmohan Gandhi) Myron Weiner wrote the following in the same vein: "The Assamese often think of themselves as a 'forgotten' and 'neglected' state within the Indian Union and as a neglected people in danger of being overwhelmed by migrant peoples and absorbed by neighbouring states." (*Sons of the Soil* by Weiner). Because he scripted these words, he had been even accused of conspiring to incite the people of Assam. Be that as it may, even after four decades of making these observations, the situation vis-a-vis illegal migration from neighbouring countries, has deteriorated further with New Delhi still looking the other way. But few senior Assamese journalists like Kirtinath Hazarika, Prafulla Barua, Kanaksen Deka, Dhirendranath Bezbarua, etc., did not lag behind in informing the reading public about the serious threat to the identity of the indigenous people of Assam. In fact, during the movement few newspapers like "Dainik Asom" and "Dainik Janambhumi" were put under strict censorship, thereby repeating the mistakes of the infamous Emergency days. Not that few other Assamese journalists like Dr Hiren Gohain and Homen Borgohain etc., did not oppose the Movement; but their opposition mainly pertained to the fascist elements involved in the movement. However, they did not deny the centrality of the core issue of the Movement. In fact, Dr Hiren Gohain subsequently qualified his stand by putting it on record that such a mass uprising cannot take place without some valid reasons. On the other hand, Dr Gohain's and Borgohain's bitter criticism enabled the leadership of the mass agitation to remain on guard against those who were constantly trying to impart a violent turn to the non-violent agitation.

Most of the journalists who came from outside Assam for reporting on the Assam Movement were highly educated persons; but their outright failure to appreciate the real character of the movement, amounted to sheer intellectual poverty. They themselves did not understand the implications of their superficial and at times, false reportings. True, the agitation centered round the issue of illegal alien migration; but at the same time, it amounted to an all-out revolt against the traditionally weak servile and myopic leadership of the state intent only upon self aggrandisement which the national media either did not understand or did not want to highlight for reasons left to the reader to deduce. Briefly speaking, they saw everything but observed nothing.

I was this time transferred to Patna Jail where, I was told, better medical attention would be available and also that I would be confined in a cottage of the Patna Medical College. But on arrival at Patna, the superintendent of the medical college refused to make any such cottage available on the plea that no cottage was vacant and this was a white lie. In due course, it transpired that cottages were made available only on payment of heavy bribe to the superintendent. Further it transpired that these cottages were safe havens for some of the hardened criminals, including dacoits. Cottages were allotted to them on payment of heavy bribes although they hardly occupied the cottages. But if arrested for committing some crimes, they would invariably take recourse to the alibi that on the particular day the crime was committed, they or he was under medical treatment in the hospital cottage and hospital records would prove the alibi! The main accomplice in such reprehensible anti-social activities was invariably the Superintendent. All concerned knew it but nobody could proceed against such malpractices—obviously because of strong political patronage the Superintendent could boast of. So, no cottage was available for me and I was accommodated in a barrack which was already full to its capacity with 14 convicts of murder cases. What an irony of fate! A Class I security prisoner was compelled to share a barrack with 14 murderers! The superintendent of the jail could not be blamed as he had no alternative available to him. An extra cot was brought in and I thanked my stars as I did not have to sleep on the ground littered with wastes and droppings of varied sorts. The less said about it, the better for me to adjust with what had suddenly befallen me.

Of the 14 convicts, eight were old persons. One such old convict had his two sons and two nephews undergoing the same sentence. As it transpired, all these murders resulted from disputes over land and none of them had any regrets for what they had done!

Otherwise they were kind hearted persons. In fact, they took it upon themselves to look after my comforts and needs. Amongst them was one Atta Khan, an Afghan citizen who had not heard from his family for the entire period of 17 years he had been in the jail. How painful and cruel a system is still prevalent in independent India's prisons! One of the convicts had also got the B A degree. By the evening of my arrival at Patna, I was down with high fever, but other inmates of the barrack immediatley got busy with nursing me and this was something one could not expect from the jail officials. One of the convicts fitted the mosquito net while another was fanning me. Still another convict started pouring cold water on my head. What was more touching, was that they arranged within themselves to maintain night-long vigil over me, lest some emergency occur. I was really astounded to find such kind hearted persons among these murderers. It seemed that the law failing to deliver their dues, they were constrained to take the law into their own hands.

Anyway, experiencing the anxieties amongst these murderers for my welfare, I was inclined to discard what Oscar Wilde had written while in prison :

"The vilest deeds like poison weeds
Bloom well in prison air:
It is only what is good in Man
That wastes and withers there:
Pale anguish keeps the heavy gate,
And the warder in despair."
As he had written once that
"Something was dead in each of us
And what was dead was Hope."

Even here too, Wilde proved himself wrong when subsequently he wrote the following:

"This too I know—and wise it were
If each could know the same

That every prison that men build
Is built with the brick of shame
And bound with bars lest Christ should see
How men their brothers maim."

The real truth is that hopes never die, may be they remain concealed in the human heart. Altogether 1,219 prisons of India are proving Wilde right every day. V. R. Krishna Iyer, the retired judge of the Supreme Court sounded similar feelings when he wrote the following: "Our prisons are human warehouses of tension and terror, alienation and sadism, rule of iron and wageless workers with pervasive zoological process. This prison sub-culture hardly heals, rarely humanizes, never restores dignity."

On 6 May 1981, Premkanta Mahanta who was my senior staff officer when I was the DIGP, Border, addressed a letter to all the MPs of the country. The letter will speak for itself. The letter is reproduced below without any editing :

An Appeal to the Hon'ble Members of the Indian Parliament

Sir,

How sheer conspiracy and personal jealously of colleagues can ruin a person, Shri H. K. Bhattacharyya, IPS since dismissed, is a glaring example. He has been dismissed from service and detained under the NSA on serious charges of having link with the Assam agitation and a so-called extremist group. As a very close associate of Sri Bhattacharyya during the tenure of his office as DIG and mine as SP of the Border Organisation I can assert that he was never connected with the agitation over the foreigners' issue not to speak of extemist groups, if any. During his tenure in the Border Organisation the work of detection of foreign nationals was taken up earnestly which, when obstructed by some vested interest, gave rise to the agitation. When the agitation gained momentum and got wide publicity in the early part of 1980 many journalists of all India repute dashed to Assam for collection of various data about the magnitude of the influx of foreigners into the North Eastern States. Some of these journalists, I clearly remember, were directed from the higher authorities to the Border Office for collection of these data. Of course at times some leaders of the organisations spear-heading the movement also approached the Border Police Organisation for various data, who, however, were not obliged except with information of general nature. He had no acquaintance, not to speak of intimacy, with the agitation leaders at the early stage. It was the Government at whose behest Shri Bhattacharyya was compelled to come in closer touch with the agitation leaders. Some instances of this kind were: on one occasion he was asked by the highest authority of the State Government to contact the AASU leaders, after a talk had failed in order to bring them back for further discussions with the Central Home Minister who even postponed his return to Delhi for a day. On another occasion during a deadlock Shri Bhattacharyya had to oblige the highest authority of the country by helping RK Dorendra Singh the then Chief Minister of Manipur to establish contact and have informal discussions with the agitation leaders at Guwahati. Once he was even summoned to Delhi when a negotiation had almost failed, to make use of his not unfriendly relations with the Assam leaders. Thus in many more ways it was the Government who got him closely acquainted with the agitation leaders. He did not do it voluntarily. Had he succeeded, he would have, perhaps, been rewarded. Now, should he be punished for the failure in spite of his best efforts? Is it fair to make him the scapegoat for the failure of the Government to come to a settlement due to obstacles put by some vested interests? Was it not he as DIG (Range) who successfully maintained law and order in the teeth of many odds enabling the last Parliamentary elections to be held in Cachar? When Shri Bhattacharyya came to limelight and became important in course of the agitation as stated above, some of his rivals and jealous colleagues in the department suffered from serious heart burning. They were eagerly waiting for their turn to come. The opportunity came in a big way when the main two persons who felt grossly affected due to deletion of quite a large number of foreigner's names from electroal rolls of their constituencies came to power as the Chief Minister and the Home Minister of the puppet government of Assam. Shri Bhattacharyya, a loyal and sincere public servant has been made a victim of a heinous conspiracy by means of false and fabricated documents.

Viewed from personal angle his dismissal from service and detention under the NSA may not appear to be of any national significance. But it is a case which has proved that Police can even make a man a woman and a woman a man. Here lies the danger. Unless the existing procedure of preparation and maintenance of dossiers by police is suitably modified the liberty of the citizens will always be in jeopardy. This power given to police for larger interest of the State will always have the danger of its being misused by mean and unscrupulous persons in power against their personal rivals. It is high time that it be made obligatory for police to keep a "Judiciary Cell" constituted for the purpose, intimated immediately when a person is brought under surveillance. This will prevent the police from fabricating back dated false documents as is in practice now to suit their or their unscrupulous masters' unholy designs.

May I appeal to the Hon'ble members of the Parliament to take up the case of Shri H. K. Bhattacharyya as a test case and to press the Government to form a Committee of the House to scrutinize it for the sake of justice and equity? If done, I am sure this case will bring out many more things of national interest to light.

Dated,
Guwahati,
the 6th May, 1981

Yours etc.
(Prem Kanta Mahanta)
Retd. Superintendent of Police
Assam

The letter speaking for itself, I prefer not to offer any further comment on the matter.

My advocates JP Bhattacharyya, Prasanta Kumar Goswami, etc., were reported to have made strong protests against the conditions in which I was confined. As a result, Nripen Das, the Registrar of the High Court, was deputed to ascertain the ground realities. Nripen Das found that I was confined in a barrack where convicts of murder cases were kept. He also found that the jail doctor, namely Dr Kalwar, did not follow any of the instructions given by Dr CP Thakur, the cardiology specialist of the Patna Medical College. Besides, he took my statement also about the hardship I had experienced in all the jails I had been confined to so far. Dr Kalwar had betrayed his motive when he was insistently enquiring of me whether I was a Bengali or an Assamese. Das took the statement of the superintendent of the medical college also who did not hesitate to take shelter under so many lies. Das had carried with him the High Court's order to accommodate me within 19 May 1981 in one of the cottages of the medical college after making necessary security arrangements. Thus, the superintendent was compelled to accommodate me in a cottage under heavy police guards. But troubles did not cease there either. Because no arrangement was made for my food nor were the prescribed medicines made available to me. Thank God, my younger brother Anil and my eldest son Sanjeev had arrived on 18 May 1981 to meet me. Their presence eased up the situation to a great extent. On 21 May 1981, my lunch was sent from where I did not know. My son detected some particles of mercury mixed with the rice and prevented me from taking the food. The matter was reported to both the doctors who were in charge of my treatment. They, too, smelt a rat and assured my brother and son that they would personally take care of my food.

I was told that my transfer to any of the Assam jails would depend on what Nripen Das would report to the High Court. Obviously, it was his report which caused my transfer to a jail in Assam. Ultimately, I was transfered to Nagaon special jail via Calcutta and Silchar jails. Surprisingly, the conduct of the jail officials in Calcutta and Silchar jails was congenial and sympathetic. Nagaon jail was still better.

Immediately after my arrest, I had expressed my deep faith in our judiciary. But great disillusionment was in store for me. When I heard about one of the two judges who were hearing my writ petition in the High Court, I had smelt a rat as also my lawyer, senior advocate J.P. Bhattacharya did. In all fairness, he should not have agreed to take up my case as in the recent past, he used to drink and play cards with me at more than small stake. That being so, how could he take up my case unless he had something up his sleeve. No wonder I received a copy of the following letter written by one Anjan Kumar Barua which addressed quite a few questions. I, however, do not have the slightest intention of voicing any contempt of the court. I am simply quoting facts. The said letter is reproduced below without correcting any grammatical mistakes, if there be any:

Justice Versus Propriety

Sir,

May I recall the commendable service rendered by a few lawyers of the Guwahati High Court Bar at this critical juncture of state. All the Habeas Corpus cases filed in the Guwahati High Court were argued by them without charging any fee—even at times spending money from their own pockets. They have been successful in obtaining release order of almost all deteneus except in three cases. May I, in this connection request hon'ble members of the Bar to ponder over some very basic and important questions involving liberty of citizens.

It is well known that delay defeats justice and justice hurried justice burried. Citizens are at a loss for not being able to understand as to why Habeas Corpus cases take such long time to be disposed of by the Guwahati High Court. Recently, Gujarat High Court disposed of the Habeas Corpus petitions within seven days of the detention order. Do our lawyers raise very complicated questions of law while arguing their cases? I happened to pose this question to a very eminent lawyer of Supreme Court. He was surprised to hear that hearing of a Habeas Corpus case continued for more than fifteen days and the Judgement was reserved on conclusion of arguments. According to him hearing of cases of such nature must not take more than two days and Judgement must be delivered on the very day the hearing is concluded.

He is of the opinion that there is no scope of raising complicated questions of law as the Supreme Court settled all such questions of law in last thirty years. Few instances will reveal a very sorry state of affairs. Hearing of a batch of six Habeas Corpus cases commenced on 20 January and continued till 11 February 1981 in the Guwahati High Court. Hearings of another batch of five cases started on 5 March and the judgement was delivered on 19 March 1981. The Habeas Corpus petition of Shri HK Bhattacharyya, DIG of Police came up for hearing on 16 March 1981, which ended on 10 April 1981 and the judgement was reserved. Thereafter, Bihu Vacation of the High Court ensued. Even on reopening day, i.e., 20 April 1981, the High

Court did not deliver the judgement. Reportedly Shri Bhattacharya was lying seriously ill in Ranchi Medical College during this entire period. Lawyers maintained silence. Hon'ble Judges did not give any explantation for this delay in their judgement. Justice suffers. Detenu laments in his dingy prison hole. Lawyers claim that they have never asked for adjournment in Habeas Corpus cases. Once it was adjourned only to facilitate inspection of muffasil courts by the Hon'ble Chief Justice (Acting). To the Hon'ble High Court, it appears, inspection of lower court is much more important than the liberty of citizen languishing in jail without trial. Records show another serious and important question of propriety.

On 20 April 1981 the State of Assam bade farewell to Shri L P Singh, Governor of Assam, under the Presidentship of Mr Justice D Pathak, Chief Justice (Acting). The farewell was addressed by Mr Justice K Lahiri showering rich compliments upon the Governor as reported in the newspapers. The farewell was followed by a dinner hosted by the chief minister of Assam. Reliable sources confirm that all the judges of the Guwahati High Court attended the said farewell and dinner keeping the judgements in Shri Bhattacharya's case and the Press case undelivered, wherein fundamental rights, namely, liberty and freedom of speech of citizens are involved. The chief minister of Assam has lot of stakes in these two cases. She is personally involved in the matters.

Today everybody in Assam considers that Shri Bhattacharyya's detention is malafide. Reportedly, Shri Bhattacharyya as DIG Border, detected about 14,000 foreign nationals in the constituency of Mrs Anwara Taimur. But unfortunately Shri Bhattacharyya is not in a position to prove the said facts in the court of law. His only fault is that he faithfully and religiously implemented the government policy. The chief minister approved the detention order of Shri Bhattacharyya and disposed of his representation filed against the detention order. Legality of both statutory actions of the Chief Minister is questioned by the detenu in his Writ Petition. Hon'ble judges were to decide the legality of such actions of the Chief Minister while disposing of the case. Incidentally, both the law points were decided against the detenu. Shri Bhattacharyya's case was not listed for judgement in the cause list of 21 April 1981. A supplementary cause list was published and the Bench was constituted at 2 pm on 21 April 1981 to deliver the judgement. Petition was dismissed rejecting all the points raised by the detenu. On the same day few more Habeas Corpus cases, including that of Shri Bharat Narah, were heard by the High Court.

All the detenus were released within two hours of hearing of their cases with impressive and illuminating judgements holding all the points in favour of the detenus. Does it give an impression that Hon'ble High Court is maintaining 'balance' between the Government and the litigant public? In the circumstances was it proper and fair on the part of those two Hon'ble Judges to attend the said farewell dinner? On the face of the doctrine of equality, would it have been possible for the Hon'ble Judges to refuse to attend the dinner hosted by family members of Shri Bhattacharyya if they were invited to? By the time Hon'ble Judges were served with sumptuous dinner at the State expense, the State served the dinner to the detenu with two potatoes, a bowel of rice and two onions. Today, India is taking singular pride in upholding democratic values. On the morning of 20 April 1980 itself two Hon'ble Judges of Guwahati High Court took oath in the name of God and Constitution of India. It seems they violated their oaths before the ink of their signatures on oath paper had dried up.

Justice must not only be done but it must also appear to have been done. Justice is not a cloistered virtue. There cannot be absolute Justice. Finality has to be attached somewhere. Though the verdict of the Court cannot go in favour of both the parties involved in a case yet justice can and must be done to both parties. Being a student of law and hoping to join the Bar very soon, I am really disturbed with the feeling expressed in this letter.

I am not aware of any precedent if any High Court Judge had even presided over or addressed farewell function of the Governor. My ignorance may be excused. Moreover, where is the occasion to bid farewell to Shri LP Singh? He has not retired as yet. Even today he is the Governor of North-Eastern Region States. Only difference is that he will solve problems of the North-Eastern Region from Delhi, which he could not do staying at Shillong in the last eight years. If Hon'ble Judges had not attended the farewell party even then also the verdict of the case with all probability would have been same. In that case the deteneu would not have had any occasion to make any grievance in that respect.

On the pain of transfer spree, if independence of judiciary is to be sacrificed at the altar of the Executive, the cause has to be taken up by the ever vigilant Bar. Judges settle the controversies between two or more litigant parties but an independent and fearless Bar is a Judge of the Judges. Judges cannot escape the verdict of the Bar. After all, Judges are also human beings with all the limitation. Bar must be able to keep the Judges within their bounds. Hon'ble Judges must be aware of fair and constructive criticism made against their conduct by the citizens. It goes without saying that Bar must act as the watch dog if not black hound, of the independence of judiciary. If Bar fails, Bench is sure to fail. Bar is the twin brother of Judiciary.

Therefore, I appeal to the good conscience of the Hon'ble members of the Bar to play little more serious attention to the problems mentioned above.

Yours faithfully
Sd/ Anjan Kumar Baruah
Gauhati

After going through the letter again and again, I felt as if this was the end of the road. My writ petition was dismissed on 21 April 1981, thereby compelling me to prefer an appeal to the Supreme Court. Only after carefully deliberating within myself for quite sometime, I decided to let my countrymen know the fate of a security prisoner detained without trial.

In all fairness, here I must mention that the two Hon'ble judges hearing the petition filed by the '*Assam Tribune*' group of newspapers did not attend the aforesaid farewell meet and the landmark judgement delivered by them in this context, had earned them large scale acclamation throughout the country.

On receipt of Anjan Barua's letter, the Bar Association of High Court had expressed deep anxieties over the entire matter in the shape of a resolution adopted in its executive committee and had forwarded the same to the Chief Justice of the High Court. The Bar Association could not have done anything better under the circumstances. In any case, Anjan Barua had raised some relevant questions in respect of propriety and sense of values, so important for maintaining dignity. However, at personal level, I had to cope with another problem : I was entertaining the hope of making my eldest son a lawyer; but after what happened to me and particularly after having gone through Anjan Barua's letter he decided not to study for the legal profession. He also decided against going for any government job, although I was sure that he would have come out successful in competitive examination.

During this period, another extremely undemocratic development added another black chapter to Assam's parliamentary history: Governor LP Singh rescued the Taimur government even after it suffered a defeat on a cut motion tabled in the context of the budget presented by Taimur government. Taimur did not resign and the Governor rescued her by issuing an Ordinance. *Indian Express* had written, inter alia the following in its editorial column on 6 April 1981: "Never have the ordinance making powers of a Governor been used quite in the way the Assam Governor, Mr LP Singh, rescued Mrs Taimur's minority Government from its well-deserved fall. ----- By any standard of parliamentary practice, the ministry should have been dismissed forthwith on suffering defeat on a cut motion." ----- It was further observed in the same editorial column that --- "The Governor, in effect, has usurped the functions of the Legislative Assembly which alone, or Parliament, in the event of dissolution of the Assembly, can legitimately authorise the expenditure of a state from the consolidated fund. ------" The reader may kindly recollect that I had already dwelt upon the non-development of democratic tradition in our country. Anowara Taimur seemed to have taken a cue from what Hitler had said to his colleagues on the eve of invading Poland that, "I shall give a propagandist cause for starting the war. Never mind whether it is plausible or not. The victor will never be asked, later on, whether we told the truth or not." Unfortunately for her, Taimur lost!

That "Crisis needs no rehearsal" has been amply proved by the course of the Assam Movement. The indigenous people of Assam have, briefly speaking, resorted to this mass movement for fear of losing their identity and existence like the indigenous people of Tripura. Four aspects of their troublefree existence must be taken care of. These are political, economic, social and cultural aspects.

Even if one of these aspects is ignored, the Movement in the ultimate analysis, will be deemed to have failed. And exactly this is what happened under the self-seeking leadership of the AGP. The current state of affairs can by no means guarantee that the political power will remain in the hands of the indigenous people of the state. On the economic front, the prosperity of the rural economy cannot be achieved in the face of the rapid fragmentation of holdings which cannot cater for the need of modernisation of the agriculture sector. The only way out seems to organise the agriculture sector on co-operative basis. But in order to develop the full potentials of the co-operative system, co-operative leadership must not be identical with political leadership so that vested interests may not get the upper hand; unfortunately since the days of Sarat Sinha ministry, this most important aspect of co-operative movement is being ignored at the altar of partisan interests whereas in advanced countries like Denmark, Sweden, Norway, etc., mostly dependent on their co-operative sectors, have developed their co-operative leadership independently of political leadership. Be that as it may, unless the purchasing power of the villager is enhanced, it will be very difficult to sustain free growth of small-scale industries manufacturing consumer goods. The entire exercise should target processing Assam's raw materials within Assam instead of exporting these raw materials to outside Assam.

In lonely confinement, I could not help brooding over these matters. But I could not compose a self-contained discourse on Assam's economy for want of necessary data and literature. As such, I decided that I would certainly reflect on this issue in due course. (which I did).

After going through the judgement of the Guwahati High Court, I did not expect much relief from the Supreme Court either but did not object to filing an appeal in the Supreme Court, lest my lawyers might feel hurt. In the Apex Court, V.M. Tarkunde, the famous human rights activist argued my case. But the hearings in the Supreme Court were not without hassle. The hearing was adjourned for facilitating the visit of Siddhartha Shankar Ray, the lawyer of the respondent, to London where his father-in-law was lying sick and I was granted parole for the period of Ray's absence. I had never asked for parole but when I had asked for parole after my mother died, the authorities were very reluctant to grant me parole! Only after some senior citizens of Guwahati pressurised the government, I was granted parole for three days only. Then again these senior citizens approached the government to extend my parole so that I could remain with my family till the vedic rites were completed. As such, I got parole for 13 days.

The High Court while disposing of my writ petition had, at least, given reasons for turning down my prayer. In the Supreme Court my lawyers while arguing my case, had raised as many as nine constitutional points before the hon'ble judges. If I did not have the right to freedom, I should not have been in any case deprived of the benefit of knowing why these nine constitutional points raised by my lawyers were not valid in the eyes of the law. Even my lawyers could not give me any satisfactory reply as to why the hon'ble judges prefered to remain silent on these nine counts. According to my lawyers, the judges would have had no alternative other than restoring my right to freedom if they would have given their judgement even on one of these nine points. To substantiate why I feel aggrieved, the judgement is reproduced below :

In the Supreme Court of India
Crl. Appellate Jurisdiction
Crl. Appeal No. 542 of 1981
Hirannya Kumar Bhattacharyya—Appellant Vs
Dist. Magistrate, Kamrup and ors—Respondents.

Judgement

After hearing learned counsels for the parties at very great length we are of the opinion that no interference with the impugned order is called for. The appeal is dismissed and the order directing the government to release the appellant on parole is revoked.

New Delhi — sd. A. D. Koshal
Dated November 18 — sd. Balakrishna Eradi
1981 — sd. R. B. Misra

So, it appeared that if I was released on parole for facilitating S.S. Ray's visit to London, I would not be a threat to the national security; but otherwise I was! Such self-contradictory positions taken by the government simply exposed the irrational nature of the grounds of my detention. As such, I am reminded of what David Thoreau had said: "The law will never make man free; it is men who have got to make the law free. They are the lovers of law and order who observe the law when the Government breaks it." Hopes for the separation of powers in the administration ensuring the right to freedom and a vibrant democracy were thus soaked in the desert of bureaucratic manipulation and malpractices.

In Hazaribagh jail, I had developed acute pain in my left foot—possibly because of the defective cot which compelled me to sleep, resting on the left side only. This deteriorated into severe spondylitis while in Nagaon jail. On the advice of two orthopaedic specialists from GMCH, I was removed to Guwahati Central Jail for better treatment. So it was from this jail that I was released on 28 January 1982 after completion of one year of detention.

The first moment of freedom made me feel how soft was the air outside and how wide the sky! But what was more astounding, hundreds of people, including several hundred students had assembled outside the jail gate to receive me with loud cheering and greetings. They did not allow my eldest son to take me home in the car he had brought. Hundreds had swollen up to thousands outside the jail campus for taking me in a procession to Cotton College. So, I had to walk with them, using a walking stick for easing out the pressure on my weak left foot. The Police tried unsuccessfully to disperse the crowd. But we reached Cotton College and then taken to B Borooah College. At both the places few student leaders made very emotional speeches and hailed my uncompromising spirit as also my contribution to unmasking the serious problem of illegal migration from Bangladesh.

That the police tried to disperse the procession, amounted to my fresh confrontation with the administration the moment I came out of the prison. On the other hand, that I was escorted by a huge procession amounted to getting actively associated with the public life of Assam without any such immediate intention on my part. I could arrive at my residence at 2 pm, only to find that intelligence surveillance had already been mounted over my residential campus. I felt like loudly shouting out in Kipling's language that, "Decency is a fraud and shame. There is nothing clean or pure or wholesome under the. ----"

Thus started my tryst with an unknown and uncertain future.

12

In Uncharted Waters

As mentioned in the last chapter, I was launched into Assam's public life without any intention on my part to do so immediately. Because my immediate concern was to ensure a steady source of income through honest means. But that was also not to materialise so easily.

My release from the prison on 28 January 1982 was followed by a series of ovations held all over the Brahmaputra valley, thus involving me more closely with the anxieties and worries of the people of Assam without, however, intending to get involved in politics. Most of these ovations were organised by units of the AASU. As I could understand these meetings were organised for creating awareness amongst the people against the implications of unabated infiltration from Bangladesh as well as to organise the people. Talks and speeches veered round, by and large, the following points in addition to analysing the respective local problems.

a incessant illegal influx of foreign nationals from Bangladesh and Nepal into Assam;

b the danger of being overwhelmed by such influx;

c the government's apathetic attitude to the problem of illegal infiltration;

d the vote-bank politics of all the political parties;

and

e total lack of development since Independence.

In 1982, I had to address many meetings all over the Brahmaputra valley sponsored by AASU. In fact, I proved to be a great crowd-puller, possibly because of the tremendous sacrifice I had to make and extreme hardship I had to undergo. Besides, I was invited as a special guest to the annual session of the Axom Xahitya Xabha, the largest non-political literary organisation of North-east India, held at Diphu in April 1982. I considered it to be a great honour for being invited to such an august and huge gathering of thousands of people. Besides, I was not only elected to the executive committee with highest number of votes to my credit but also appointed as the founding convener of the Jatiya Nyax Puji (National Trust Fund). The objective of this fund was to make the Sabha self-dependent, economically independent of government aids. I held this office consecutively for four terms and was also elected to the Executive Committee of the Sabha for three consecutive terms which afforded me rare opportunities of working with literary luminaries like late Sitanath Brahmachoudhury, late Dr Birendra Kumar Bhattacharya (a Jyanpith awardee), late Prof Jogesh Das, etc. Because of their proximity, I developed an abiding interest in literary activities.

After the Diphu session of Axom Xahitya Xabha, I was nominated as the Sabha's representative along with late Hitesh Deka, to the executive committee of the AAGSP. It was only after such nomination to the Executive Committee of the AAGSP that I got directly involved in the movement and never before as many had alleged so. There is no denial that the movement centred round a highly sensitive political issue. That being so, the Sabha, a non-political cultural organisation, could have refrained from being active member of the AAGSP and instead supported the mass movement from outside. The Sabha had its own image and dignity to uphold and AAGSP certainly was not the best forum for this purpose.

In fact, on few occasions I had requested to be relieved of this charge and on each occasion Dr Nagen Saikia, the general secretary of the Sabha and a personal friend of mine, persuaded me to continue as the Sabha's representative. I still entertain strong doubt as to how the Sabha promoted its own cause by being a member of the AAGSP. Still worse, the Sabha's opinion was never obtained while preparing the draft of the Assam Accord. To be precise, it was totally ignored. From the very beginning, the then AASU leaders were betraying fascist tendency in the various discussions held in the meetings of the AAGSP. They refused to put up with any opposition to any of their proposals put up before the AAGSP. Instead, they found it convenient to expel from the AAGSP any inconvenient members, including senior leaders like Nibaran Bora, Atul Bora, Jatin Goswami, etc. They certainly appeared to have some hidden agenda as was proved subsequently. Besides, rivalries and bitter feelings between AASU and AJYCP did not contribute the least to creating a healthy ambience. I was particularly opposed to frequent calls of all-Assam bundh, thereby simply attracting the ire of the then leaders of AASU who from the very beginning betrayed total lack of adherence to democratic norms. From the time of the State Language Movement of 1960, Assam's atmosphere has continued to remain agitational at the cost of real development. As an insider of the AAGSP, I could feel that the entire exercise was to keep the agitational ambience alive instead of trying to arrive at a mutually agreeable solution, in spite of the sufferings of the common man and losses suffered by the student community. Even at this early stage, the nascent leadership of AGP, was ignoring the functioning of democracy at micro level, thus demoting democracy to the status of a bonded handmaid in order to promote the image of few AASU leaders who subsequently entirely betrayed the cause of the movement. The cunning bureaucrats of the central government did not fail to take advantage of this inbuilt contradiction in the functioning of the AAGSP, as was proved while preparing the final draft of the controversial Assam Accord. This tendency of ignoring the opinions of selfless grassroot workers has been evident even in well organised political parties like Congress(I) and the BJP also. In fact, the introduction of the concept of high command in political parties is presently making a total mockery of democratic functioning. The very concept gives birth to the 'personality cult', thus paving the way to camouflaged fascism in the name of democracy. Ultimately, the will of one person prevails, regardless of the opinions of millions. All powers are concentrated in one hand. Even the election of the leader of respective Parliamentary Party has to be okayed by the so-called high command; else, it would amount to dissidence! While writing the biography of Hitler, Robert Paine wrote that, "The moral to be learned from the life and death of Hitler, is a very simple one: no man can be trusted with power. To be endurable, power must be shared to the widest possible extent; the single ruler defeats the purpose of our common humanity. When the chief executive is powerful enough to overwhelm parliament, when he rules by edict and executive order, when he attempts to exercise the rights that properly belong to the community, then he places himself in the position of Hitler.-----" In the present situation of Assam, once more one may recall what Paine had written: "The small Hitlers are around us everyday, tormenting us with their promises, rejoicing in our weaknesses, demanding our trust, our votes and our lives, while remaining totally indifferent to everything except their thirst for power.-----"

13

Elections of 1983

Having exposed the fearful phenomenon of lakhs of Bangladeshi nationals getting themselves enrolled as voters in Assam, I was totally committed to the cause of the movement without the least intention of getting involved in active politics As such, I worked with full dedication for implementing the AAGSP's programmes for furthering the cause of the Movement.

All the leaders who had gone to participate in the Delhi talk of 5 January, were arrested at Borjhar airport the moment they disembarked from the aircraft, thereby committing another unholy act by breaking a well set democratic convention. That is to say, those who were invited to participate in the discussion, were denied the time-honoured convention of safe conduct for such participants. However, I got myself busy in association with the younger generation of student leaders by whirling all over the valley for holding anti-election rallies as per plans chalked out by AASU and AAGSP. I was ready to leave for Sibsagar on 14 February 1983 for holding anti-election rallies; but I was again arrested on the night of 13 February 1983 under the

NSA and flown off in an IAF aircraft to Silchar. At Silchar jail, I met Hiten Goswami, another student leader, also under detention. Hiten's company certainly mitigated the boredom of loneliness, besides his company giving me an insight into the mindset of the progressive section of the student community, although he also appeared to have lost his progressive zeal once he became a minister. Be that as it may, Hiten was particularly wedded to the policy of forming a joint front of all the students of the entire North-east, a policy still being pursued by the AASU. But such a front has so far failed to work out an amicable settlement of so many interstate boundary disputes, although they are united in voicing their opposition to the unabated influx of illegal migrants from Bangladesh. This organisation bears the name of North East Students Organisation (NESO). Samujjal Kumar Bhattacharyya, the adviser of AASU, is the present president of this organisation.

The forcibly held elections of 1983 had created a serious law-and-order situation and unprecedented mass opposition to such arbitrary action of the CEC. As many as 8,800 Central government employees were airlifted from outside Assam for manning the polling stations. Such action of the central government had evoked sympathies for Assam all over the country. It is worth mentioning that the state government employees of Bihar had refused to come to Assam for helping in holding the elections. The state government employees of Assam remained absent from their offices between February 5 and 22. Some prominent Muslim citizens of Assam also issued an appeal for refraining from participating in the elections. The government did not remain silent either; it deployed about a lakh and half police and para-military forces to confront the agitating people and in the process, more than a hundred agitationists lost their lives in police firings alone. At times in the face of grave provocations the agitationists had also become violent and such violence resulted in the death of more than 200 persons, apart from the massacre of thousands of people at Nellie. The agitations had mainly targetted the activists of Congress(I) and the activists of the Left parties. Election campaigns could be conducted only in areas dominated by immigrant Muslims. Indira Gandhi used to conclude her electioneering speeches by uttering— "Khuda Hafiz". Abdul Ghani Khan Choudhury of Congress(I) went one step further by inciting the immigrant Muslims in an electioneering speech delivered at Moirabari on 10 February 1983 in the following words: "------ If Hindu kills one Muslim, the Muslims should retaliate by killing three Hindus and the government would support you. -----" No wonder that violence erupted subsequently in full vehemence, culminating in the ghastly massacre of Nellie. Thousands of innocent people lost their lives, many villages were burnt down and many more thousands uprooted from their hearth and homes. The ghastly scenario reminded one of the riotings on the eve of the partition of the country! Nellie massacre could take place despite advance information available to Assam Police as depicted by Arun Shourie in an issue of *India Today* (forgot the date of the issue).

That the elections turned out to be a mere farce is proved by the fact that some of the constituencies did not record even one per cent turn out, although in immigrant Muslim areas, the turn out was more than 25%. Hiteswar Saikia of Congress(I) was sworn in as the chief minister but the agitationists refused to extend the recognition due to a CM and instead, termed his government as an illegitimate government. On the other hand, the clashes taking place in the context of the election caused bitter ethnic divisions resulting from machinations by the anti-Movement vested interests.

The CEC had turned a totally blind eye to the abnormal rate of increase in the number of voters of Assam. During 13 years between 1957 and 1970, the number of voters increased by 12,08,446 whereas during eight years between 1970 and 1978, the increase was by 22,82,671 voters. Obviously, many of those who had crossed over during the Bangladesh war did not go back and instead managed to enroll themselves as voters in Assam. Now because they had voted in elections held in India, they were claiming to be Indian citizens! This is how the CEC had made a total mockery of the ROP Act. The phenomenal growth of Assam's population has thus been fully reflected in the bewilderingly bizarre increase in the number of voters registered by the Election Commission of India. Our system had never made it impossible for lakhs of alien citizens to register themselves as Indian voters. In fact, the experiences of 1980 should have sufficed for the CEC to abstain from holding the bloody election of 1983.

The betrayals perpetrated by the Election Commission of India on the people of Assam are no less pronounced than those of the successive Central and the State Governments. In fact, the role of the Election Commission in preventing such distortion of the ERs has never been adequate. Not that everybody had remained a mute spectator like the statutory bodies. This author himself had addressed an open letter to the Chief Election Commissioner of India, duly pointing out the large scale distortion of the ERs and the letter, released to the press, was published in a number of dailies published from Assam, albeit without attracting any reaction from the Commission. The letter reproduced below will speak for itself.

"To
The Chief Election Commissioner Of India, New Delhi,
&
The Chief Electoral Officer, Assam, Guwahati

27 October 1992

Dear Sirs,
Namaskar,

We are constrained to draw your pointed attention to the following and demand that you clarify your position vis-a-vis the points raised below.

Lately, lot of controversies have been raised and apprehensions voiced in respect of cleansing the electoral rolls of Assam of foreign voters. It has been alleged that the Election Department of our State has succumbed to the influence exercised by the State Government with the result that the guidelines issued by the Election Commission for deleting the names of foreign nationals from the ERs have been totally ignored. On the other hand, the Chief Minister has totally denied any such interference. We, the Indian citizens of Assam, have a right to know whether the Election Department of the State is discharging its duties in faithful obedience to the aforesaid guidelines.

In the All Parties Conference held on 22 September, assurances were given that these guidelines would be strictly implemented; but it seems the CEO had found it more convenient to forget these assurances. Else, why would he remain silent about the allegation that the guidelines issued by the Commission had not been circulated among the Deputy Commissioners and the Electoral Registration Officers? If the allegation is correct, then this amounts to a total betrayal of the people of Assam, if not a heinous crime committed on them. The Chief Election Commissioner and the CEO owe it to the people of Assam to clarify their position on the following counts also:

1. What prevents the CEC from identifying the infiltration-prone constituencies on his own, instead of passing on the buck to the State Government? With little application and objective analysis, it should be possible for the CEC to determine these constituencies from his own office records. We are ready to furnish the names of these constituencies, but will he accept them?

2. The Commission has betrayed the people of Assam time and again. In the past, it has gone back on many of its own assurances and this time seems to be no exception. For, the Commission seems to be intent upon converting a simple operation into an unnecessarily complex problem for reasons which cannot be considered constitutional and to be in conformity with their constitutional duties. Both the CEC and the CEO must be aware of the provisions of the Assam Accord, which stipulate that all the post-1971 foreign infiltrators should be deported. That they have not been deported is another matter; but what prevents the Commission from accepting the 1971 (1972?) ERs as the basis for weeding out the names of lakhs of foreign nationals from the voters' list, is not explicable. If the Commission is true to its salt, then they would even now refrain from accepting the 1990 rolls as the basis for preparing the 1992 draft rolls. Even after doing so, it can certainly atone for its sins by comparing the draft rolls whose names do not figure in the 1971 rolls. This, however, will not apply to the children of the Indian voters enumerated in the 1971 rolls as they have by now attained the age of 18 and over as well as those genuine Indian nationals who have since taken up residence in Assam. It will be also pertinent to point out that there is absolutely nothing sacrosanct about the 1990

rolls. Despite all these, if the Commission yields to political design of the party in power by treating the 1990 rolls as the basis for correcting the current draft rolls, then this will be nothing short of total abdication by the Commission, besides being another sin committed on Assam and her people. The Commission also possibly cannot afford to ignore the threat held out by the fundamentalists promoting the cause of the Bangladeshi infiltrators that if need be, they can throw out the Saikia government within "five minutes".

3. Do the CEC and the CEO also, like a particular lobby, consider that foreign nationals illegally registering themselves as Indian voters and Indian voters belonging to the religious minority community are identical? If not, then they better say so instead of remaining silent on such claims being constantly put forward by the fundamentalists with transborder inspiration.

4. Between 1958 and 1969, about 3,10,000 foreign infiltrators were deported from Assam under different laws of the land. This figure also includes about 2,50,000 infiltrators deported under the PIP scheme. Besides, between 1978 and 1980, another number of about 10000 foreign infiltrators were deported from Assam. Both the CEC and the CEO will certainly agree with us that these deportees cannot be voters here by any stretch of imagination. Names of these deportees were not deleted from the ERs even during AGP rule also. Will the commission now make it bold to assure the people of Assam that all the names of these deportees will be deleted from the 1992 rolls? This is the minimum the Commission can do without raising any fresh controversy. The Commission may also do well to note that taking advantage of the existence of these names in the ERs, many fresh infiltrators are reported to have assumed many of these names and been exercising voting rights. All the names of these lakhs of deportees are available either with the DIGP (Border) or with the respective Police Chiefs of all the districts of Assam unless these have been destroyed at the instance of the ever manipulating fundamentalist politicians who had in the past captured power in the state.

5. Successive Chief Election Commissioners have been categorically admitting for years on that the ERs of Assam contain names of foreign nationals; but surprisingly, the Commission has never considered the question of initiating necessary action on its own for deleting the names of foreign nationals from the ERs, although the Commission has the power to do so under the relevant law without taking any dictation from the state government. That being so, how does the Election Commission expect the people to believe that its independent constitutional status has not been sacrificed under political pressure? On this count also, the Commission owes an explanation to the country in general and to Assam in particular. If this time also, the Commission sabotages the process of preparing a correct voters' list excluding the names of foreign nationals, then this will be an act of treason in the face of the silent invasion of Assam by millions of Bangladeshi nationals with active support from their government and politicians of this side of the border. All said and done, the Commission cannot afford to be a party to the diabolic action of suppressing the Commission's own instructions and this is where the Chief Electoral Officer of the state has to assert his independent status.

While anxiously waiting for a reply to clarifications on the points raised above, we conclude by quoting from a statement made by the then External Affairs Minister Mr Atal Bihari Vajpayee on the floor of the parliament on 2 November, 1978:

"It has come to the notice of the Election Commission from time to time that large-scale inclusion of foreign nationals in the electoral rolls, specially in the north-eastern region, has been taking place.

In August, 1975, the Ministry of Home Affairs instructed all the state governments that the state criminal department may be instructed to take immediate steps to check the electoral rolls, and if they discover the names of foreigners in the rolls, the fact may be brought to the notice of the concerned Electoral Registration Officers for getting such names deleted from the electoral rolls. The Commission has also issued instructions to the electoral officers of the states and Union Territories concerned that if it is found that a large numbers of foreigners have managed to get their names registered in the electoral rolls, recourse should be had to provisions of Section 22 of the Representation of the People Act of 1950 for getting the names of such persons deleted from the electoral rolls on the ground that they are not Indian citizens."

What prevents now both the CEC and the CEO from taking recourse to this provision of the law and thereby end all controversies once and for all?

Thanking you.

Yours faithfully

Hiranya Kumar Bhattacharyya
Beltola, Guwahati."

Instructions as mentioned by Sri Vajpayee in his above quoted statement were issued by the MHA on 2 August 1975 when the 'National Emergency' proclaimed by Indira Gandhi, was in operation in full swing. The Government of Assam, despite having fully supported the ongoing 'Emergency', not only failed to take full advantage of the situation arising out of the proclamation of 'Emergency' but also instead, totally hushed up the above-mentioned circular issued by the MHA. The top Police official concerned found it more covenient to look the other way, lest he might incur the displeasure of his Congress bosses. Of course, he was amply rewarded in due course! Nor did the MHA ever follow up the matter, let alone ensure the implementation of its own directives. Needless to emphasise that Assam lost a golden opportunity.

The press-media were also crying hoarse over the matter highlighted in the above-quoted letter. A press report published in *The Sentinel* is reproduced below:

"Govt. ensures neat burial of CEC gidelines

Enumerators get vague orders on making draft rolls

By a Staff Reporter

Guwahati 23 October: The State Election Department has taken up the preparation of draft electoral rolls without having undertaken the enumeration work as laid down by the Chief Election Commissioner in respect of identifying the foreigner infested constituencies first. On the other hand, none of the over a dozen guidelines issued by the State Chief Electoral Officer to the Deputy Commissioners and Electoral Registration Officer, etc. has a word on foreign nationals and vaguely asked the enumerators to "include names of eligible citizens who are members of the household or are ordinarily residents in that house," etc. Meanwhile, the other State Governments have already identified foreigner-infested constituencies as asked by the CEC.

The State Government and the Chief Electoral Officer have not circulated the guidelines of the Chief Election Commissioner among the Deputy Commissioners and the Electoral Registration Officers. The CEC guidelines (details of which were published in *The Sentinel* on 18 October at page 3) have been kept by the Government and the Chief Electoral Officer though the State Government is required not to interfere in the works of the Election Department. Meanwhile, the works on the preparation of the draft rolls are going on in full swing.

The first instruction of the CEC guidelines has specifically asked the State Government to fully implement the instruction in respect of first identifying the constituencies with substantial population of foreign nationals. But now that the enumeration works have been stated to be over to take up the preparation of draft electoral rolls, the CEC guidelines seem to have been given a neat burial by the Chief Electoral Officer and the State Government.

The CEC guidelines, it may be noted, were issued after it was widely published that illegal infiltrators from Bangladesh had swamped vast areas in neighbouring states and the Government of India decided to convene a conference of Chief Ministers to discuss the problem. The guidelines were issued to the governments of the North-Eastern states, West Bengal and Bihar.

They laid down that after having identified the foreigners

dominated constituencies, such areas covered by each polling booth in such constituencies had to be identified. It was only after such identification that the enumeration was to be taken up. The CEC also fixed 31 August as the date for completion of the identification process.

When asked if the State Government would start the identification of the foreigner-infested constituencies a senior official told *The Sentinel* that the State Government had no data or records to show which constituency was foreigners-infested. However, if the Chief Election Commissioner furnished such data, the State Government would immediately start the work to identify such constituencies, he said. It was only after the draft rolls were published that the exact position could be ascertained; he said and suggested that before the position was ascertained, it would not be proper to act on the CEC guidelines.

On the other side of the scenario, the State Election Department is still waiting for a positive decision from the State Government on the CEC guidelines. "We are still waiting for the Government to first identify the constituencies with large foreigner population," Election Department official told *The Sentinel*. He agreed that much time had already been wasted by now.

The State Government has not informed the CEC that it had not implemented its guidelines. It may be recalled here that a meeting of all political parties convened by the State Government on 22 September, had lent its full support to the CEC guidelines and asked the State Government to implement them fully.

What, however, has baffled the concerned citizens is the Government's explanation that it had no data or records to identify the constituencies with substantial foreigner population. The CEC guidelines were the only rational and correct ones under the circumstances, but with the non-implementation of the very first instruction contained therein by the State Government the whole exercise has been a non-starter.

The Election Department is, meanwhile, working within its

limitations to publish a revised voter's list. It has already appointed six officials.

It may also be noted here that the CEC has not asked for any information from the State Governments whether its guidelines had been implemented or not till today.

Thus the tug of war between the Commission and the State Government has been continuing with the result that the main issue has been lost sight of. It may not be out of place to mention here that the State CEO was himself present in the All Parties conference held on 22 September 1992 and as such, he cannot be unaware of the State Government's consent to implement the aforesaid guidelines. Thus it transpires that the CEO was more committed to tow the line of the State Government than to implement the guidelines of the Commission, lest he might be harassed subsequently by a vindictive State Government!

This is not the only instance of the Election Commission shirking its responsibility and failing to follow up its own instructions. Even prior to this, during the Assam Movement, the Commission had gone back on its words and commitment. Indira Gandhi might have asked it to bend little bit but it preferred to kneel down in a hurry! Be that as it may, the following developments may be more illustrative:

Following the fall of the Janata Government at the Centre, the Commission found it convenient to change its stance. On the eve of the general elections of 1980 necessitated by the fall of the Janata experiment, the Commission issued an instruction to the State Government as released by the State Government in its press-note number 88 dt. 18/9/1979 in the following words:

"The Commission have instructed that no person whose name was included in the electoral roll should be eliminated on the ground of citizenship as the process of establishing whether a person is a citizen or not is time consuming."

Because the process is time consuming, the foreigners must be allowed to vote! What a self-defeating argument! Thus the entire process/exercise was reversed in favour of the alien infiltrators who were straightaway lifted to a platform wherefrom they have since been arguing in the following vein: "Only citizens have the voting right. Since we have been voting so long, we are certainly citizens." However, in order to stave off the emerging controversy, the Commission issued the following statement:

"The Commission has further advised to take up scrutiny of Electoral Rolls after the ensuing General Election is over, with reference to the question of want of citizenship of any elector included therein in a systematic manner having regard to the provisions of Section 22 of the Representation of People Act 1950 and general instructions issued thereunder. Action as per the instructions of the Election Commission is being taken."

As it turned out subsequently the statement was made only to soothe public resentment. The promise was never honoured.

A few prominent persons took up the matter with Sri SL Sakhder, the then CEC. Sri Sakhder had come to Shillong towards the end of the month of May, 1982. Though he was very reluctant to spare any time for such discussions, Captain Williamson Sangma, the then Chief Minister of Meghalaya, displaying keen interest for a peaceful end of the Assam Movement, persuaded Sri Sakhder to meet the following persons at the Inspection Bungalow of Meghalaya State Electricity Board at Burnihat: HK Bhattacharyya, (the author), Indrajit Barua, Prafulla Kumar Mahanta and Bhrigu Kumar Phukan. The day was 29 May, 1982. During the discussion, Mrs Sabita Goswami, a leading journalist of the state, was also present. Sakhder was all praise for the Assam Movement. He appeared to be more royal than the king! We discussed the entire range of issues involved in cleansing the ERs of the names of illegal migrants. Sakhder gave the impression of being inclined to accept all our submissions and suggestions. In fact, his appeasing tone roused Indrajit's and my suspicion and we insisted that the details of our discussions should be reduced to writing so that the decisions arrived at, would not be forgotten. On the plea of shortage of time, he could not wait for the exercise to be completed and on our repeated insistence, Sakhder ultimately suggested that the matters discussed and the decisions arrived at might be sent to him in the form of a letter which we sent after few days. The letter is reproduced below for the benefit of the reader:

"H. K. Bhattacharyya
The Wilderness.
Beltola, Basistha road.
Guwahati- 781005 (since changed to 781028)
Date : June 4 1982.

To
Shri SL Sakhder,
Chief Election Commissioner of India, Nirvachan Sadan.
Ashok Road, New Delhi- 110001.

Sir,

Kindly allow us to thank you for sparing your most valuable time on 29 May last at Burnihat (Meghalaya) when you accorded us and our friends the privilege and honour of being able to meet you and talk to you freely and frankly.

In that meeting, we had a threadbare discussion about the revision and correction of electoral rolls of Assam as well as the present circumstances.

You may kindly recollect that the points discussed in the meeting were as follows:

1. You were kind enough to appreciate that the Assam problem is not one of LAW & ORDER as it has been made out to appear.
2. The electoral rolls of Assam prepared for the last general elections including the draft rolls of 1979 did contain the names of a large number of foreign nationals, numbering lakhs, if not a few millions.
3. It is not possible to prepare correct electoral rolls without inviting and disposing of objections in this regard in Form No. 7 as prescribed in Rule 13(2) Registration of Electors Rules 1960. Further the scope of eliminating the names of all foreign nationals from the electoral rolls by means of objection filed in Form No 7 being extremely limited and inadequate to meet the existing situation, recourse has perforce to be taken

to the mandatory provisions of Section 22 of Representation of the People Act 1950 (Act 43 of 1950).

The Election Commission would therefore issue guidelines for taking action under Section 22 of the ROP Act-1950 well in advance so that the plea of non-availability of time cannot be taken as was done by the State Government vide its press Note No 88 of 18 September 1979 (Copy enclosed).

4. The final electoral rolls required under section 21 of the ROP Act 1950 and Rule 22 of the RER 1960 cannot be prepared without disposing of all the pending objections, numbering about 6 lakhs filed after publication of 1979 draft rolls, which is precisely the reason why the final electoral roll for 1979 could not be published till now.

5. The stand of the Election Commission as explained by you is very clear on the matter. On more than one occasion, the Election Commission had instructed the State Government to proceed forward with the revision and correction of rolls. But the State Government has willfully ignored the Commission's instructions in this regard so far. That it has done so is evident from the fact that (i) it has transferred two successive Chief Electoral Officers without the knowledge & consent of the Commission, and (ii) despite the Commission's repeated instructions it has kept the post vacant for over a year. These omissions and commissions of the State Government have clearly proved its callous and indifferent attitude towards this vital matter. The State Government has shown that it could not care to flout the Election Commission's lawful directions and orders.

6. Elections in Assam cannot be held without publication of the final electoral rolls as required by Section 21 of the ROP Act 1950 and Rule 22 of the RER 1960. The publication of the final electoral rolls must logically result in the inclusion of the names of Indian citizens to the exclusion of the names of all foreign nationals, as required by our Constitution and our law. It is also imperative that all necessary steps as laid down by law are taken so that foreign nationals are not enumerated as voters in Assam in future.

7. For the purpose of deletion of names of persons who are not qualified to be electors, not only all the objections filed in Form No 7 shall have to be disposed of, but also the mandatory provisions of Section 22 of the ROP Act 1950 shall have to be invoked to cover the large number of pockets of foreign nationals spread all over Assam—particularly the riverine islands and the border areas—from where the likelihood of objection being preferred by a person whose name is already included in that roll and countersigned by another person whose name is also already included in that particular part of the roll in which the name objected appears, is practically nil for obvious reasons.

   To enable the Electoral Registration Officers to take action under Section 22 of the ROP Act-1950 under their own motion or otherwise, the Election Commission would be pleased to take into account any enumeration or inclusion of foreign nationals as electors.

8. The Commission will not hold elections anywhere in Assam until and unless the process of exclusion of names of foreign nationals from the electoral rolls is completed as required by law. The plea of non-availability of sufficient time to delete the names of foreign nationals from the electoral rolls, or a so-called need to fullfill constitutional obligation, will not be resorted to, as was done by the State Government in 1979. You were also kind enough to say that the Commission would satisfy itself through its own independent machinery whether it is really possible to hold free & fair election as required under the law, which process, you said, is voluntary process that cannot be imposed on the people against their will.

9. The Election Commission certainly did not authorise or allow the imposition of curfew to enable any particular candidate for certain Lok Sabha constituencies to file nominations in 1979. Curfew orders were resorted to, in the face of AASU's stiff resistance, in quite a few constituencies to enable the Congress candidates to file nominations! There cannot be any such permission in future either. In fact, you very much appreciated that such a step is not conducive to hold a free &

fair election, and also mentioned that such a step may lead to annulment or countermanding of such elections.

10. It was very kindly clarified that the Commission does not intend to hold elections only in certain specific constituencies in the State to the exclusion of certain other constituencies as such a procedure is not permissible under the law.

11. Various statements recently made by certain spokesmen and high dignitaries of the Government including a Union Minister of State have nothing to do with the independent and impartial functioning of the Election Commission, and as such, these statements do not reflect the views of the Commission in any way whatsoever.

12. Assam Govt. Press Note No 88 of 18 September 1979 mentioned that the inclusion of name in an electoral roll does not necessariy entitle the person to claim the right of citizenship. You have also kindly clarified that this does not *ipso facto* entitle such a person who does not have the primary qualification of being an Indian citizen to the right of franchise perpetually just because he might have voted in the past. In fact, to allow non-citizens the right of franchise is a sacrilege of our Constitution and election laws.

Sir,

We have attempted to put before you the sum and substance of our discussions with you on 29 May 1982. We feel greatly relieved that your considered opinions on the matter have coincided with our humble views. We shall deem it a great honour and privilege to receive your valuable reply and comments thereon. The disposals of objections filed in Form 7 and the application of Section 22 of the ROP Act 1950 by the ERO may not cover all the cases of foreign nationals, the situation being what it is. We have every apprehension that political pressures will be exerted and manipulation attempted by vested interests. We have raised this vital point because we have bitter experience of such happenings. In this connection, it may perhaps not be out of place to point out that Mrs. Anowara Taimur in 1979 rushed inside the chamber of a particular Asst. ERO with a batch of her rowdies while hearing of objections was in progress, not only to disrupt the proceedings but also to threaten the Asst. ERO to drop the proceedings. This is precisely the reason why we had suggested the use of an electronic computer to ensure the correct preparation of electoral rolls in a foolproof manner. The use of computer would rule out the possibility of any manipulation in respect of pinpointing the names of all foreign nationals. It would also overcome all the difficulties that may be presented by the time factor. We sincerely and earnestly pray that you would kindly consider our humble suggestion and do the needful in this matter also.

With kind regards,

Yours sincerely,

Sd./ (H. K. BHATTACHARYYA)

Sd./ (Indrajit Barua)"

Not remaining content with merely sending the letter by post, Indrajit Barua went to Delhi and met Sri Sakdher in pursuance of our prayers made to him at Burnihat. In reply, the Secretary of the Election Commission sent us a letter which is reproduced below.

From : Secretariat of Election Commission of India.

Letter No. 23/1/82 dated 10 June 1982.

To

1. Shri P. K. Mahanta,

   President, All Assam Students Union.

   Guwahati University Law Students Faculty, Guwahati, Assam.

2. Prof. Ajit Kumar Sharma M. P.

   Suwagpur, Guwahati- 781008, Assam.

3. Mr. H. K. Bhattacharyya

   "The Wilderness"

   Beltola, Basistha Road,

   Guwahati- 781005

4. Mr. Indrajit Barua.

C/o H. K. Bhattacharya.

"The Wilderness" Beltola, Basistha Road.

Guwahati- 781005

Subject : General Election—Assam

Sir,

I am directed to refer to your letter dated1 June 1982, 4 June 1982 and today that the Legislative Assembly has been dissolved and the state is now under President's Rule. The question of holding general elections to the Legislative Assembly would arise only if and when it is indicated to the Commission by the Central Government that the Commission might proceed witht the holding of the elections and that the Centre would revoke the President's Rule. In that event, the Commission will first have to revise the electoral rolls in the state with reference to the 1 January of the year in which the revision would be taken up as the base and they will be published as a draft roll. Adequate time will be given to raise objections to any entry in the electoral rolls. As and when objections are filed on any of the grounds mentioned in the law including the ground of want of citizenship they would be dispossed in accordance with the provisions of the law.

As regards the question of disposal of objections and application under Section 22 of the Representation of People Act, 1950 by the Electoral Registration Officer is concerned, I am to say that those objections seeking deletion in the electoral roll as finally published would also be disposed in accordance with the provisions of the law.

As regard the holding of elections to the 12 vacancies in the House of the people from Assam, the above observations hold good.

Yours faithfully

Sd./ (K. GANESH)

Secretary

Delhi was too far to reach the homilies performed at Burnihat! It may be noted that there was nothing to prevent the Commission from disposing of about six lakhs objections, pending since 1979, during the President's Rule which was then in force. It seems the Commission either did not want to displease the Congress(I), that is the "Infiltration Lobby" or was scared by the enormity of the task! All the promises made to us were left behind at Burnihat itself. In fact, these objections were never disposed of despite the fact that according to the provisions of the relevant law, the Commission was legally bound to dispose them of. Indrajit Barua and late Girin Barua, then president of the Assam Jatiyatabad Dal, had again written to the Commission on the same matter; but there was no positive response. Indrajit ultimately filed a writ petition in the High Court to get the aforesaid Press Note No 88 (Civil Rule No 7/83) cancelled. However, before the writ petition and the aforementioned six lakhs objections were disposed of, the infamous elections of 1983 were pushed down the throat of Assam! That is, of course, another black chapter of the Indira Gandhi's reign. In fact, Indira Gandhi neither understood the character of the Assam Movement nor did she ever try to make a correct assessment of the situation then prevailing. She was totally blinded by her partisan interests and when her flatterers met, the Devil had gone to his dinner!

The betrayal perpetrated by the Election Commission on Assam by forcibly holding the election in 1983, left behind a long trail of bitter legacies still (2000 A.D.) bedevilling the community life in Assam. It, however, succeeded in achieving the following:

1. Bringing to power a Congress(I) Government in Dispur;
2. Fostering sharp communal and ethnic division in Assam, thereby feeding fat the 'divide & rule' policy of the Congress(I) so religiously borrowed from the British;
3. And enabling the immigrant Muslims including lakhs of infiltrators to assume a more aggressive posture in a better organised manner.

The Assamese people refused to recognise the legality of the Saikia

Government installed through this elections in 1983. The indigenous people including the Assamese Muslims had mostly abstained from voting while the immigrant Muslims including the infiltrators had come out in thousands for voting. The Freedom Fighters' Association of Assam had appointed an unofficial Commission of Enquiry headed by Justice Sri TU Mehta, the retired Chief Justice of Himachal Pradesh High Court with late Ganesh Chandra Phukan IAS (Retd) and late Prof. Raihan Shah as other two members of the Commission to enquire into the barbaric holocaust caused by this election. Despite the Government's directive for not co-operating with the Commission, altogether 6000 memoranda were submitted to the Commission and 600 persons from various walks of life had appeared before the Commission for recording their statements. The Commission had, in categorical terms, attributed numerous incidents of large-scale violence before, during and after the elections to this forcibly imposed illegal election. Unknown to the rest of the country, the findings of the Commission which constitute a vivid account of the happenings of 1983 in Assam, are lying somewhere unattended. In any case, these findings of the Commission will continue to be a vast reservoir of information for the historians of contemporary Assam. Some of the important findings of the Commission were as follows:

The Commission, having drawn attention to the evenful year of 1980, pointed out that the Assamese people had conveyed their message to the Central Government in no uncertain terms by not allowing elections to be held in 12 out of 14 Lok Sabha constituencies. (Elections were held in two constituencies of Barak valley where the Assam Movement had no impact.) On the other hand, the Government had itself admitted that the situation in Assam was not normal by virtue of its orders dated 26 November 1981, 25 May 1982, 25 November 1982 and 25 November 1983 which had under Section 3 of the Assam Disturbed Areas Act, declared large areas of Assam as disturbed areas. The Commission was of the firm opinion that the situation prevailing in the months of January and February, 1983 was by no means favourable for holding elections. The Commission had also recorded that, "We also cannot avoid the conclusion that the party in power at the Centre ordered elections with the sole object of capturing power and was determined to go through the process by availing of the services of tame bureaucracy and savage police." (Mehta Commission's Report : page 74:4.1). The Centre was insisting from the very beginning that 1971 should be the cut-off date for detecting the foreign infiltrators. As such, the Commission very relevantly raised the question as to why the long intervening period between 1979 and 1982 was not utilised for deleting the names of the alien voters. This writer had also pointed out to the Commission that even the name of about 3 lakhs foreigners already deported were not deleted from the ERs. (Ibid: page 74). AGP government also took no action in this regard. Sri Ajit Kumar Sharma, MP, had succinctly recorded his statement before the Commission in the following words: "When the Union Government arbitrarily ended the negotiations with AASU and AAGSP at Delhi on 5 January, unilaterally announced elections on 6 January and put under arrest all leaders of the Movement at Borjhar airport on their way back home from Delhi, it revealed its evil intentions so long harboured, against the people of Assam and at once imposed a situation of confrontation between the Government and the people of Assam. The Election Commission played a subservient role to the Government and started the process of election, the Governor and his Principal Adviser, the Chief Secretary and the Chief Electoral Officer of Assam acted as political agents of the Union Government and carried on a conspiracy to hold elections in the face of warning given by almost all other senior officers of the Assam Government." (Ibid: page 80-81).

Elections were to be held in three stages on 14, 17 and 20 February 1983; the elections held on 14th proved beyond all shades of doubts that the situation was not conducive to hold free and fair elections. Out of 61 constituencies where elections were held on 14th February, large-scale violence was witnessed in as many as 18 constituencies and in another 15, as many as 100 polling stations could not be established. Then just before the second phase of elections, a serious armed clash took place on 16 February 1983 at Goalpara between some jawans of Assam Police Battalion on the one hand and some jawans of CRPF and Rajasthan Police on the other; resulting in the death of two CRPF jawans, three Rajasthan Police jawans and one havildar of Assam Police. Forty Assam Police personnel were subsequently dismissed from the force. Simmering discontentment against the inhuman repressive measures unleashed against the native people of Assam was already evident amongst the officers and employees of the State Government and the aforementioned ghastly clash amongst the Police forces of the same country was one of the most unfortunate manifestations of such widespread discontent. Even then, the Election Commission continued to be nonchalant: King Nero was still playing on his violin! On 17 February 1983, elections were to be held in 37 constituencies; but elections could not be completed in 16 of these constituencies. Even then, the Commission remained silent and was determined to go ahead with the elections to be held on 20 February 1983. It may be noted that just before the elections of 20 February, large-scale rioting, arson, and murders coupled with inhuman atrocities had taken place at Nellie, Gohpur, Samaria Satra, etc. Even on 20 February 1983, elections could not be held in 11 Assembly constituencies. Many of the voters were reported to have been transported in Police vehicles! Even some mobile polling centres were also reported to have functioned! There was no constitutional compulsion to hold elections on 17 and 20 February as already the electoral process was completed in 61 constituencies on 14 February 1983. No doubt, the Election Commission had assumed the role of the chief priest of Indira Gandhi's "Naramedha Yojna"! Within the city of Guwahati, even the non-Assamese voters did not venture out to the polling stations on the date of polls. The Mehta Commission has most aptly observed, "even if the third round of poll was wholly adjourned in time, much of the bloodshed could have been avoided. "(Ibid: page 108). Abdul Ghani Khan Choudhury was Indira Gandhi's main agent for perpetrating this unprecedented communal holocaust. During the electioneering campaign, he had boldly given a call at a meeting held at Mairabari in Nowgong district that "--- if Hindu kills one Muslim, the Muslims should retaliate by killing three Hindus and the Government would support you". Needless to mention that Ghani Khan went scot-free.

The Mehta Commission has further observed that taking advantage of this forcibly imposed election, some anti-social elements had engineered the serious clash between the tribal and non-tribal people in Gohpur area. The Commission has most relevantly pointed out that though prior to 1983 elections the Assam Movement had reached its peak, there was no clash between the Movement activists and the foreigners' but this election opened the floodgates of serious clashes. Appearing before the Commission, prominent Assamese Muslim personalities like Fazlul Rahman, Hamidur Rahman, Nusen Ali, Abu Sama, etc., had stated that the Congress leaders spearheaded by Indira Gandhi herself had threatened the immigrant Muslims openly that unless they voted for Congress(I), the Assamese leaders would drive them out from Assam. To quote the Mehta Commission: "The most important factors contributing to this great situation is in my humble opinion, the mad pursuit of Prime Minister Indira Gandhi and her party to install a Congress(I) Government in this state at any cost." (Ibid : page 133). Even those immigrant Muslims who had appeared before the Mehta Commission had admitted that 990 immigrant Muslims had lost their lives at Nellie and another 584 of them at Barbari only because of this cursed election.

The tremendous momentum generated by the Assam movement had certainly reduced the pace of fresh infiltration from Bangladesh; but the return of Indira Gandhi to power in 1980 gave a fresh fillip to the Infiltration Lobby. And immediately after her return to power, the immigrant Muslims including the infiltrators betrayed a tendency for engaging themselves in open clash with the native people of Assam. In 1980, they attacked a number of Assamese villages in North Kamrup and rendered about 5,000 people homeless, thereby compelling them to take shelter in relief camps. In April, 1980, Indira Gandhi visited Assam and instead of trying to come to terms with the Movement leaders, she tried to organise the minority communities on the basis of religion and language with the result that the AAMSU observed a "Demand Day" on 26 April 1980 at Barpeta. They had the audacity to hoist the flag of Bangladesh while rending the air with the slogan "Jai Bangla"! Almost simultaneously, hordes of Bangladeshis attacked some villages of the native people in Nagaon district and rendered 1,500 people homeless besides setting fire to the houses of 300 families. One should have no doubt that these were well-planned incidents of organised violence. On the other hand, 43 MLAs were won over and despite not commanding a majority in the Assembly, Mrs. Anowara Taimur was sworn in as the Congress(I) Chief Minister of the state. During her short tenure of stay in power, Anowara Taimur had unleashed such a reign of terror that many knowledgeable persons could compare the atrocities committed by her with only those of the Burmese invasion in the first quarter of the 19th century. True, Assam was spared the agony of Taimur Lang's barbarous invasion; but equally bitter memories of Mrs Taimur's reign of short duration will continue to haunt the Assamese mind for a long time to come. In fact, during her short reign, Dispur had assumed the look of some Islamic country's capital, thereby possibly throwing a hint of the shape of things to come in case the Assamese failed in their struggle for survival. Mrs Taimur's atrocious activities had even stirred the conscience of the neighbouring states so much so that Jubehu Lule, the president of the Naga Students Federation came forward to extend their support to the Assam movement. Besides, Stanley Nichols Roy, a prominent leader of Meghalaya was constrained to observe that in case the Assam movement failed, then the entire North-east would face a very serious crisis for existence and how prophetic he has proved over the years! AASU's refusal to accept 1967 as the cut-off date offered by Indira Gandhi for detection/deportation and insistence on 1951 to be the cut-off year, would subsequently undermine the entire cause of the Assam movement.

Even after the elections were over, the aggressive role of the immigrant Muslims did not show any signs of abatement. Those who were victims of violence at Samaria and Gohpur were of indigenous stock while those subjected to violence at Nellie were of Bangladeshi origin. The immigrant Muslims had started the violence in a planned manner. Bangladeshis had first murdered eight tribal children in Nellie and the Nellie massacre took place as retaliation. The clashes between the native people and the foreign infiltrators had assumed such serious proportion that under the Samaguri Police Station eleka alone, 30,000 native people were rendered homeless on 22 February 1983 and 22 Assamese villages were demolished by arson! Indira Gandhi lost no time in attracting the attention of the international media to the Nellie massacre while totally undermining the large-scale atrocities, unprecedented in free India, suffered by the Assamese people.

And all this was allowed to happen despite strong pleas made by, not only the Assamese people but by national political parties like the BJP, Janata Party, Lok Dal etc., for not holding the elections. Many prominent national leaders like Atal Bihari Vajpayee, Jaswant Singh, Late Raj Narain, Madhu Dandavate, Shyamnandan Misra, Late Charan Singh, Late HN Bahuguna, Late Karpuri Thakur, etc., had made fervent appeals to Indira Gandhi for postponing the elections; but she would not listen to anybody, not having forgotten as yet the ignominy she had suffered in the general elections of 1977. Sri Vajpayee and Sri Dandavate had even raised the demand in the Political Affairs Committee of the Parliament for postponing the elections. Sri Sethi, the Union Home Minister could hardly understand the raison d'etre of such a demand. On the other hand, the leadership of the Movement had appealed to all the national and regional political parties to boycott the elections. In response to the appeal, the BJP, the Janata Dal and the Lok Dal from amongst the national parties and all the regional parties boycotted the elections while the Congress(I), the Congress(S) and the Left parties participated in the elections. None of the Congress leaders, including Indira Gandhi could do any electioneering campaign in non-immigrant areas. With the induction of many more additional battalions of CRPF and BSF, entire Assam was imparted the look of a battleground.

Assuming that the election was not held forcibly, then what would have happened might be summarised as follows:

1. There would not have been a Congress(I) Government in Assam;
2. Indira Gandhi might not have had a chance to wreck vengeance on "Agitational Assam" and
3. Above all, the barbaric holocaust could have been avoided.

As against this, the fall-outs of the elections have not only torn apart the social fibre of the age-old composite society of Assam but have also now been threatening our national integrity. To quote Dr Hiren Gohain, a leading intellectual of the state: "The overall approach of the centre to the problem ridden states of the North-east is to destroy the local popular base of the leadership opposed to it. Puppet regimes, or something very like them, are being propped up everywhere with plenty of Police *bandobast*, CRP deployment and army operations. There is an intensive drive to divide tribes and races against one another. Civil liberties have suffered. In Assam alone, more than eighty Police Station areas are under the Disturbed Areas Act. This kind of basis for Government invariably breeds an irresponsible and cynical kind of corruption which turn the local people even more against these Governments. ***Terrorism is the desperate resort of rebels brought up against the wall.*** (Emphasis mine). (*Assam: A Burning Question*, page XXIX by Dr Hiren Gohain).

On the eve of Indira Gandhi's electioneering campaign, 36 persons had already lost their lives to police bullets while campaigning for boycotting the election. As the election was drawing nigh, the number of casualties resulting from Police/CRPF firings had crossed the 200 mark! On 14 February 1983 alone, 50 persons had been killed by the army in Darrang district. Instead of "Jai Hind", Indira Gandhi used to wind up her electioneering speech with "Khuda Hafiz"!

Before completing the topic of the infamous elections of 1983, we must put on record, for the sake of fairness, that the majority of the Assamese Muslims of the Brahmaputra valley had boycotted the elections. Even 62 prominent Muslims of Guwahati, in a joint appeal, had called upon the Muslims of Assam not to participate in this illegal election as well as not to get instigated by the communal utterances of the scheming politicians. In fact, Ataur Rahman of Titabar, Kadir Ali of Sipajhar area and Mehnur Ali of Barama had to sacrifice their lives in the process of resisting the efforts for holding the elections. This apart, the tribals, the tea-labour community and the Bengali-speaking Hindu people of the Brahmaputra valley had also responded in overwhelming majority to the boycott call.

To revert back to the extent of infiltration, we shall do well to note how some of the Congress(I) leaders, despite their subsequent volte-face, had reacted in the past to the never-ending flow of infiltrators:

As the Assam movement was gaining momentum, late Hiteswar Saikia wrote an article captioned "The Foreign Nationals problem in Assam" which was published on 20 December 1979 in *Nagarik*, an Assamese weekly, since defunct, and then edited by Sri Homen

Borgohain. The article had highlighted almost all the data discussed in this book besides dwelling on the apprehensions of the people of Assam caused by large-scale infiltration of Bangladeshis. He had even drawn attention to some international conspiracies for de-stablishing the situation in the entire North-East by fomenting acts of violence. Like many others, he had also pointed an accusing finger against late Sadullah for promoting the migration of Muslim farmers from East Bengal while, at the same time, reflecting on the land hungry characteristic of these migrants. He also referred to the Census Reports, which were replete with data indicating the much higher growth rate of Muslims in Assam, West Bengal and Tripura. Analysing the population growth of Assam religionwise between 1951 and 1971, Saikia throws light on the phenomenal increase in Assam's Muslim population. He also enumerates the steps taken by him in this context as the Minister of State for Home as well as the role of the PIP scheme. He has even claimed in the very article that he had resisted as the state home minister the Centre's proposal to wind up the PIP scheme. He had sounded words of caution in no uncertain terms against this growing menace. He had, however, advocated 1971 to be the cut-off year in specific terms by offering specific suggestions for detecting the post 1971 infiltrators.

Let us also have a look at how some other Congress leaders felt about the problem in the last decade of the last century:

Five general secretaries of The North-Eastern Congress(I) Coordination Committee, namely RC Chiten, BB Dutta, DD Pugh, HK Bora and Liansuama had submitted a memorandum to the Prime Minister Sri Narasimha Rao in July, 1992 during the latter's visit to Guwahati, highlighting the seriousness of the problem of infiltration into the North-Eastern States from Bangladesh. Some of the observations made in the memorandum as reproduced below are not only most revealing but these also bear out our own observations:

1. Referring to the repression of minorities in Bangladesh, it was stated that, "The atmosphere of general repression of all minority communities makes them look forward to India as a haven of refuge---."
2. "Apart from the chronic influx of people in search of work

and food, fundamentalist forces find it a fertile ground to utilise the leverage of aid, etc. for anti-secular and anti-India campaigns----."

3. Commenting on the partition of the country, the memorandum admits that, "the assumption that partition would solve the Hindu-Muslim question and that, on both sides, Hindu and Muslims would be able to live in peace and unity, proved to be unreal."

4. "To remind ourselves, the religious minorities, which accounted for 29.7% of population in the area comprising East Pakistan (now Bangladesh) in 1947, were reduced to 14.6% of the total population in 1974, the influx period being 1947-71.----- Riots and killings have yielded place to other means of oppression. Minorities today find that they are seldom able to protect their faith, property and women. Reports of forced marriages and conversions have been pouring in----."

5. "Between 1971 and 1981, Bangladesh Census Records show a reduction of 39 lakhs in the minority population,---- Between 1981-89, 36 lakh religious minorities were missing from that country." The memorandum further points out that, "In 1972, there were 7.5 lakh Bihari Muslims in the camps in Dacca. As a result of mediation by Saudi Arabia only 33000 of them were accepted by Pakistan. At present, there are less than two lakhs in the camps, where have the rest gone?"

6. "Shri MM Jacob, Union Minister of State for Home Affairs, said in parliament in December 1991, in reply to a question, that there were one lakh Bangladeshi nationals in Delhi and 5.87 lakhs in West Bengal."

7. Making many other relevant observations on matters already discussed by us, the memorandum adds that, "From the above we may infer:

   There are infiltrators—though it is a difficult task to examine the precise number.

   The infiltrations are not only by minorities of Bangladesh but also from the majority community—Muslims. In absolute terms, the number of Muslims crossing into India is likely to be much larger than that of non-Muslims.

An ideological support is given to the phenomenon by the Islamic fundamentalists creating the vision of a larger Islamic country comprising Bangladesh and the entire North-east where its economic problems will be solved and security ensured.

There is a direct co-relation between the rise of fundamentalism and increase in influx."

8. Before concluding, it is pointed out that, "Unfortunately the Government of India appears to be suffering from a half-hearted approach or no approach to this challenging problem. The External Affairs Ministry has not done the job it should have done. The concerned desk has virtually been a non-functioning one. For years, the practice has been if anything appears to be wrong there, ask Mr So and So of West Bengal who was in the limelight at that time. The desk is not asked to come forward with its findings. It is not realised that the problem is too deep for an active politician, however talented he is, to understand without the help of expert watchers. It is also not realised that the problem is not merely of West Bengal but of others as well.

So, these are the observations of some of the most prominent Congress leaders of the region; but they are fighting shy of confronting the problem, obviously because they do not want themselves to demolish their own vote banks. To quote John Earl's Jacobian character: "---the affectate traveller who hath seen all and perceived nothing."

Unfortunately, the present leadership of the AGP, which had spearheaded the Assam Movement on the foreigners issue, may be today, without any fear of valid contradiction, placed in the same category as these Congress leaders blinded by their greed for political power!

No specific steps have yet been taken to determine the correct figure of Bangladeshi infiltrators staying in Assam. On the basis of principles adopted during Census, the number of Bangladeshi infiltrators may broadly be determined as follows:

1. According to government records, five lakhs foreigners came to Assam between 1947 and 1950 and another two lakhs had come without being registered. These seven lakhs had multiplied into 12.20 lakhs by 1982.
2. On the other hand, 49.75 lakhs came over between 1951 and 1982 and they must have multiplied up to 66 lakhs by 1991.

Of course, these figures include both Hindus and Muslims. That is to say, the number of non-Indians in Assam by 1991, had crossed the mark of 78 lakhs and by the end of the century, to this number must be added not only the progenies of these 78 lakhs but also the fresh infiltrators still coming in a torrential flow in the absence of any effective preventive measures.

However, it will be wrong to assume that all these illegal migrants are Muslims as one is wont to do. The analysis of the Census Reports and ERs of Bangladesh presents an altogether different picture. The records of the Election Commission of Bangladesh would prove that a sizeable percentage of the illegal migrants was non-Muslim. On the eve of the parliamentary elections held in Bangladesh in June, 1996, the Commission had removed the names of 12 lakhs of Bangladeshi citizens from the country's ERs because they were absent from Bangladesh. Again in 1991 the ERs of Bangladesh had 6,21,81745 voters; but the Commission had to delete the names of 61,65,567 voters from the ERs while revising the ERs in 1995 because these people were no more residing in Bangladesh. Where these 61,65,567 Bangladeshis have disappeared? Noteworthy is that fundamentalist forces were in power in Bangladesh during this period. According to their own Census records, 39 lakhs people of minority community could not be traced between 1971 and 1981 and another 36 lakhs were missing between 1981 and 1989. Obviously all these 75 lakhs Bangladeshi nationals of minority communities had found their way to India and added to the burdens of Assam, Arunachal, Tripura and West Bengal. At the same time, the progressive increase in Assam's Muslim population also bears a tell-tale story: In 1951, Assam had a Muslim population of 19,81,857 returning an increase by 56.51%

over the Muslim population of 1931. Again in 1971, Assam's Muslim population was recorded to be 35,92,124, the increase being 80% during the intervening period of 20 years. Again in 1991, Assam's Muslim population was reported to be 63,73,204, an increase of 77.42% over 1971. Thus during 120 years between 1871 and 1991, Assam's Muslim population of 86,193 of 1871 had reached an all-time high of 63,73,204 in 1991 and by now, given the weak-kneed policy of successive Assam governments, including two AGP governments, it must have recorded a much higher rise. I have been a witness to this abnormal phenomenon during my service life as well as after retirement with no means at my disposal to stem the rot excepting efforts for creating awareness amongst the indigenous people. What were the consequences of my such efforts have already been highlighted above.

Now back to the days of 1983: My second detention was also based on false allegations. No mention was made in the grounds of my detention about so many meetings I had addressed for boycotting the elections which on the face of it should have been valid grounds for detention. So many secret meetings alleged to have been held by me, were the main grounds whereas I never participated in any secret meeting. In fact, there were no efforts on the part of official agencies for collecting factual intelligence. In any case, this time I was released by the High Court after about five months.

As I look back, I developed a feeling that it was strategically wrong to boycott the elections of 1983. Because, AGP contested the elections of 1985 held on the basis of incorrect ERs not cleansed of the names of alien voters. The ERs of 1991 also suffered from the same fault. ERs must be cleansed of alien names before the NRC is updated and this is what the present leadership of AASU and AJYCP has been insisting upon and the agitational atmosphere is once again gaining momentum. Briefly speaking, the entire matter revolves round the game of power politics.

AAGSP was gradually being bypassed by a handful of student leaders and/they were reported to have been carrying on secret negotiations with the representatives of the central government. The movement had also betrayed symptoms of losing its momentum.

Which is why, the then leadership of AASU was in a hurry to get rid of the stalemate.

Meanwhile, I was finding it very difficult to make two ends meet. I had an old Ambassador car. Even if I would have sold it off, it would not have brought in any adequate fund for sustaining any long term venture. So on number of occasions, I started driving the car myself as a taxi. It is an illegal practice to drive a private car as a taxi; but I had no other alternative for meeting day-to-day household expenses. In order to avoid detection, it was only in the evening that I used to pick up passengers at the Paltan Bazar area. But one evening, Indrajit Barua practically caught me redhanded. He was very sorry for this state of affairs and seriously advised me to take up some productive project with the help of loan from some bank. It was really a bitter experience to get such a loan sanctioned as I did not have anything to offer as a security against the loan. After PG Barua, the then managing director of the Assam Tribune group of newspapers came forward to stand as guarantor, the bank sanctioned the loan. My cousin brother, Ramendra Narayan Bhattacharya (now no more), who was a consultant engineer, helped me to set up a unit of small-scale industry for manufacturing tablewares using Urea Formaldehyde Moulding Powder supplied by the Assam Petrochemicals Ltd. The project proved to be a very viable one with good percentage of profits from the sale proceeds of the products. I had even extended my marketing net to Calcutta, Bangalore. New-Delhi, Patna, Meghalaya, Nagaland and Mizoram, etc. In fact, 70% of the products were sold outside Assam. Briefly speaking, this venture brought me financial stability, although ultimately I had to close down the unit in December, 1992 for want of raw materials. The Assam Petrochemicals Ltd. discontinued the production of the moulding powder on some flimsy grounds; but meanwhile I had enough savings for sustenance. The sale proceeds of the machineries also begot me considerable amount.

14

Glimpses of A New Venture

During my school and university days, I used to write short stories and articles on socio-political problems; but I had practically unlearnt all about it during my days in the police. During my solitary confinement in Hazaribagh jail, I had started writing a diary which was printed as my Prison Diary with the help of Jogesh Sharma, the owner of the Saraighat Press and an intimate friend of mine since my school days. It was a voluminous book extending over 600 pages. Altogether 2,250 copies were printed and all the copies excepting few retained by me, were sold out within 29 days. The book has since gone into a third edition. During my second detention also in 1983, I wrote another Prison Diary extending over 240 pages and covering wider range of socio-political and administrative problems. This has also gone into its second edition. In addition, I started writing articles in the regional English and Assamese dailies and weeklies. Thus, I became an eassyist of sort. These books and articles had certainly attracted public attention and gradually mine became a known name in the literary world of Assam. Homen Borgohain, late Kirtinath Hazarika and PG Barua were constantly goading me to write short stories and novels also. In fact, PG Barua of *Assam Tribune* group, also published a collection of my short stories. But it was because of constant pressure from Homen that I took to writing novels, including a detective one. One of the novels written by me and extending well over 300 pages, has also gone into a second edition. The book written in English reflecting on the problem of illegal transborder migration, titled as *The Silent Invasion* had attracted readership even from outside Assam and India. I feel that if I had retired from service in normal and due course, I would not have been possibly known as a writer but only as a retired IPS officer! Though some of my works have been acclaimed, I do not claim to have achieved any literary distinction mainly because I was not fully dedicated to this particular academic discipline.

Most of my literary exercises centred round socio-political issues and struggles of the indigenous people for survival with their identity intact. However, my efforts for writing a novel about the changes in personal and social life the globalisation has ushered in, is yet to end. Hope I can achieve this before I have to call it a day. My close association with Dr Birendra Kumar Bhattacharya, Prof Jogesh Das and Kirthinath Hazarika cultivated in me an abiding interest in creative literary works. Once accompanied by Birenda, I was coming back from Howly after attending some meeting; but about 40 km before we reached Guwahati, we were stranded for more than three hours as the road was blocked because of some serious accident. As we talked to the villagers who had assembled there but not known to us, we could feel that they were getting fed up with the lingering character of the Movement. In fact, this was the state of affairs in 1984. As we were held up, we discussed various matters during this long period; but what enthused me most was when Birenda told me, *inter alia*, that "Bhattacharjee, at the end of the day, the people will remember only by what you leave behind in writing---." Now in 2014, having realised that 'public memory is proverbially short' I wonder how prophetic was Birenda!

Meanwhile, the top echelon of AASU leadership had become so much adept in intrigue-based politics that they had ensured the expulsion of all their potential rivals in days to come from the AAGSP.

They could not lay their hands on me despite their best efforts. Some of them did not even welcome the idea of the unification of the two regional political parties of Assam. Still some of us had failed to understand their real intention which transpired only after the signing of the Assam Accord followed by the formation of the Axom Gana Parishad (AGP).

The peak of the movement was reached while resisting the elections of 1983 pushed down the throat of Assam. Unfortunately, it also witnessed the multidimensional ethnic chasm which further complicated the socio-political equations in Assam, besides darkening the face of Assam in the context of her proverbial communal harmony. Above all, the momentum of the movement also betrayed symptoms of losing its genuine tempo and this must have alerted the scheming leaders of AASU. Besides, they had also meanwhile attained the age of constitutional eligibility for contesting elections. Hence the hot haste for bringing the movement to a conclusion irrespective of what the Government of India was ready to concede. And a national convention was held at Jorhat towards the end of 1984 without, however, drawing up any list of priorities and formulating the next step forward. However, the intention of the AASU leadership to organise a political platform on their own had become clear and with this intention, they drafted the Assam Accord without taking the AAGSP into confidence in collaboration with the cunning bureaucrats of the Union Government.

15

Assam Accord: A Stillborn Baby

Hue and cry is still being raised for the implementation of the Assam Accord even after 27 years of signing it. Ridiculously enough, the AASU had to sign another agreement on 5 May 2005 with the Union Government for implementing the Assam Accord with, however, no worth-mentioning result following.

The much-vaunted Assam Accord had promised much but delivered nothing till date even after 27 years. It will be quite in order to point out that the objectives of the Assam Movement were not to establish an Indian Institute of Technology (IIT), two universities and to revive few sick industries. Even after 27 years, the problem of illegal trans-border migration could not be solved. Rather, the possibility of detecting and deporting the illegal migrants has been becoming more remote with the passage of each day whereas various data and so many census reports of India and Bangladesh clearly indicate that the rate of such illegal migrants has assumed serious and ever expanding proportion as were envisaged and contemplated by Sadique Khan and Abdul Momin, two eminent persons of Bangladesh. As a result, the indigenous people of Assam irrespective of their language, caste, creed, religion are gradually becoming a minority in many Legislative Assembly constituencies.

The turn of events had since exposed the fact that Rajiv Gandhi never intended the Assam Accord to solve the problem of illegal migration from Bangladesh, his only intention seeming to be, as it transpired subsequently, to defuse the Assam Movement. However, the Accord certainly paved the way for the contemporary AASU leadership to capture power at Dispur almost immediately after the Accord was signed.

Interesting to note that the same leadership did not accept 1967 as the cut-off date for the detection of the illegal migrants whereas they accepted 1971 as the cut-off date in the Accord. This was because in 1980 they had not attained the age of Constitutional eligibility for contesting elections! Still worse, no time frame was fixed for updating the NRC which should have been the main basis for detecting illegal migrants.

I do not have the slightest hesitation to emphasise that the Assam Accord amounted to a deed of total betrayal perpetrated by Prafulla Mahanta and his colleagues on the people of Assam. The draft of the Accord was never discussed or analysed in AAGSP. Delegates of the AAGSP were flown to New Delhi in two special aircrafts on 14 August 1985 and kept practically confined to a guest house of the Home Ministry since their arrival at New Delhi. The draft of the Accord was simply read out at 11 pm., without giving any chance to anybody for examining the clause of the Accord and all were rushed to Rajiv Gandhi's residence for signing the Accord! Dissatisfaction was writ large over faces of all the delegates and in fact, some of the delegates boycotted the Accord-signing ceremony.

And today, in the absence of any definiation of the Assamese people as stipulated in the Accord (which should have been indigenous people) the most important clause of the Accord pertaining to constitutional safeguards against being overwhelmed by illegal alien migrants, has remained confined to the file, besides cultivating enough scope for politicising the entire matter. True, the current leadership of AASU is crying hoarse for implementing the Accord; but they cannot boast of the same credibility which AASU leadership enjoyed during the days of the legendary Assam movement only because of the betrayal perpetrated by Prafulla Mahanta and Co. Mahanta formed two governments in 1985 and 1996 but did nothing worth mentioning for implementing the Assam Accord. Incidentally, BJP despite being a participant in the Assam Movement, also let down the people of Assam when it was in power in New Delhi for six long years.

The non-implemention of the Assam Accord had been indirectly contributing to the growth of militant activities. Besides, no serious and sustained efforts were in evidence for educating the people about the political, economic and cultural implications. The legendary Assam movement had conceived much but practically delivered nothing excepting giving birth to a stillborn baby in the shape of the Assam Accord. But its adverse fallouts have been bedevilling the public life in Assam only because the Movement leadership, being motivated by sheer selfish interests, lacked not only in farsightedness but was totally bereft of any objective perspective, both long and short term.

Axom Gana Parishad's current agitation for implementation of the Accord is nothing but another attempt at taking the people for another ride up the garden path. Its loss of credibility is the greatest hurdle. The people of Assam are eagerly waiting to see if the pro-talk ULFA group can still salvage something on the basis of their charter of demands. Still in the context of the present ambience, their efforts are also seen as rear guard action only.

Assam is burning. Despite all the betrayals perpetrated on her, she is still crying hoarse to sound to the rest of the country that neither she is suffering from a 'persecution-mania' nor is the crisis exaggerated. This is not a class-war. Nor is it a war-cry sounded by the so-called 'Assamese middle class' as many of the theorists and westward looking progressivists would like to depict. Class war or no class war, every individual as is natural, endeavours to preserve and promote his identity. And this trend or instinct for self-preservation gets magnified whenever a particular state or a particular ethnic group or groups or an entire range of peoples, encounter the threat of being politically, culturally and economically extinct.

Thus ended a glorious struggle of the people of Assam in a very inglorious manner. RN Ravi, a retired Special Director of the IB and lately an essayist of eminence, expressed his opinion in the following words: "A discerning glance at the Accord illuminates its amateurish character and the queer pitch. It was designed to doom. Of the 15 clauses in the Accord only four are somewhat relevant to the issue while remaining 11 are preambles and peripherals like good intentions of the government and the prime minister, promises of economic development, clemency to the protagonists of the agitation, etc. The core concern was mischievously obfuscated in the thicker of irrelevancies and lollypops." (*Assam Tribune*, 30 September 2012). There is no denial that the direct legitimisation of the IMDT Act, reduced the core issue into a non-starter. Still worse, none of the ethnic groups were taken into confidence while preparing the draft of the Accord as if to prove the charge of Assamese chauvinism!

As I look back, I am inclined to believe that the historic movement did more harm than good to Assam's composite society. Most adversely affected was the academic world of the state. During the movement period, continuous agitational programmes kept the students away from their classes for months on end. On the other hand, they had to pass their examinations. So the adoption of unfair means during the examinations on massive scale became the order of the day and that too, not without the blessings of few teachers and overlords of the academic world. Let me quote an example: My own brother was an examiner of some answer papers of LLB examination. The Dean of the faculty himself had approached him for ensuring the success of some candidates! No wonder my brother returned all the answer papers without evaluating them and refused to be an examiner in future. But the movement had presented a grand opportunity for disciplining the student community because the sway of the AASU leadership over the entire student community was so complete that it could have easily banished for good the adoption of unfair means in the examinations. Students of ordinary calibre were awarded first class in their BA/MA examinations besides many others getting their degrees without ever attending their classes. The movement leadership was in need of huge fund for sustaining a movement of such long duration and funds were collected from all conceivable sources. Complaints of coercion and intimidation were also heard frequently. True, huge amounts were collected but no account was ever submitted in any of the meetings of the AAGSP. Thus, the principle of accountability in respect of using public funds had become a casualty from the very begining of the movement and as it turned out subsequently, the tradition was carried forward by the AGP government. In fact, the collection of fund for the movement had become a source of income for a number of young activists with the connivance of their senior colleagues for reasons not in need of any clarification. Thus the urge for easy, unearned money had gradually grown deep roots in the midst of the young generation which ultimately proved extremely detrimental to the growth of a clean public administration under the young rulers of the AGP. The accountability in public life is the cornerstone of a strong democratic edifice and its absence breeds not only corruption at all levels of the administration as had precisely happened during the AGP rules but also created compulsive circumstances for betraying fascist tendencies. Also it is certainly not difficult to discern a strong co-relation between adoption of unfair means in examinations instead of putting in hard labour for acquiring knowledge necessary for success in examinations and acquisition of the benefits of unearned easy money. Both these malpractices are two sides of the same coin. And today in Assam, these two factors have combined to totally destroy the work culture of the young generation, thereby also creating more opportunities for the illegal migrants to infiltrate into various economic sectors. Worst of all, the lure of unearned money had totally paralysed the functioning of the second AGP government elected in 1996. The degradation of academic pursuit brought in its train all-pervasive moral degradation also and held its full sway during the tenure of both the AGP governments. Not that the Congress(I) government was any different; but it could, at least, boast of some matured heads.

The government employees played a major role in imparting the gigantic proportion the Assam movement had assumed. The Xadau Asom Rajyik Karmachari Parishad (XARKP) (All Assam State

Government Employees Union) had held total sway over the state government employees during the entire period of the movement as the AASU had done in case of the student community. The Parishad had kept the state secretariat totally paralysed continuously for 17 days. Its dictates had become as good as inviolable laws for the employees. Still the Parishad cannot claim to have done any better than the AASU. During the movement, it could have, its control over the employees being what it was, worked towards developing a healthy work culture free of corrupt practices, amongst its members numbering few lakhs while also ensuring that the members of the public were not harassed in various government offices; but nothing was done. In fact, the Parishad has not till date thought in terms of disciplining its members to the advantage of the toiling millions whereas it would have been so much easier to do so as a widespread patriotic fervour had swamped the entire atmosphere. Such constructive programmes could not, however, claim any pride of place in the Parishad's agenda. Nor did the Parishad think in terms of restraining the state government employees from putting the self before the interests of Assam and her people, particularly in respect of denying any opportunity to the illegal migrants for settling down in Assam. Few illustrations may be in order: A Bangladeshi cannot operate a rickshaw or a push-cart in Guwahati without the active connivance of some employees of the municipal corporation. A Bangladeshi national can never dream of encroaching upon forest land without the knowledge of the employees of the forest department. A Bangladeshi national can never get a plot of land registered in his or her name without the connivance of some employees of the revenue department. Well, if we have to document the entire range of such pro-Bangladeshi but anti-national activities of the government employees without any interference from the Parishad, the list would be rather unending. To cut a long story short, one can posibbly without any fear of contradiction assert that the Karmachari Parishad despite its dominating role in the Assam Movement, could neither make any concrete contribution towards solving the 'infiltration problem' nor could it do anything to prevent further infiltration excepting, of course, ensuring that one of its prominent leaders got a berth in the first AGP Ministry and another became an MLA. In fact, none of the AGP MLAs and MPs thought it to be their moral responsibility to resign on grounds of not implementing the Assam Accord and for failing to prevent fresh infiltration, let alone devoting themselves to devising measures for solving the problem. Such inaction has further substantiated the charge that the movement leadership spearheaded by the contemporary AASU leadership was never serious about the matter, their sole preoccupation being to construct a platform which could catapult them to power. Their success was confined to maintaining a well-camouflaged chism between ground realities and the image of the contemporary leadership of the AASU which the present AASU leadership was finding very difficult to erase. No doubt, their credibility and hold over the imagination of the people have suffered a serious beating. After all, AASU was in the forefront while signing the Assam Accord in August, 1985 and since then quite a few presidents and general secretaries of AASU have come and gone without ensuring the implementation of the Accord. As such, not only AASU's but also the common man's confidence in the Centre has been thoroughly shaken and the present AASU leadership cannot be blamed if they are thinking in terms of another agitation and this time for implementing the Assam Accord. A press report published in *The Assam Tribune* newspaper on 13 August 2000, also points to the same direction. Some excerpts from the report may enlighten the reader further.

"Govt. encouraging militancy by not implementing Assam Accord"

GUWAHATI, Aug 12-- The signing of the historic Assam Accord to facilitate detection and deportion of foreigners from Assam will complete 15 years on 15 August and the leaders of the All Assam Studentss Union (AASU) which spearheaded the six-year long movement, have now alleged that the government is encouraging armed struggle by not implementing the Accord, which was the result of a democratic movement....

The AASU President, Sri Prabin Boro, said that till date the AASU has been putting pressure on both the State and the Central governments for the implementation of all the clauses of the Accord. But at the same time, he said that the organisation would not be able to wait for ever for the implementation of the Accord. He said if the Accord is not implemented immediately, the AASU would be forced to 'rethink' on the Accord....

The AASU general secretary Amiya Bhuyan alleged that... If the government fails to implement all the clauses of the Accord within a specific time frame, the people of Assam will completely lose faith in all forms of democratic movement, he added.

The AASU adviser Samujjal Kumar Bhattacharyya pointed out that the threat posed to the identity of the indigenous people of Assam by the silent invasion of foreign nationals is now more dangerous than the time when the Accord was signed and this happened because of the failure of the government to implement the Accord. Now the demographic pattern has been changed because of unabated influx of foreigners while the agents of the Pakistan Inter Services Intelligence (ISI) have also started to come into the State along with the foreign nationals, posing a grave threat to the country as a whole, he said, "The State and the Central government betrayed the peace loving people of Assam by not implementing the Assam Accord for 15 years. The government should make its stand clear whether the people have to launch armed struggle to preserve their identity," he said. Sri Bhuyan alleged that the Central Government played a discriminatory role by not implementing the Accord to protect the identity of the indigenous people of the State. The ruling BJP, in its election manifesto, promised to scrap the IM(DT) Act but till date the promise has not been fulfilled.

Sri Bhattacharyya said that the failure of the Central Government to protect the border is a crime. He further said that the Government sealed the Indo-Pak border but no such step has been taken to seal the Indo-Bangla border. He demanded that Army should be deployed to seal the Indo-Bangla border as was done in case of the Indo-Pak border. (The present scribe invites the reader's attention to similar views expressed by the Governor of Assam in his report to the President.)

Sri Bhattacharyya reminded the AGP leaders that.... He alleged that, the "AGP leaders are now reluctant to speak about the Accord fearing that they might lose the vote of the foreign nationals...." (*The Assam Tribune*, 13 August 2000)

The above quoted statement of the AASU depicts a clear picture of what has not only been presently agitating the minds of the Assamese people but also a picture of the gathering clouds full with potentials for plunging Assam into another holocaust of unknown and unforseen character and intensity. True, 'North Block' will not decipher the coded message now and will ultimately resort to following the path of Indira Gandhi which had so far succeeded only in alienating the people of this region.

While exposing the deficiencies of the movement leadership, particularly of AASU's, one must not also ignore the fact that the Assam Movement had ushered in an era for building up a cordial atmosphere for welding the loose joints of the ethnically divided age-old composite society of Assam presently facing a common danger of being overwhelmed in all respect by the Bangladeshi nationals. But that was not to be, because of Mahanta's hidden agenda of capturing power and unleashing a campaign for naked and shameless self-aggrandisement. In fact, as it transpired, the question of ethnic diversities-related issues of ethnic aspirations and apprehensions certainly did not receive the priority it deserved while Mahanta had assumed the role of the self-styled president of the AAGSP only because he was then the president of the AASU and not because everybody concerned wanted him to guide the proceedings of AAGSP which, at least, presented some semblance of coming together, a facet Mahanta & Co. had neither the farsight to appreciate nor the broadmindedness to free itself from the caste-Hindu middle class grip over the deliberations about the emergent socio-political situation.

The turn of events has now exposed the fact that Rajiv Gandhi never intended the Assam Accord to solve the problem of infiltration ffrom Bangladesh, his only intention seeming to be, as it transpired subsequently, to defuse the Assam Movement. However, the Accord certainly paved the way for the contemporary AASU leadership to capture power at Dispur. Even while selecting the candidates for the post-Accord Assembly elections, Mahanta & Co. betrayed absolute lack of farsightedness in as much as the claims of most of the leaders of various ethnic groups and Assamese Muslims, were ignored. Else, much of the ethnic problems and violence faced by Assam today could have been avoided. The non-implementation of the Assam Accord over last 15 years has also bred hesitancy on the part of the militant secessionist outfits to come forward for a negotiated settlement. In other words, both Delhi and Dispur have lost their credibility, the most important factor in such situation.

Assam has been facing a silent invasion for decades on end with the eyes of the invaders focussed on the game of numbers. That Assam's hydra-headed problem of infiltration form Bangladesh, lately aggravated by the subversive activities of the ISI, is a threat to the security of the entire country and her territorial integrity, cannot be overemphasised. Assam is an ancient land with very rich heritage and culture. Her demography, socio-economic equations and political stability have already been subjected to severe strain and ISI's appearance on the scene has not made matters easy either. Clearly ISI's game plan has been to:

1. Avenge the creation of Bangladesh.
2. Destabilise the situation in the entire North-east.
3. Organise terrorist activities.
4. Spread anti-India feelings and above all,
5. Promote Muslim fundamentalism with the help of millions of uneducated, illiterate Bangladeshi infiltrators.

16

Two AGP Governments

With the change of guards at Dispur, I was gleefully basking in the sunshine of hopes for turning a new page in Assam's history without any premonition of the greatest betrayal ever perpetrated against Assam. In fact, India had resorted to a new experiment by entrusting power to the young generation with Rajiv Gandhi in New Delhi and Prafulla Kumar Mahanta in Assam replacing the old guards but both failed. Rajiv, though a pilot of aircraft, tried to be a politician without requisite experience. Mahanta's case was little different. From the presidentship of AASU he was catapulted to the topmost seat of power of the state without any administrative experience at his command. Some of the teachers who had helped AASU in carrying on the six-year-long agitation, took the role of Mahanta's advisers. The experienced bureaucrats were totally ignored. Even an efficient and experienced administrator like Jatin Hazarika was shunted off from the post of home secretary. The results were there for everyone to see. The student activists who were left out of the electoral fray, were now hell bent upon extracting their respective "pound of flesh". Briefly speaking, it became a free for all. Mahanta and his colleagues in his cabinet totally forgot why and how they had captured power. They totally forgot to implement whatever little there was in the Assam Accord in favour of the historic movement. The issue of infiltration was pushed under the carpet. Mahanta, his wife and cabinet colleagues, AGP MLAs with rare exception and many AGP activists embarked on a spree of sheer self-aggradisement. Some of them became millionaires overnight. In the process, the administration was banished to the back bench. Assam has been a multi-racial, multi-lingual state for ages and the tendency to ignore these historical facts, was evident even during the Assam Movement and now after capturing power, the AGP leaders made it bold to ignore this vital issue of Assam's public life both in their words and deeds and such intention certainly did not go down well with the leaders of the various ethnic groups. Not that AGP did not have senior leaders capable of foreseeing the consequences of such suicidal pursuits. Leaders like Paragdhar Chaliha, Dinesh Goswami, Ataur Rahman, Dr Nagen Saikia, etc., were totally ignored nor any efforts were made to organise the party at the grassroot level with the result that dedicated cadres capable of sustaining the party during lean periods, did not surface at all. The leadership of the party has been monopolised by the same set of leaders till date whereas other political parties have been trying to induct new and young blood into their respective ranks.

To be very precise, there is nothing much worth-writing about the two tenures of AGP rule excepting its misrule, corruption, salacious conduct, nepotism, personal misconduct and intra-party rivalries. Worst of all, CM Mahanta himself got involved in so many scandals—both financial and salacious. Even his legally married wife was seen on a public road to have been involved in a hand to hand fight with a woman whom Mahanta was alleged to have married secretly in some temple in Maharashtra. Poor woman was married and then divorced because of such scandal. This woman was accused of amassing properties disproportionate to her known source of income and she was presently undergoing imprisonment for such corrupt practices. The reader may draw his or her own conclusion as to how she came to be in possession of such properties. As if that was not sufficient for scandalising the Chief Minister, his unholy alliance with some anti-social cliques were unearthed in the shape of the "Letter of Credit" scandal involving the misappropriation of more than rupees four hundred crores from the public exchequer. In fact, he was to face criminal prosecution in this context but the Governor refused to give requisite sanction for his prosecution for reasons not yet made public, although it was not difficult to surmise that BJP-led NDA government's anxiety to save him from such ignominious fate was at the root of non-availability of such sanction. Why the BJP-led union government was anxious to save him is another issue which will be hinted upon in due course. Taking the cue from the CM himself, some of his cabinet colleagues also started making money by committing fraud on the public exchequer. As far as I remember, the scandal involving the Seed Corporation of Assam and the scandal centering round the supply of tubewells in agricultural sector, had made headlines in the media. Most of them had come empty-handed from the university hostels to Dispur and today quite a few of them were seen to have owned palatial buildings in Guwahati, Nagaon, New-Delhi and reportedly in few other cities of the country. Thus a parallel economy of black money polluted the entire functioning of the AGP government. Mahanta's style of functioning had never convinced me that he would ever make a good administrator. His leadership quality left much to be desired as had been the case with all self-seeking power-mongers.

Meanwhile, the law-and-order situation was gradually going out of control. The memories of atrocities committed in the context of the elections held in 1983 coupled with the disappointment emanating from the Assam Accord, had motivated the ultras to adopt a more militant attitude not only against the central government but also against the non-Assamese large business houses with ULFA taking full advantage of the non-performing AGP government. The ultras went on a fullscale extortion spree and Mahanta's government was simply an onlooker. To start with, they had targetted only non-Assamese business houses but gradually they gave up the practice of making such distinction, thereby provoking the ire of the Assamese business houses and the urbanised Assamese middle class also. The climax came when Surendra Paul, a tea baron and close relation of Swaraj Paul, was assassinated. On this occasion, the Central Government was fully alerted as Paul's murder caused widespread panic in the tea circle, particularly amongst the tea companies still boasting of enough foreign involvement. Chandrasekhar was then the Prime Minister, New Delhi was really fed up with such lawlessness and dismissed the Mahanta government. A wrong impression had been created that the AGP had swept the poll of 1985; this was not true. The AGP had managed to get majority by capturing 71 seats that too, after largescale rigging. A number of voters had managed to vote 7/8 times either by hoodwinking the polling officials or with their connivance. The Left parties were practically wiped out excepting that CPM bagged two seats. But the ugly head of communal politics became quite evident with the emergence of the United Minority Front (UMF) winning in 17 seats. The BJP, the Janata Party and the LokDal had each drawn a blank. The people had hailed the advent of regionalism in Assam's politics, only to be thoroughly disappointed subsequently for reasons already hinted upon. Mahanta could never boast of his vision for the future of Assam. His party had no well thought out economic agenda. Though the appointment of the Jain Commission had created some hope for revamping the economy of Assam, its report practically remained confined to the files with no visible efforts made to implement the reccomendation of the Commission. In fact AGP had neither the time nor the talents to appreciate the significance of the Commissions' reccomendation. They concentrated more on issuing licence for wine shops. Today Assam has the highest number of wine shops in the country in proportion to her population. Touts surfaced in hundreds for begetting contracts, various licences and the likes for their clients. In the process and above all, the respect for law and prescribed rules was thrown to the wind resulting in considerable flight of capital from Assam. In fact, I had personally dissuaded at least two industrialists from shifting to Ahmedabad. They are doing fine now. It will not be an exaggeration to claim that some of the AGP leaders died of complications created by wrost kind of alcoholism. The use of alcohol and narcotics assumed a menacing proportion during this period with all the adverse consequences to follow.

No wonder, the AGP was thrown out of power in the general elections held in 1991. The Congress(I) formed the ministry with Hiteswar Saikia as the CM. He certainly imparted some semblance of administration but the very day he assumed office, some employees, including the general manager of the Guwahati Refinery were kidnapped by the ULFA. They demanded the release of some of their colleagues languishing in jail in return for the safe release of kidnapped persons. Saikia had to relent and complied with the request of the ultras, thereby boosting the morale of the militant outfit. But Saikia was a past master in executing the "divide & rule" policy and did not take much time in causing a split in the ULFA leadership. Some of the leaders of ULFA were taken to Delhi for holding the first-ever negotiation with, however, no worth mentioning result of the negotiation excepting that some of the leaders who went for talk did not return to ULFA and instead, chose to set up their own business ventures, both fair and foul, with the connivance of Saikia. Obviously, Saikia was following a policy of carrot and stick. Following the dismissal of Mahanta government in 1990, "Operation Bajrang" was conducted against the ULFA in Lakhipathar area and during the tenure of Saikia ministry, "Operation Rhino-1" and "Operation Rhino-2" were conducted for flushing out the ULFA from its hideouts. Such enterprises by Saikia government compelled ULFA to seek hideouts outside India in both Bhutan and Bangladesh. The "Operation All Clear" conducted jointly by the Indian and the Bhutanese armies flushed out the ULFA boys and girls from Bhutan and in the encounter while on flight, many ULFA cadres lost their lives, many were captured and quite a few were missing, never to be found again. Subsequent developments and the failure to inform the public about the fate of the missing cadres, intensify the suspicion that they were eliminated after capturing them alive—a blatant example of ghastly murder by any standard of inviolable human rights and norms of civilised society. According to media reports, they were handed over to Indian army but their whereabouts were never made public. If ULFA was a terrorist organisation, then those who caused the disappearances of these missing cadres, were no less terrorists in their conduct. It is significant to note that one of the clauses of the Charter of Demands of ULFA, presently negotiating with the Union Government, is to make available the details of the whereabouts of these missing cadres. Their eviction from Bhutan made it imperative for ULFA to organise fresh hideouts in Bangladesh, then under the rule of Khaleda Jia known for her anti-India stance actively promoted both by the Jamiat and the ISI. However, the scenario underwent perceptible changes after Seikh Hasina came to power.

Saikia's tenure was certainly not a glorious one. Corruption skyrocketed at all levels of the administration and the commercial world. Government jobs were, for all practical purposes, put on auction sales. In this context the greatest damage was done in respect of primary school teachers and the education department topped the list of wrong-doers, a legacy left behind by Saikia yet to be cleansed. The disgraced AGP leaders were outdone in this respect by Saikia's performance which may be termed as a pyrrhic victory over the AGP, only to be overshadowed during AGP's infamous second tenure. Meanwhile, the AGP had resorted to an apologetic stunt by repeatedly announcing that the people should pardon them for their mistakes which were the result of the lack of their administrative experiences and that they would never commit these mistakes again if they were brought back to power and given one more chance to serve Assam. They blamed the Union Government and the IMDT Act for their failure to do anything meaningful in the context of transborder illegal migration—the core issue of the Assam Movement.

On the eve of the elections in 1991, as a result of the intra-party rivalries and unseemly quarrels agaist each other, the AGP split into two parties with senior leaders like Dinesh Goswami, Bijoya Chakraborty, Bhrigu Kumar Phukan, Pulakesh Barua, Brindaban Goswami, etc., choosing to form the "Natun Axom Gana Parishad (NAGP)". At this time, there were as many as five aspirants in the undivided AGP for the chair of the CM, proving to be a major factor in split of the party. The people really felt outraged with such self-seeking agendas. Unfortunately for the NAGP and the state also, Dinesh Goswami lost his life in a motor accident during the election campaign. His untimely and premature death not only deprived the state of a very able parliamentarian but also NAGP's venture for removing Mahanta from the saddle of power received a great setback. The lure for power and money, possibly more for money, made them all blind to the ground realities and consequently their relevance in the public life of Assam was also put on a downhill journey. Above all, the image of regional politics took a severe beating. It will be really a Herculian task to restore the glory it had cultivated during the Assam Movement. In fact, many of the ethnic tribes have meanwhile promoted their own parties and the hope for an all-Assam regional party surfacing again receded further to the background. In fact as one looks back, one is inclined to surmise that the authoritarian trend betrayed by Mahanta can hardly be conducive to promoting regional politics in a multi-ethnic state like Assam.

True, Hiteswar Saikia will never be remembered as a great chief minister; but his sworn enemies will also admit that he was a great politician. In this context, his greatest achievement was to revive the moribund Congress(I) Party in Assam. Many observers thought that Congress(I) was a spent force in Assam without, however, considering that Hiteswar Saikia was a force to be reckoned with. Saikia had no peers in contemporary Assam politics so far manipulative strategy and persuasive skills were concerned. Added to this must be his inborn humility and soft-spoken vocabulary while concealing his uncompromising determination. The fascist character of the Assam Movement had made it impossible for the Congressmen to move about freely—let alone promoting political activities. Hiteswar Saikia rescued them from such banishment from Assam's public life and facilitated the rejuvenation of Congress(I) in Assam. In fact, the above mentioned fascist style of functioning paved the way for Congress(I), to return to power. As such, Saikia's greatest achievement was, inter alia, the gradual restoration of a peaceful atmosphere in Assam which was totally destroyed during the tenure of the first AGP government.

As a strong supporter of the Assam Movement, I have no reason to wax eloquent in praise of a Congress(I) CM but at the same time I cannot distort historical facts. In fact, he had foreseen that a peaceful solution of the Assam Movement must centre round 1971 as the cut-off date. His recommendation in this context was accepted by Mrs. Gandhi in toto and he worked behind the scene while scripting the Assam Accord. Then he resigned after the Accord was signed and thus facilitated the entry of AGP into the arena of power politics where, of course, it proved to be totally inadept. On the other hand, Saikia may also be credited with ridding Assam politics and administration of domination by the so-called high caste Hindus without imparting any semblance of sectarian consideration unlike Sarat Sinha. To cut a long story short, it may be safely observed that after Bharat Ratna Bordoloi, he had succeeded in emerging as the leader of the entire North-east.

The second tenure of AGP rule between 1996 and 2001 was not less inglorious than its first tenure. The plea for pardon as mentioned above, certainly swayed public opinion to some extent in favour of AGP; but that might not have sufficed to see AGP back in power. The sudden demise of Hiteswar Saikia on the eve of the election, in fact before the election campaign had come to an end, proved to be the deciding factor in favour of AGP. Even then AGP could not score decisive victory in as much as it failed to achieve a majority on its own in the House. As I had hinted upon earlier, AGP had no ideological background nor did it have any scruple. Now it turned to the Left parties who were the main target of their irrational attack during the movement. Left parties also did not hesitate to extend their support—possibly with a hope to recover what they had lost during the Movement. Even, Pramod Gogoi of CPI became a cabinet minister in Mahanta's second ministry. Still worse, Abdul Muhim Mazumdar, who was the main architect of the IMDT Act, was also inducted as a cabinet minister! Is there any further need to elaborate AGP's unscrupulous compromises? Above all, nothing prevailed on AGP to burrry their inglorious past record in blatant violation of their promises to the people. Here I am reminded of a statement made by Bangabandhu Sheikh Mujibur Rahman in his unfinished Memoirs: "One should never work for national development with unfit leadership, unprincipled leaders and cowardly politicians on one's side. That results in more harm than good for the people of the country." Though made in a different context, this statement holds good for all patriotically oriented persons. Possibly, those who became ministers and MLAs of AGP in 1996, had apprehended that this was the last chance for them to loot the public exchequer as was proved by subsequent developments. They surpassed all past records of corruption at the government level. They once again forgot all about the issue of illegal migration from Bangladesh and simply remained satisfied with blaming New Delhi for inaction on this life and death question of Assam's identity and existence. They never got over the hangover of the malignant fallouts of their first tenure in power and they would never get over that under the present leadership.

A comparision between Hiteswar Saikia and Prafulla Kumar Mahanta had become unavoidable because on both the occasions

Mahanta had succeeded Saikia without ever imbibing the positive qualities of Saikia, particularly in respect of dealing with opposition camps, be it the media or political opponents. It was during the second tenure of Mahanta's rule that senior journalist like Naresh Kalita of Agradoot group of newspapers was sent to jail twice, purely as vindictive measure. Mahanta had even invoked the provision of the NSA to detain Naresh in prison without trial for 78 days after keeping him in police lock-up for five days. Again Jitumoni Bora, another budding journalist of the same concern, was arrested and sent to jail, apparently on the basis of some concocted allegations. Thus, Mahanta cultivated permanent animus against a section of the print-media. Though Mahanta could capture power in 1996 mainly because of media's tirade against Saikia's corrupt regime, it did not take Mahanta much time for rubbing the media on the wrong side. Not remaining content with harassing Naresh and Jitumoni, he turned his attention to Ajit Bhuyan, a senior and respected journalist known for his voice of protest against injustice, violation of human rights, encroachment upon states' powers by the centre and depriving Assam of her legitimate dues. It appeared as if Mahanta was out to teach a lesson to the media. On the other hand, media leaders had not diagnosed the treacherous character of Mahanta and his camp followers and as a result, they were now realising how low a treacherous chief minister could stoop down to. Ajit Bhuyan was repeatedly arrested in quite a few cases and the malicious intent became very clear when efforts were made maliciously for implicating Bhuyan in the "Sanjay Ghosh murder" case also. Despite being taken seriously ill, he was not released from custody. It was only after the Supreme Court intervened, he was admitted to the Dibrugarh Medical College for treatment. Not remaining content with such untold harassment, he was compelled to appear in the Assembly and reprimanded and that too, in the context of a case, the investigation of which was yet to be completed. Besides Press reports, Ajit Bhuyan himself had narrated to me these facts of his woes. Such vendetta may satisfy personal ego against an uncompromising journalist and the urge for nakedly displaying one's power; but it never helps in building up a healthy ambience for the society at large. At any cost, Ajit's voice of protest had to be put down! But could really Mahanta do that? It would be wrong to assume that the people were only mute spectators as would be evident from the result of the general elections held in 2001 when AGP could win only 20 seats with both CPI and CPM drawing a blank. Thus the hope of the leftists for recovering the lost ground also evaporated. In fact, by 2001, AGP had lost the potential for fielding its candidates in all the 126 Legislative Assembly seats. It could field its candidates only in 77 constituencies.

There is more about Mahanta's lack of trustworthiness: In the elections held in 1991, AGP was victorious in 19 seats only with NAGP winning only in five seats. Possibly, this was the reason for unification of both the warring factions of original AGP well before the election of 1996; but in Mahanta's second ministry, none of NAGP's winning candidates found a place. Even, Bhrigu Kumar Phukan, once a most-trusted colleague of Mahanta, was not given a ministerial berth. Mahanta had started clipping Phukan's wings from the days of his first ministry. That is to say, from the very beginning Mahanta did not want to share power with anybody—a sheer exposition of his fascist way of functioning, the root cause of AGP's downhill journey.

Parag Das, another journalist of eminence, was assassinated immediately after Mahanta assumed power for the second time and thus started an unending chain of murders. The chain of secret killings, following the murder of his cabinet colleague Nagen Sharma, constituted the darkest chapter of AGP rules. Some other colleagues of Mahanta were also subjected to violent attacks. Biraj Kumar Sarma, Joynath Sharma, Hiranya Konwar, Pradip Hazarika, Kumar Deepak Das, etc., who were subjected to such violence were all AGP leaders. This apart, two ministers, namely, Chandra Mohan Patawari and Kamala Kalita lost a brother each to ULFA's bullets. Even attempt was made to blast off Mahanta's convoy also once. But why this orgy of violence against AGP activists? ULFA had gone all out to ensure AGP's victory in 1996. Then why this volte-face?

Having ensured AGP's return to power by large-scale rigging and sheer terrorisation in the countryside, ULFA considered itself to be in the seat of power and launched upon an extortion spree never witnessed before and also started resorting to frequent violence in case of any resistance encountered in their unlawful operations. Briefly speaking, Assam was again drifting towards total lawlessness with very grave consequences likely to follow unless preventive measures were taken in time. The adverse fallouts of such lawlessness became very evident in respect of two very vital sectors of the developmental process: (1) Flight of capital, and (2) heavy brain drain. The first one hardly requires any elucidation. Simply speaking, there was no ambience for fresh investment. However, the second point certainly needs little explanation: The academic atmosphere having been totally destroyed, the brilliant students in general and the pupils of well-to-do families in particular started leaving Assam for pursuing their studies outside Assam to places like Delhi, Madras, Bangalore, Mumbai, Pune, etc., and a sizeable section of these students preferred to stay away from Assam, thus depriving Assam of the services of her talented children. Even the performance of students studying in Assam during these years of lawlessness, in all-India competitive examinations was nothing to write home about as compared to today's situation, whereas most of the boys and girls who had gone away from Assam have done wonderfully well in their respective profession and fields of research and other fructitious activities. It is a pity that most of these boys and girls have developed a loathsome aversion to Assam, their motherland. Even on the family front, parents are finding it very difficult to arrange suitable matches in Assam for their highly educated children with the result that many of them have found it more convenient to go for interstate marriages. I have my own doubt how far such matches will promote national integration with corporate houses intent upon extracting their 'pound of flesh', thereby banishing the issue of national integration to the back-burner.

The lawlessness of aforesaid nature had certainly adversely affected, to a great extent, the revenue earning sectors of tea, oil, coal, timber, etc. and the development of international tourism. All these developments certainly alarmed the Central Government. On the other hand, Mahanta had not also forgotten the ignominious dismissal in 1990 of his first ministry before the completion of the full tenure. As such, he could hardly afford once again to remain impervious to the lawlessness let loose all over the state. No doubt that he himself had created this Frankenstein, which would, destroy him unless he destroyed it. The arithmetic was thus very simple and he was a man who could stoop down to any extent for self preservation. So, not remaining content with "Operation Rhino- 1" and "Operation Rhino-2", he is reported to have imitated a strategy resorted to in Punjab for eliminating militant secessionism, by killing the dear and near ones of ULFA leaders. Ajit Bhuyan himself confirmed to me that some faces of Assam Police personnel were seen while raiding his residence for eliminating him. Even the judicial commission appointed to investigate into the series of secret killings during Mahanta's second term in office, had occasions to point out the participation of uniformed personnel in quite a few such killings. The significant casualties in such operations were Mithinga Daimary's (ULFA's publicity secretary) entire family, Raju Barua's (ULFA's second in command) quite a few close relations, Arabinda Rajkhowa's (ULFA's chairman) brother Dimba Rajkonwar and many others, including some innocent persons not any way related to ULFA leaders. Apparently, the strategy was twofold: To put pressure on the close relatives of ULFA leaders and cadres to prevail upon their relations to desist from their unlawful activities and secondly, to strike a terror amongst the members of the public so that nobody dared to offer shelter to any member of the ULFA. The rumour doing the rounds is that a team was formed under an IGP for committing these secret killings, although nothing has been conclusively proved in this context. This has been the darkest chapter of Assam's socio-political history. In the name of counter-insurgency measures, these extra-judicial killings were alleged to have been done with blessings of Mahanta, as dictated by a particular lobby from New Delhi and active co-operation of the SULFA members who had become target of ULFA's violence; they were being killed mercilessly by their erstwhile comrades. These 'secret killings' took place between 1998 and 2001 during the second term of Mahanta's chief ministership. Mahanta was holding the home portfolio as well.

Ananta Kalita who miraculously escaped "secret killing" despite being shot from point-blank range, stated before the Saikia Commission that he and his friends were being pressurised to quit AJYCP and join the Assam Yuva Parishad, the youth wing of the AGP. Ananta was seriously injured but escaped death by the skin of his teeth to expose the conspiracy of Mahanta and his colleague, Nurul Hussain. In its report, the Commission indicted both Mahanta and Hussain in no uncertain terms and recommended to the government an award of compensation of of Rs. five lakhs to Ananta Kalita. What more evidence is required to unveil the inhuman trait in Mahanta's character?

It is no surprise that since the secret of "secret killings", remained no more secret, it has been impossible for AGP to return to the centre stage of Assam politics and the Congress did not fail to fill up the resultant vacuum in all the elections held after Mahanta's second term of office. On the basis of Saikia Commission's findings, the people, the media and all concerned had valid reasons to suspect that Prafulla Mahanta, the CM and GM Srivastava, the IGP (Operation), few other pliable police officers and a handful of gullible and prominent SULFA leaders were responsible for all these secret extra-judicial killings. Saikia Commission had further hinted upon an unholy nexus between the police and the SULFA. But the matter did not end there. Many of the SULFA activists who were active participants in these killings, were also subsequently eliminated by the ULFA and some by the police for silencing their voices, so that they might not disclose vital information before the Commission. Surprisingly, most of these heinous crimes were not registered in the police stations concerned and if registered, they were not investigated.

Saikia Commission's reports revealed many truths unpleasant for Mahanta, Srivastava and many others. Mrinal Talukdar, Utpal Borpujari and Kaushik Deka in their jointly written book captioned "Secret Killings", have quoted some of the Commission's findings as follows:

After almost 30 months the report of the Commission found similarities amongst all these killings and also suggested some measures to stop future occurrences. The similarities are:

- In almost all the killings, the victims were related to senior leaders of the ULFA. All the police inquiries met with dead end and there were no arrests, no inquiries and every killing was hushed up.
- Almost all the killings took place around midnight so that assailants could escape easily and could not be identified.
- In all the killings, assailants covered their face with black hood. However, except Ananta Kalita, nobody survived

to tell the final moments of the killings and the nature of killings.

- In most of the killings .32 and .38 bore weapons were used. Both of them are prohibited and can be used only by security forces.
- The recovered materials like cartridges and weapons were not sent to forensic laboratories for ballistic tests. Even if those, which were sent, were sent very late and often reports were never collected.
- The vehicles used in the killings were either Maruti Van or Tata Sumo. They did not have number plates or had them covered. None of the vehicles were seized by police. It gave birth to suspicion that government vehicles were used for the killings.
- In some areas the regular police patrol party went missing mysteriously on that particular night when the secret killing took place.
- Army was involved everywhere. There was proof of collusion between Assam Police and SULFA. An extra-judicial killing force was created in the form of the SULFA. The modus operandi was to first pressurize the relatives to persuade the ULFA leaders to surrender. When it failed, their activities were monitored closely and one fine night they were eliminated.
- There was strong public resentment against the Unified Command Structure and the then Chief Minister Prafulla Kumar Mahanta.
- There was initially a murmur and then SULFA members were openly accused of carrying out those ghastly murders. There were clues but they were never investigated properly.
- There was no use of modern and scientific methods of inquiry like sniffer dogs, ballistic and forensic examination of finger prints and empty cartridges recovered at the crime spot. The state government did not send any condolence message to any of the victim's families.

- No monetary compensation was offered to any of the families of the victims. They were eliminated just because they were related to ULFA leaders.
- There was enough indication that the entire episode was remote controlled by someone and that could be the then Home Minister of Assam who happened to be Prafulla Kumar Mahanta.

As I was scripting this portion of my discourse (10 May 2013), a judgement of the Guwahati High Court further exposed the corrupt practices indulged in by both the AGP and the Congress governments. The appointments of hundreds of teachers without observing any of the prescribed and obligatory rules, commenced during the first term of AGP government and once the flood gate was opened by Mahanta's government, such irregular appointments assumed a gigantic proportion during the Congress regime between 1991 and 1996. Now in May, 2013 Guwahati High Court has set aside all such appointments of about 9,000 teachers as illegal. Unfortunately, those who were responsible for making these appointments are more likely to go scot-free. This is another glaring example of how the accountability of public servants has been reduced to a mockery.

Let us now have a look at how the strategy of the two main Left parties of Assam for regaining their lost ground by allying with AGP worked out. The relevant election results of six general elections held between 1985 and 2011, will present a tell-tale story with no need for any minute analysis:

1985 : AGP = 71, Cong(I) = 25, Cong(S) = 4, UMF = 17, CPM= 2.
1991 : Congress(I) = 66, AGP = 19, NAGP = 5, CPI = 4, and CPM = 2.
1996 : AGP = 58, Congress(I) = 34, CPI = 3, and CPM = 2.
2001 : Congress(I) = 71, AGP = 20 out of 77 candidates fielded by the party, CPI = 0, CPM = 0.
2006 : CPI=1, CPM=2, AGP=24, AIUDF=10, and Cong(I) =53, BPF=10, BJP=10

Congress formed the ministry with support of BPF and independent MLAs.

2011: Congress(I)= 79, AIUDF=18, BPF=12, AGP=9, CPI=0, CPM=0, BJP=5

I was yet to reconcile to the fact that I was summarily dismissed from the IPS entirely on concocted allegations. So I made an unusual request to the first AGP government in writing with a prayer to institute an enquiry into all these allegations against me. Had it done so the cat would have been out of the bag and I would not have to wait till May, 1995 for getting back all my dues. However, my father was not there to offer his blessings to me on this occasion of vindicating my stance. He had already expired on 28 September 1985. The letter written by me to the AGP government is reproduced below which will speak for itself. :

To,

Sri Prafulla Kumar Mahanta, The Chief Minister of Assam, Sri Bhrigu Kumar Phukan, The Home Minister of Assam, Sri Surendranath Medhi, The Law Minister of Assam.

Sirs,

Most humbly and respectfully, I write to submit before you the following few lines for favour of your consideration and necessary action.

I was arrested under the NSA on 29 January when I was, still in service and on leave for treatment of my heart ailment. I was subsequently dismissed from the IPS on 27 March 1981. My detention under the NSA and subsequent dismissal from the IPS were based on maliciously false and fabricated allegations. I was never given any chance to explain my conduct nor was any enquiry held into the allegations against me, which were mainly fabricated at the instance of a colleague of mine.

Interestingly enough, the intelligence agencies of the state and of the Central Government had nothing to report against me. The aforesaid colleague of mine, at the instance of some political leaders and in collaboration with few other senior and junior officers, fabricated the false allegations against me and fed the Central Government with wrong and false information, thereby ensuring my dismissal from the IPS.

I understand that your benign Government have recommended to the Central Government to reinstate me in service. But unfortunately, the Central Government seem to be lukewarm to the proposal. As reported in the press, a parallel is being drawn between my case and the case of ex-DIGP of Punjab, Shri SS Mann, which is in reality non-existent; because I was never involved in any specific case or in any criminal case. As you will kindly appreciate that my arrest at that time was mainly aimed at spraying cold water on the enthusiasm of the state Police Officers for detecting and deporting foreign infiltrators.

Meanwhile, I had filed a title suit also in the Asst. District Judge's Court for my reinstatement in service. The previous government had contested the case. The case is still subjudice. It is not known what stand your government is likely to take in the case. But it may be self-contradictory on the part of your government to contest the case on the basis of the written statement furnished by the Saikia government entirely on false allegations—particularly after you have recommended to the Central Government to reinstate me.

In order to remove all these confusions, may I request you to kindly cause an enquiry into all the allegations against me on the basis of which I was detained under the NSA and then furnish the findings to the Central Government, and if necessary, submit an additional written statement to the Asst. District Judge on the basis of these findings. Irrespective of the fact whether I am reinstated or not, I am sure such an enquiry will, at least, remove the stigma attached to me for my alleged anti-national activities. I have had already two heart attacks. Your kind gesture towards the above-quoted line of action will, above all, allow me to die a happy man.

Thanking you.

Yours Sincerely

(H. K. Bhattacharyya)

The reaction of Mahanta government was nil. It missed a grand chance of exposing the misdeeds of Anowara Taimur and Samar Das perpetrated during the brief stint of Anowara Taimur at Dispur. As days passed on, I was convinced that Mahanta did not want my reinstatement in service. Only after my persistent requests, the home department sent a two-line letter to the MHA for reconsidering my case. The bureaucrats of the MHA did not fail to discern the casual manner in which the two-line letter was written. But I must put it on record that Ataur Rahman, once my senior colleague, who had become a member of the Lok Sabha as an AGP candidate, tried his best to ensure my reinstatement. He facilitated my meeting with the PM VP Singh, Union Home Minister Mufti Muhammed Syeed and both of them had agreed to do whatever was possible, but none of them even cared to go through the file concerned. Dinesh Goswami, the Union Law Minister, kept the relevant file pending for more than six months and meanwhile the days of VP ministry were getting numbered. Only Chandrasekhar, who was PM for a short period, consulted the MHA officers who had come up with the plea that there was no precedent of rescinding a Presidential order! Then how could hundreds of officers summarily dismissed during the Emergency of 1975, could be reinstated? Before Chandrasekhar could address this issue raised by me, he too went out of power. Interestingly enough, after he had formed his own political party, Chandrasekhar had sent his emissaries to me with an invitation to join his party! It seems he did nurse some good will for me.

Anyway, AGP never devoted itself sincerely to promoting regional politics. All the time its leaders were busy with power-politics so much so that AGP had split into three different parties: the NAGP, the Trinamul AGP under Atul Bora and AGP (Progressive) under Prafulla Kumar Mahanta—only to be unified again on the eve of one or the other election. Briefly speaking, AGP reduced itself into a party of opportunists weded to the motive of sheer self-aggrandisement. Mahanta's insenstivity to public opinion and so many media reports were certainly the portent to shape of things awaiting AGP.

The AGPs downhill journey has already been amply illustrated. Before I conclude this chapter, I feel obliged to portray a historical account briefly of the ethnic alienation and their sense of deprivation. Peaceful co-existence of so many tribes and races, etc. had been, in the past, the key to Assam being a self-sufficient, conflict free land. But the advent of the British with sheer colonial purposes, changed the scenario. Their colonial exploitation created a class of deprived people. For example, the cases of the Moran and the Matak tribes may be cited. They were driven out of their age-old settlements without any compensation for the sole purpose of making suitable plots of land available to the British tea planters. This is how many big tea gardens owned by British companies had surfaced in today's Tinsukia district. Nor were they provided with the benefit of modern education. So the educative sensitivity necessary for voicing their demands, was conspicuous by its absence while facing so many British Commissions appointed for liberalisation of the administration. Nobody from amongst them were competent enough to represent their cases before these Commissions. Unfortunately, no other leaders also took up their cases in 1919, 1929 and 1935. No wonder that the Moran community proved to be a very fertile ground for recruiting cadres of the ULFA.

Gradually most of the ethnic tribes formed their own associations. In 1933, a powerful organisation of the backward ethnic tribes surfaced in the shape of 'Tribal League' which, besides trying for the all-round development of the respective tribes, had clearly intended to strengthen the larger Assamese identity. Late Bhimbar Deuri, Rupnath Brahma, Bhramarchandra Saikia, Dambarudhar Saikia were the torch bearers of these moves. In 1929 while submitting a separate memorandum to Simon Commission, they had clearly announced that, "We the Bodos can by no means call ourselves other than Assamese." (as quoted by Indibar Deuri in one of his very enlightening articles: *Axom Andolan: Pratisruti aru Fala sruti, page 287*). Then why the gradual development of mutual mistrust and acceleration of ethnic divisions? The Assamese middle class (Caste?) has been accused of ignoring the demands of these backward communities while the latter had invariably veered round the larger interests of the Assamese society whenever any crisis befell the larger Assamese society. The so-called Hindu caste stratum of the Assamese society has, therefore, been frequently accused, rightly too, of failing to rise above their caste consciousness. Bhimbar Deuri had in no uncertain terms had, while speaking in the Assam Assembly, said that, "The right of every community to have a share in administration, a right of every community to serve the province, or to serve the people at large--" (Ibid, page 288).

In the wake of the Freedom Movement of the 40s of the last century, the Assamese middle class leadership of the Congress had called upon the tribal leaders to join the Movement. Bhimbar Deuri's response to the call was in the following words: "If Swaraj is to come, it must come to each and every section of the populace." Then came the infamous 'Grouping Scheme', jeopardising the very identity and integrity of Assam. Once again, the tribal society rose to the occasion and presented their voice of protests unitedly with the Assamese middle class against this grouping scheme of the Cabinet Mission (1945–46) in the larger interest of the Assamese society. Unfortunately, most of the promises made at this time for rapid development of the tribal society remained unfulfilled. As a result from about 1967, demand for seperate political identity started surfacing with full vehemence. That their legitimate dues were once again ignored by the AGP government has already been discussed earlier. Not remaining content with depriving the tribal society of its dues, the hegemonistic attitude of the AGP government assumed a distinct shape when on 28 February 1986 it notified that the Assamese language would be compulsory for all non-Assamese students as the third language. Also the same government stipulated, also in 1986, that the knowledge of the Assamese language would be necessary for appointment to any state government job. Obviously many educated tribal students would thus not be eligible for state government jobs. As such, the young generation of the Assamese middle class also failed to impart the requisite broadmindedness towards building up, if not reviving, the traditional composite society of Assam. The tribal people had never failed the Assamese middle class whereas the latter has failed them again and again.

Meanwhile, six other ethnic communities, namely, Ahoms, Koch-Rajbongshis, Chutias, Mataks, Morans and Tea Tribes/Adivasis have been agitating for many years for getting the status of a scheduled tribe. They feel marginalised not only in economic spheres but also in respect of representation in the administration and the legislasture in proportion to their numerical strength.

The grant of scheduled tribe status to these communities is sure, if nothing else, to safeguard the legislative constituencies reserved for them, against being captured by hordes of illegal migrants from other countries. No doubt, the issue of self-determination is at the root of all these demands accentuated by a long history of deprivations and undermining their right to survive as distinct identity.

For about last four decades, Assam has been witnessing agitation of varied magnitude, both democratic and aggressively violent, for establishing distinct ethnic identity and ensuring self determination. Karbis are agitating for an autonomous state under Art. 244 (A) of the Constitution while the Dimasas are agitating for a seperate Homeland to be called 'Dimaraji'. Both these two movements have frequently been turning violent. Violence against other ethnic groups like the Kukis, the Hmars and Zemi Nagas has been a regular feature. Also clashes between the Karbis and the Dimasas are also not uncommon. However, the formation of the Bodoland Territorial Council has certainly reduced the incidences of violence, although a faction of the Bodo militants continues to be adamant about a sovereign Bodoland. In the BTC area also, there have been frequent clashes between the Bodos and the Koch-Rajbongshis as also between the Bodos and the imigrant Muslims. Most of these clashes have their origin in the most vital issue of land alienation.

From my school days, I have noticed that most of our tribal schoolmates were very much conscious of their all pervasive backwardness. As I look back now, socio-economic safeguards for all the ethnic tribes do not seem to have been determined by a universal standard, thereby engendering the oft-repeated charge of discrimination and ethnic rivalries. Having deliberated within myself about all these controversies, I am firmly convinced that if a tribal leader from amongst Chhatra Singh Teron, Capt Williamson Sangma, Nichols Roy, Lolit Doley, Rupnath Brahma, was made the chief minister of Assam at the opportune moment, most of Assam's problems emanating from tribal discontent and disillusion would not have surfaced at all and even if it did, it would have been easier to deal with. I really find it difficult to comprehend why leaders like BP Chaliha, Debeswar Sharma, Mahendramohan Choudhury, Bipinpal Das, Omeo Kumar Das etc., could not visualise the benefits of such a political strategy. Dr Nagen Saikia had informed me recently during a conversation on this issue that as the Hill State Movement was in progress, Koka Nilmoni Phukan had suggested that Capt. Sangma should be made the CM; but nobody listened to him.

It will be an unending affair if we also have to delve into all the multifarious grievances of the ethnic tribes of Assam. So to cut a long story short, their basic demands have since crystalized to the following :

1. The numerical strength of some of the ethnic tribes of Assam is so low that they can never expect to have any say in the legislative activities of the state nor do they have any chance of their voices being heard in any other platform. In order to allay their apprehensions of losing their distinct identity, there should be a legislative council for ensuring their representation in the legislative activities. This will be the Upper House of the Assam Legislative Assembly.
2. Primary education in their respective mother tongues.
3. Constitutional arrangements for safeguarding the Tribal Belt and the Tribal Blocks.
4. Such measures must ensure prevention of land alienation.
5. Scheduled tribe status to the six ethnic communities already mentioned above.
6. Separate Cultural Directorate for indigenous tribes and communities along with an Ethnic Sahitya Academy.
7. Foolproof measures for allocation of funds for each ethnic group.

In other words, measures for safeguarding their political, economic development and cultural rights are imperative.

Though I have dealt with this matter in the context of the situation prevailing in Assam and her society, unfortunately, the same state of affairs holds good in the case of the depressed class of Bihar, UP, MP, Haryana, Rajasthan as also some parts of the South. Even the stigma of untouchability is yet to be fully effaced. As such, the emergence of the Bahujan Samaj Party seems to be a logical conclusion. The oligarchy of the Brahmins and the ruling class of yore, is still fighting against the democratic forces of the largest democracy of the world. Even as recently as 1989, the Scheduled Caste and Tribes (Prevention of Atrocities) Act had to be added to the book of statutes!

While whirling through the Brahmaputra Valley in 1982 for addressing so many meetings, I had occasions to meet many tribal leaders and freedom-fighters. Then also I could feel the restive mood of the tribal leaders. As I recall those days, I am reminded of how quite a few of my dear and near ones had treated me almost like an untouchable after my release from the jail—obviously for fear of attracting the wrath of the vindictive authorities. But one of my nephews aged about 13/14 and a student of Class VII, used to give me company unhesitatingly. He was Nitul who, as a young activist of the Assam Movement, used to address these meetings and he had become very popular with the people mainly because of his oratory skill. No wonder that in due course he blossomed into a high class, crowd-pulling orator. And that Nitul has today proved himself not only as a superb orator but also as a very successful minister of Assam. He is Himanta Biswa Sharma, an eye-sore to those aspiring for the chair of the chief minister. He had learnt how to develop grassroot level contacts. So far, his greatest achievement has been to create a modern vision for the two departments under him, viz., the Departments of Health and Education.

So far freedom-fighters are concerned, I was dumb-founded to learn that some of these freedom-fighters had aquired the brand of freedom-fighters by sheer fraud. In the narrowest sense of the term, I might have also claimed the status of a freedom-fighter: In 1942, I, then aged about 11, had joined a procession led by Sriman Prafulla Goswami, a prominent Congress leader, shouting slogans not to help the British in their war efforts by contributing men and materials, Goswami and those immediately behind him were arrested and I was one of them. I was detained in Nalbari PS for the whole day and in the evening, Sricharan Barua, the OC of the PS who was my father's classmate, handed me over to my parents at our residence with a loud retributive shouting asking me not to induldge in such activities. I had never considered that I had also contributed to the cause of the Freedom Movement by being so detained for few hours only.

17

The Rule of Law

The Rule of Law is the foundation of civic peace. To negate it is to invite disorder in civic life. Weak enforcement agencies are mainly responsible for such negation which is testified by undue delay in disposing of litigated issues and criminal cases. According to a survey conducted by Bibek Debroy in the 1990s, there were 25 million cases pending for disposal, which at the present rate, would take 324 years to be disposed of! I had already dwelt upon the naked politicisation of the Police. Lately in Assam, another dangerous trend has surfaced. On many occasions, the members of the public have taken the law into their own hands, thereby making a total mockery of the enforcement agency concerned. Recently, the Supreme Court has passed an order that the Police should video-tape the destruction of public properties (*Dainik Axom*, June 2013.) Here too, the success of such exercise will depend on the enforcement agency.

The rapid erosion of respect for law in Assam may be ascribed to the "Bundh" culture, lately gripping entire Assam and that too after both the Supreme Court and the Guwahati High Court have banned such anti-people activities. Most of these "bundhs", instead of serving any useful purpose, have been rather resulting in destruction of both public and private properties, if not lives, besides disturbing the normal course of public transaction. But till now the government has not cared to prosecute anybody either for violating the court order or for the concomitant vandalism. In fact, the violation of orders promulgated under Sec.144 of the CrPC has been making frequent mockery of the enforcement agency. The cutting of earth from the hills sorrounding Guwahati has been banned umpteen number of times; but steps taken by the police and the forest department for prosecution and prevention of such lawlessness have not been in evidence for uncanny reasons not in need of any scrutiny. Even 50 years back such a state of affairs was simply unimaginable. Again unabated flow of illegal migrants from Bangladesh has contributed volubly to the rising graph of heinous crimes. From media reports, it appears that more than 90% criminals arrested in connection with heinous crimes like murder, rape, kidnapping, rioting and arson, etc., are of Bangladeshi origin. But the rate of their conviction in courts of law does not augur well for a better state of affairs in the immediate future.

Unfortunately, no social scientist has come forward to do any research works for tracing the reasons for such lawlessness. Such researches might have resulted in devising corrective measures. Still, the fact remains that the fear of adverse political fallouts has been deterring the party in power from taking strong measures against such rampant lawlessness. This state of affairs is certainly a distinct depature from what I had witnessed during my younger days.

History has proved beyond any shade of doubt that in absence of the Rule of Law, no society has been able to be progressive.

18

BJP Days

I was not inclined to its theory of Hindutwa while joining the BJP on the eve of general elections of 1991. I was pressurised from time to time by Dr Anandeswar Barthakur, a great admirer of my father and also a close relation of ours as he had married my paternal aunt. True, BJP's five basic principles, viz, National Integration 'Democracy, Gandhian Socialism, Value-based Politics and Sarva Dharma Sama Bhava, had certainly held out some attraction to me only to be disillusioned by the Party's way of functioning. Atal Bihari Vajpayee, Lal Krishna Advani, Dr Murli Manohar Joshi, Jaswant Singh—all senior leaders of BJP had actively participated in the Assam Movement and this was how I came to know them closely while also believing what they were committing in their public speeches made during the said movement. Of course, I knew TN Chaturvedi, former-union home secretary, and Dr Joshi from before. Dr Joshi was my hostelmate in Allahabad, having occupied the room next to mine in the Ganganath Jha Hostel.

Frankly speaking, I was swayed away by the promises galore made by Vajpayee, Advani, etc., during the Assam Movement in the context of the issue of illegal migration from Bangladesh. In fact, Vajpayee had enunciated his own seven-point formula for solving the vexed problem of unabated transborder illegal migration. Possibly, the national stature and clean images of these senior leaders weighed heavily on my inner self subconsciously.

Actually, politics was never my cup of tea. As such, I had never thought in terms of joining politics; else I could have also become a MP or a MLA in 1985 when my charisma was still fresh in the minds of the people. Still I joined the BJP in 1991 for the following two reasons:

1. AGP's betrayal of the cause of the Assam Movement caused extreme anguish in me. I did not want the spade work I had done, to go in vain. I had never imagined that the AGP leaders who had spearheaded the Assam Movement, would be turncoats overnight. Meanwhile I had written so many articles published in the local print media, both in Assamese and in English with a strong plea and call for taking the bull by the horns; but this could hardly make any impact on the AGP government. The lions had deteriorated into jackals overnight! Once I confronted AGP minister Joynath Sarma and enquired of him what was happening. He replied shamelessly that,"Dada, it was one thing to agitate but another to detect and deport Bangladeshi infiltrators." Then once I met Atul Bora, the AGP minister for PWD, and suggested that any contractor found to have engaged foreign labourers without valid travel document should forfeit his security deposit and be blacklisted for ever. Remaining silent for few moments, Bora held out more surprise for me. Bora replied that such a step would entail serious communal trouble without, however, amplifying why did he apprehend such an eventuality. I simply wondered if this was the same Atul Bora who had not hesitated to mete out rough treatment even to Indira Gandhi! I silently walked out of his chamber. My disillusionment was total. I gave up all hopes of AGP doing anything about the issue which had brought them to power. Many more similar talks proved equally abortive. On the other hand, Chief Minister Prafulla Kumar Mahanta and Home Minister Bhrigu Kumar Phukan had no time to spare

any thought to the issue which had catapulted them to the seat of power. Their patent reply for public consumption used to be that because of the IMDT Act, they were handicapped in taking any action on the matter without, however, informing the public if they would take any action for the repeal of this unconstitutional and discriminatory Act. What pained me most that even senior leaders like Dinesh Goswami (Law Minister in VP Singh cabinet), Paragdhar Chaliha, Muhiram Saikia (another minister in VP's ministry), Bijoya Chakraborty, etc., also preferred to remain silent. AGP ministers had neither the will nor the talent for coming to grips with such a politically complicated problem.

2. Having already gone through a tortuous period with a dark cloud looming large in the horizon of Assam, I could not remain silent only because all other involved in the matter remained silent. I still had deep faith in the commitment of Vajpayee, Advani, Dr Joshi, etc., and therefore, turned to the BJP with the hope that they would certainly respond to the issue with the seriousness it deserved and convert it into a national issue. If nothing, I could at least inform the rest of my country about the threat to the country's integrity, if I could be elected to the Lok Sabha. In fact, I had already collected a huge store of data for placing before the Lok Sabha. So after the schedule for the General Elections of 1991 was announced, one evening I telephoned Atal Bihari Vajpayee in presence of PG Barua (presently Editor of the *Assam Tribune*) and Dr Dulal Chandra Borkotoky and requested him to nominate me as the BJP candidate from the Guwahati Lok Sabha seat. He very much welcomed me and gladly approved of my request. He further advised me to set up as many candidates as possible in the Legislative Assembly's seats, of course after getting clearance from the Party. Both PG Barua and Dr Borkotoky also heartily supported my intention. The state unit had not yet made any arrangement for setting up any LAC candidate. During the electioneering campaign, it transpired that the BJP had no organisational network at all excepting few activists confined to few localities of Guwahati

city. Then only I realised why Mr. Vajpayee had asked me to set up candidates in the LACs. On the other hand, some of the party activists from Guwahati and the Barak valley not only did not welcome my entry into the Party but some of them had even sabotaged some of my electioneering programmes. Apparently, that I got the nomination directly from the Party's HQs., was not received warmly by them. However, Dr Anandeswar Barthakur, Ramen Deka (presently a BJP MP) and Banshilal Soni, the central observer for the state unit deputed from the RSS, had heartily welcomed me to the Party. Both Dr Barthakur and Ramen had also helped me within their limitations in organising my campaign.

Soni was soon after transferred to Orissa and those who succeeded him were mostly Hindutva-oriented, confined to few urban areas of their own choice and totally innocent of any political perspective. They used to see everything but perceived nothing. When I joined BJP, Prabin Barua was the president of the state unit of BJP. He was not an elected president but was nominated by the central HQs. The state unit had to make do with a nominated president because organisational status did not suffice for holding organisational elections of the party units at different levels. However, Barua was elected in 1993 as the state president. Barua was a disciple of Ram Manohar Lohia but not a flamboyant type. Though he was not a favourite of the elitist section of the party, he had the uncanny knack of developing grass root level contacts in the rural areas, not paralleled by any of the contemporary BJP activists. I, personally, had learnt quite a few lessons from him in this context which had helped me in organising the BJP network in the *eleka* of Guwahati LS seat in particular.

I not only lost the election in 1991 but also forfeited my security deposit. The party had given me only Rs. 50,000/- towards my electioneering fund, a ludicrously low amount considering the extensive area under the Guwahati LS seat. The campaign caused heavy financial strains on the small-scale industrial unit (SSI) I had set up for earning my livelihood. In fact, I had to close down the unit after running it successfully for seven years.

Analysing the segmentwise result of the election, I realised that unless the rural areas were organised, Guwahati LS seat would remain beyond the reach of the party. I was soon after nominated as the President of the Kamrup district unit of the BJP. On the ground, I found that nine out of 10 Assembly segments, could not boast even of any semblance of organisational set-up. It proved to be a herculian task to organise the nine Mandal committees, mainly because of paucity of fund and non-availability of transport. The state unit did not have a single vehicle. Organisational drives implied extensive tours for developing personal contacts. As such, I had to use the Gypsy jeep of my SSI unit and that too, at my own cost. The party was not in a position to bear the cost of fuel. In the process, my Gypsy was reduced to a tattered condition and I had to go for a new Gypsy which I purchased with a loan from the Punjab National Bank, the financier of my SSI unit. However, I succeeded in establishing party network in eight out of the nine LACs put in my charge. In Chhayaon LAC earlier, I failed to do anything worth mentioning. At least, now I was in a position to spend the night in interior areas with party workers I had recruited, instead of retiring to government IBs or circuit houses. I take particular pride in this achievement because the countryside was witnessing an anti-BJP wave in the wake of the demolition of the "Babri Masjid". But this was not the whole story. Having appreciated my oratory skill and finding that I was using my own jeep for organisational work, Prabin Barua dragged me to far-flung areas of the Brahmaputra valley extending from Jonai to Dhubri and Ledo to Goalpara. Not being in a position to afford the services of a driver, I used to drive myself during all these long tours and that too, at times spending from my own pocket for the fuel. Barua, at times, used to practically beg for the cost of the fuel! But nobody ever recognised the services we rendered to promote the party. But those who had never stepped out of the party office, had invariably profited as BJP's strength assumed a rising curve. Well, possibly that is what was meant by politics for these lotus-eaters.

I worked very hard for organising the party's network before the election of 1996 and we could field nine candidates in nine LACs; but I could never find it possible to field a suitable candidate in Chhaygaon LAC. This time I was sure to win unless ULFA had intervened at the last moment for ensuring the victory of the AGP. However, this time I did offer a tough fight not withstanding the might of the underground ULFA. But it was clear from various developments that a strong coterie of the higher echelon of the party was very active to ensure my defeat. I shall mention only two instances: Firstly, BJP candidates of certain LS constituencies, which had not the least chance of returning them, were given electioneering fund from the state fund to the tune of rupees two lakhs and more whereas I was given only rupees one lakh and fifty thousand only and that too, after repeated goading. As a result, I could not open any election office in many important areas. This time, my SSI unit was also not there to fall back upon. This is a matter of records unless already manipulated or destroyed. The financial crunch thus caused, was a main factor in failing to mobilise a sizeable section of voters who were ready to vote for me. Secondly, two important non-Assamese leaders of the state unit, went around the Nepali areas of Guwahati accounting for about 12,000 votes and spread the rumour that I was personally responsible as the DIGP (Border) for deporting thousands of Nepali migrants from Assam in general and the suburban areas of Guwahati in particular. The prominent Nepali gentleman whom I had put in charge of mobilising the Nepali vote had not only informed me about this but also furnished the registration number of the Fiat car used by them and thus it became easier for me to trace the ownership of the car.

Then came the elections of 1998. This time, an ex-army officer who had nothing to do with BJP was imported and set up in Guwahati LS constituency. His only qualifications were that he was the father of an influential journalist and the brother of an ex-MP-cum-Minister though not of BJP. This ex-army officer's name was not even known to the party workers; even

I had never met him. He lost by securing much less votes than what I had secured in 1996. After losing, he did not maintain any relation with BJP. Instead of protesting against depriving me, I had even campaigned for him. This time, Vajpayee government fell short by one vote while facing a vote of no confidence in the Lok Sabha.

A coterie of vested interests, in collaboration with some of my party colleagues, was constantly projecting me as a die-hard Assamese chauvinist. Apparently, this allegation did the damage when I was again denied the party's nomination for the elections held in 1999. Certainly, I felt aggrieved but did not voice any protest. Instead, I campaigned extensively in the areas of Nagaon and Kaliabor LS constituencies so that my loyalty to the party could never be questioned. For the first time, BJP opened its account in the Brahmaputra valley by winning the Guwahati and Nagaon LS seats. What an irony of fate: I had ploughed the field for raising the crops but I was denied the opportunity for reaping the harvest both in 1998 and 1999 although in 1999, all the five mandal committees of Guwahati LS constituency had recommended my name as their first choice. However, records were interfered with to promote the cause of someone else. Still I continued to work for the party as before, although I was gradually getting restive within myself for lack of any enterprise on the part of the Vajpayee government on the count of alien migration to the North-east. It may be noted that Vajpayee government was in power for long six years but it failed to evince any meaningful interest for stemming the rot. Assam's representative in Vajpayee's Council of Ministers did not utter even one word pertaining to the issue. My first confrontation with the top leadership of the party came in the early part of 2001 when a delegation of party activists met Vajpayee, Advani and KC Pant at Borjhar airport on their way back from Shillong after attending a meeting of the North-East Council. I was asked to speak on behalf of the delegation. I had also taken with me a note emphasising the need for foolproof presentive measures. As soon as I pointed out that the repeal of the IMDT Act was not imminent and before I could complete submitting what was in my mind, Vajpayee retorted, rather harshly, that "you must know we do not have the majority in the Rajya Sabha" without dwelling on the possibility of convening a joint session of both the Houses as was done in the recent past. I could see through Vajpayee's strategy of diverting the attention to parliamentary politics and thereby silence me. Instead of causing more discomfiture to him, I emphasised upon the following points as we had to give satisfactory reply while confronting the public during our organisational tours:

i No IMDT Act would debar the issue of an executive order for banning the employment of foreign labourers found without valid travel documents.

ii Contractors found to have engaged such labourers must forfeit their security deposit and be blacklisted for ever.

iii The names of more than three lakhs of illegal migrants already deported from Assam must be deleted from the ERs and measures taken to ensure that nobody else could vote in their names.

iv Steps should be taken to update the NRC without further delay.

v The River Police Organisation must be strengthened to seal all the riverine routes frequently used by illegal migrants from Bangladesh.

Before the discussion could be completed, it was ended as it would have been difficult for the aircraft to take off once it was dark. Ultimately, nothing transpired out of this interaction. The supremo of the party did not appreciate the possibility of creating the tremendous impact the repeal of the IMDT Act on the Indian voters of the state would have created. If it was a question of maintaining the solidarity of the NDA conglomerate then possibly one could not deny that the issue of Assam's identity and existence was sacrificed at the altar of political convenience. Even otherwise also a conglomerate of 23 parties to succeed, a past master in working out compromises was indispensable.

But all efforts for keeping the Congress out of power could not succeed as was evident in 2004 and NDA's so-called solidarity ran aground. The question which still agitates my mind is whether such style of functioning was different from Indira Gandhi's ignoring the opinions of the grassroot level party activists. Vajpayee could impose what he wanted certainly because of his charismatic personality, supreme skill of oratory and unlike Indira, the comradeship he had built up with people at large. Basically a democratic person, he was, at times, apt to ignore democratic norms. But why? His vulnerability to flattery and motivated inputs fed by vested interests appeared to have clouded his independent and unprejudiced judgement. Still the fact remains that next to Pt. Nehru, he was the most charismatic leader the country was blessed with. Like Nehru, he was the darling of the people. Though claimed in many quarters, Vajpayee's six-year-long regime was certainly not a run-away success as he had to operate under so many constraints apart from the inner conflicts of the NDA. Still, apart from his shying away from the illegal influx problems of Assam, his outstanding contributions were in the following fields:

a Sincere efforts for improving the bilateral relations with China and Pakistan, although the "Bus Diplomacy" floundered on the rocks of Kargil.

b His all-out efforts for developing the infrastructural facilities. In this context the "East-West Corridor" concept was a great boost to the developmental economy which had ultimately resulted in the "Look East" policy. That it has not fully materialised in the North-east is entirely due to the inefficiency of the Assam government and not Vajpayee's.

c The institution of the "DONER" ministry.

d Remarkable improvement in the foreign exchange reserve for pursuing the policy of economic liberalisation.

e A discernible bias in favour of the rural economy.

f The Pokhran experiment

g A positive turn to Indo-US relationship.

19

Little Digression

As the chapter on my BJP days was about to come to the end, some excerpts from the Census Reports of 2011 were published in the newspapers which were quite ominous from the point of view of the distinct identity of Assam. Lest I forget later on to refer to such developments, I am giving below a brief account of this ominous portent.

As reported, the national decadal growth of population between 2001 and 2011 is 17.7% whereas the growth of population in 14 of 27 districts of Assam has recorded a much higher growth than the national growth. As for instance, Dhubri district has recorded a growth of 24.40%, Marigaon 23.3%, Goalpara 22.2%, Darrang 22%, Nagaon 21.9% and Karimganj 21.4%. This could not have happened because of migration from other Indian states. Besides, these districts are most illegal migration-prone districts. While the percentage of agricultural labourers has increased from 13.2% in 2001 to 15.4% in 2011, the number of peasants has decreased from 39.1% to 33.9% during this period. This implies that the employment of agricultural labourers has recorded a rising trend and the source of such recruitment is now anybody's guess particularly in view of the abnormal growth of population in above-mentioned districts. Unfortunately, the Census Officer concerned has not bothered to furnish any analytical forwarding note as was done in the past. For some mysterious reasons, the rate of birth has not also been compared with the growth rate of population 'The Bodos not concealing their extreme anti-illegal migrants attitude, if not activities, the Bodo dominated district of Kokrajhar has recorded lowest growth rate of population of 5.2%! Will it be wrong to conclude that in the other districts referred to above illegal alien migrants find shelter easily? No wonder that the demand for a Muslim Autonomous Council is gathering momentum.

20

Back to BJP Days

The fallouts of Borjhar meeting could by no means have been favourable for me. Because I had committed a great crime by voicing our grievances against the central leadership frankly and that must have sufficed to reduce me to a *persona non grata*.

But the final confrontation came in 2001 on the eve of the LACs elections in Assam. Meanwhile, Sunil Shastri the younger son of Lal Bahadur Shastri, was deputed to Assam by New Delhi to oversee the functioning of the BJP in Assam. Sunil Shastri proved to be a very upright man and a keen observer of the party's affairs as he was blessed with rich faculty of developing deep insight into the problems. On the other hand, the organising secretary of the state unit deputed from the RSS could not boast of any political insight. He was dreaming of capturing political power in the state with the help of an unholy alliance with AGP. In fact, nothing could have been farther from the ground realities. AGP's was a sinking boat. (In fact, AGP's downhill journey since 2001, is yet to be arrested with only nine LAC seats won in 2011.) Shastri discussed this issue of alliance with AGP threadbare not only with me but other knowledgeable party activists also. I had submitted my observations, not once, but twice in writing with firm caution that any alliance with AGP at this juncture would be suicidal for BJP in Assam, Shastri gave me the impression of being in full agreement with me but he could not boast of any RSS background. The organising secretary, a RSS Pracharak was, however, infallible for the high-ups of the party's hierarchy. My plea for not having an alliance was based on the following:

AGP had lost all credibility because of its lacklustre and corruption-ridden performance. Both BJP and AGP had to draw upon the same segment of voters. BJP had already made significant inroads into AGP's vote bank and as such, there was no point in dishing out some relief welcomed by the AGP. It would simply amount to administering oxygen to a gasping AGP. If analysed from 1991 onwards, it would appear that the percentage of BJP votes were gradually increasing while AGP's was rapidly decreasing. There should be no hurry and the vacancies left behind by AGP would naturally be filled up by BJP. Above all, the voters were not prepared for the eventuality of such an alliance. The alliance would create the impression that BJP was ignoring all the charges of corruption against AGP in general and against Prafull Kumar Mahanta in particular. His extra-marital relation had already made him a "persona non grata" with a considerable section of the electorates. In fact, on 8 April 2001 when the alliance was finalised he was one of the most hated men in Assam as subsequent events had also proved. While scripting this alliance, BJP bosses forgot to appreciate how much AGP had alienated itself from the people. Its failure or unwillingness as the case may be, in respect of holding Panchayat elections, had totally alienated AGP activists from the grassroot level workers who had surfaced in the euphoria of the Assam movement.Those who remained were by and large rootless drop-outs from schools and colleges or half-educated/ uneducated fortune hunters whose only aim was to get rich quickly. With such standards it would have never been possible for them to sway the voting pattern for ever in their favour. Ultimately AGP, got 20 seats in place of 58 it had got in 1996. And BJP got eight seats in place of four in 1996. It would have got many more if AGP had not refused to allot some of the seats which BJP was likely to win but AGP lost. For the first time, BJP opened its account in the Brahmaputra valley so far LAC seats were concerned. Even in 2011, BJP's ascendancy was in evidence when it won five seats. In respect of LS seats also, BJP has wrested three AGP-dominated seats of Guwahati, Nagaon and Mangaldoi in 2009. Thus is substantiated what I have tried to propound above. The neglect of the party's organisational work with Prafulla Kumar Mahanta monopolising its control, AGP's decline was only a logical conclusion—a phenomenon totally ignored by BJP in its hurry for capturing power. It was clear that with the evaporation of the euphoria created by the Assam Movement, ended the ascendeancy of regional forces in Assam.

My conscience did not allow me to be a party to such an unholy and irrational alliance. I, therefore, convened a conference of the main party activists on 10 April 2001 at Nalbari. It was attended by representatives from all over the state and grave dissatisfaction was voiced by all concerned. The president of the state unit Rajen Gohain also attended the conference and pleading his inability to undo what had been done already, he preferred to remain a silent onlooker to the proceedings. I, then and there, handed over the letter of my resignation from the party to him. I was also followed by many others present there. Some pressure was exercised on me through Sunil Shastri for withdrawing my letter of resignation; but I could not humiliate myself once again by such withdrawal. After a week or two, I was expelled from the party for six years as if I did not have even the right to resign. After all, I was not a bonded labourer of the party. We raised the banner of revolt against the authoritarianism of the party by setting up as many as 47 independent candidates all over the Brahmaputra valley. True, none of us won but the message of the revolt was loud and clear. Subsequently, I came to know that a high official of a Central Intelligence agency was persuaded by vested interests to submit a report that an alliance between BJP and AGP was sure to win. Anyway, if "value-based politics" incorporated as one of its five principles in BJP's constitution, was not a hollow slogan, then it could have never accepted Prafulla Mahanta as an alliance partner. In fact, Mahanta himself would have been in the dock facing trial for looting the public exchequer unless Lt General (Retd) SK Sinha, the then Governor of Assam, bailed him out by refusing, as warranted, to accord sanction for his prosecution. Many of us have, at times, wondered if such favour was shown to him for the role he had played in the context of the "secret killings" as highlighted by Justice Saikia Commission. As Justice Chagla had most aptly observed that, "we could do with less politics in our education and more education in our politics." There could not have been a more demonstrative verdict on our political culture.

The freedom of expression is a fundamental human aspiration, the denial of which breeds dissatisfaction and lack of confidence. As I felt, such denial was a regular practice in BJP in the name of party's discipline. True, one must not criticise one's own party publicly in the media but at the same time, one must not be denied the opportunity of deliberating upon the performance and policy of one's own party. But this is what was exactly happening in BJP during my time. The dichotomic system of control—one by the high party functionaries and the other by the regional RSS functionarie—never proved, at least in Assam, to be conducive to build up an ambience of mutual confidence and co-operation. It is very difficult to work under two bosses at the same time. Besides, such a state of affairs gave rise to double standards —one for those with RSS background and the other for those without such background. I had felt this distinction ever since I joined the party. Still worse, two prominent Assamese Muslims, namely, Habibur Rahman and Nessar Ahmed, recruited to the party at my initiative, never felt at home in the party. Habibur died in a road accident. Ahmed was also seriously injured in the same accident but none of the state leaders had the minimum courtesy to look him up in the hospital. Out of sheer frustration, Ahmed ultimately resigned from the party. But this was not the end of such happenings in the state unit of the party. I was also instrumental in recruiting to the party, leaders like the famous socialist activist Atul Goswami, Dulal Barua, Bijit Saikia, Charan Narzary—all with proven parliamentarian credentials. They were all materials for chief ministership but without any RSS background. They, too, could not survive in the party. That the equation between the indigenous Hindus and Muslims in Assam was at variance with what it was in the Hindi-belt, could never be driven home to the minds of the dominant segment of the party. One could possibly well appreciate my disillusionment even after I had left the party when a dynamic leader like Jaswant Singh was expelled from the party only because he had praised Jinnah in some context! None of the leaders from Assam was considered fit to be placed in a position of national importance nor were they ever inducted into any electioneering campaign outside Assam whereas Assam could in those days boast of quite a few charismatic leaders. Even on the RSS front, most of its "Pracharaks" were drawn from the Maharashtra belt as if RSS activists of Assam did not deserve such recognition. I am told the situation has since undergone some change.

As I firmly believed that a tribal chief minister would be in a better position to maintain Assam's integrity, I had enrolled Lalit Mech of Boko area in 1994 as a party member albeit after a good deal of deliberation and persuasion. Lalit was a highly educated, honest and hardworking businessman with a strong following behind him. He never dodged the Income Tax authorities and even then, he had become very rich by dint of very hard and honest work. It was possible with his help to persuade Katiram Rabha, a well-known and universally respected freedom fighter, to join BJP. His organisational ability and reputation roused strong hopes in me and my close associates for raising a formidable tribal front of the party. But my enthusiasm was not backed from the quarters that mattered. Even then it was possible to motivate Lalit Mech to work for organising a strong tribal front. A short aside may be in order for dwelling upon Lalit's brief political career:

Though thoroughly secular in his outlooks and dealings, he proved to be a strong stumbling block to proselytizing by the Christian missionaries in his own area. Else, many more tribal people would have been converted by means fair or foul. Lalit's organisational ability was simply enviable. He had realised that the LACs of East Goalpara, Dudhnoi, Boko and Chhoygaon were the strongholds of the AGP but AGP's neglect of the backward classes of the society and of the interior areas, gave an opening to him for organising the Party's network. He started holding frequent meetings of the village chiefs (Gaonbuhras) in the interior areas, thus bringing a sizeable section of the people into his sphere of influence—all at his own cost. His such efforts rang the alarm bell for the AGP, particularly in Boko, Dudhnoi and East Goalpara LAC areas. Even he could not make a dent in the Chhoygaon LAC area, mainly because it was predominantly an immigrant Muslim area.

BJP had no labour organisation in Assam. The ice was broken when I was elected as the president of the Guwahati Refinery's Employees Union. This caught the imagination of Lalit who proposed to organise a union of the indigenous owners and drivers of trucks and buses, who were being subjected to extortion by various syndicates comprising mostly anti-social elements and proteges of dishonest political leaders. His proposal had received tremendous response from all concerned. But that was not to be: "Man proposes, God disposes".

He found that the lack of unity amongst various ethnic groups was the bane of a healthy social ambience; so, taking Dudhnoi as his starting point, he had launched upon a campaign for achieving unity amongst all the ethnic groups in general and between the Rabhas and the Bodos in particular. His such ventures had also alarmed the vested interests. Above all, AGP's very existence was threatened in southern areas of Kamrup district.

Then came the fateful evening of 19 May 1997: Lalit had a petrol/ diesel depot at Boko. He collected Rs. 20,000/- from the depot and left for his residence at village Bondapara, about 13 km to the west of Boko. This was his daily routine unless he was out on tour. On the way home, he usually used to drop in at an establishment he had started for some helpless weavers for their gainful employment; but when he did not turn up well past 10 pm, his dear and near ones became little anxious and ultimately his bullet-ridden body was recovered on the national highway, about 5/6 kms. away from his petrol depot. All his valuables including Rs. 20,000/- in cash, his costly wrist watch were untouched. It transpired that the road was blocked by laying several logs on the road and as soon as he stopped his Maruti car he appeared to have been shot dead. "Rigor Mortis" had already set in when the police arrived at the spot. He was shot dead from point blank range with 9 mm pistol. I was awakened by a telephone call at about 12 midnight and by the time I arrived at his residence it was past 2 pm.

The Prime Minister, Mr. Gujral was camping in Guwahati and when

I met him next day at the Raj Bhawan, CM Prafulla Kumar Mahanta was also with the PM. Hearing my complaint that it was a political murder, Mahanta without losing a moment retorted that it was a case of dacoity only and when I pointed out that Rs. 20,000/- and all the valuables were in tact, both the PM and the CM simply remained silent. Thus ended my dream of preparing a prominent tribal candidate for the chair of Assam's chief minister!

Lalit's cremation was attended by a huge crowd at village Bondapara, although I was the lone attendant from the state BJP. However, on the day of his "Sraddha Ceremony" followed by a public condolence meeting, I and my wife were accompanied by Indramani Bora, the state president. I totally broke down while addressing the gathering of so many thousands of people, an unmistakable testimony to Lalit's popularity and the extent of his contacts. Hardly, there was a pair of eyes which was not moist with tears. Days went by; but not a single prominent leader cared to look up Lalit's widow and four minor children who were still maintaining a close and cordial relationship with me and my family.

My close association with Lalit had afforded me an opportunity for cultivating a deep insight into the working of the tribal mind. There was hardly any public ventures between Mirza and Goalpara which did not benefit from his benevolent philanthropic activities. He was murdered in cold blood and it was made possible for the main culprit to easily escape from police custody—presumably because his thorough interrogation would have unmasked something dangerously unpalatable for some persons. Though he had escaped from police custody, he is reported to be moving about freely in Boko area. BJP was in a very politically strong position at the national level at this time; but did not consider it worthwhile to persue the matter for reasons best known to it only. BJP will take years to get a better tribal leader in Assam.

May Lalit's soul rest in eternal peace.

My stint of 11 years in BJP came to an end out of my own volition. BJP was still depending on defection from other parties, although, possibly realising its past mistakes, it had, of late, inducted some highly educated young men and professionals who might take some time to ingratiate themselves with the people of Assam. With the rise of Muslim fundamentalist organisations and their active participation in Assam politics, the emerging new leadership may find it easier to break new ground if provided with savvy, not reactionary, guidance. The threat of religious fundamentalism cannot be undone by another kind of fundamentalism. The answer lies in a rational approach while not turning the slogan of secularism into another hollow one. Above all, the system of man-management and career planning, never a strong point of BJP in respect of party activists of non-RSS background, must be made more liberal, meaningful and people-oriented. Let it not be misunderstood that my intention is to pontificate—it is not so. I, simply intend to share my experiences with the new generation of leadership. I sincerely believe that sheer aggressive demonstration, protestations confined to bitter and irresponsible criticism against whatever the party in power does, do not cause any permanent impression on the minds of people nor do rhetorical preposterous promises. Instead, constructive programmes should be spread to rural areas as was done by my late lamented friend Lalit Mech.

I wish the young generation of leadership all the success.

21

Retirement And Back To Public Life

After assessing what I had achieved during the 20 years between 1982 and 2001, I do not have the slightest hesitation in admitting that I had totally wasted this most creative period of my life, firstly, blindly putting my trust in the young leadership of Assam movement and the AGP leadership and secondly, working very hard in BJP for 11 years with no gainful achievement for the people of Assam. I was let down on both the occasions. My loyalty to the causes I was committed to, did not seem to have received the attention it deserved. On both the occasions, the leadership concerned had put itself also on trial and could not come out unscathed as already highlighted.

At times, I wonder what else I could have done. What were the alternatives available to me? I find no satisfactory answers.

I had practically worshipped Atal Bihari Vajpayee as many others did (and still do); but as I realise now, I could never reach out to his mindset. I did see early the feet of clay so far Prafulla Mahanta was concerned but failed in the other case. Now I have realised that my sense of direction was possibly too much influenced by my sense of commitment.

I was now left with enough time for focusing my attention to the home-front and some creative activities. I had a flower garden which I gradually converted into a small commercial nursery. In the process I, could employ three unemployed youths. All of them picked up the necessary skill within a very short period. The venture proved to be very profitable. But it was absolutely labour-intensive. After 8/9 years of runing it successfully, I had to close down the nursery for want of labourers and adequate supply of water. Even now, the area where I live, is yet to get the benefit of any water supply scheme. Two of these three employees have now set up their own nursery business and been earning not less than 15 to 20 thousand rupees per month. While running the nursery, I found that saplings of many flowers were being imported from outside Assam whereas, with proper dedication, these could be raised within Assam and I myself raised hundreds of such saplings. Now, many nursery owners have started raising such saplings and a number of horticultural nurseries have surfaced within a radius of 30 kilometers of Guwahati. Even many educated men and women have found it to be not only employment-generating but also quite a paying proposition, thus saving themselves from the lure of making a quick buck by questionable means. Also in my kitchen garden, I raised a wide range of vegetable crops for sale in the nearby market. But this also could not be sustained for long for identical reasons.

During this period, I wrote three novels, including a detective one and the detective one is likely to be telecast soon by the News Live channel. I had observed that a wrong impression was created about the Assam Movement as if it was a secessionist venture and at the same time, it was not known to the rest of country how Assam and her people were being overwhelmed by illegal migrants from Bangladesh. As such, I scripted a full account of the situation and got it published under the caption "*The Silent Invasion*". This book is due for second edition; but I am contemplating to expand it by updating the various developments and depicting the new and ominous magnitude the problem of illegal migration has since assumed with New Delhi and Dispur still preferring to look the other way. Surprisingly, India has not yet taken up the issue seriously with Bangladesh and the MPs from Assam have totally failed to convert it into a national issue. Anyway, I had to leave two other books half-written as I took up writing this autobiographical socio-political discourse.

Though I do not engage myself much in public interaction, many persons from cross section of the society visit me almost daily and some others exchange views with me over the telephone. After such interaction and telephonic talks, I have formed an impression that the credibility of the political leaders of Assam was never lower. Which is why it has become all the more essential that a strong leadership, even non-political, must emerge from the thinking section of the population for creating awareness amongst the common people about the inadequacy of the public life of Assam. The people of Assam must abandon the habit of ascribing invariably the faultline, rightly or wrongly, to New Delhi and instead must learn to look inward. This reminds me of a very significant and relevant observation made by novelist Desmond Bagley in one of his novels: "Surprisingly. few people are aware that more Americans fought in that war on the side of the British than ever did under the rebel generals, and that the war was lost more by the incompetence of the British than any superiority on the part of Geroge Washington". This is exactly what has been happening in Assam.

After retiring from active politics, now I am in a better position, as I feel, to take a dispassionate view of the happenings in Assam. As I find today, all aspects of Assam's public life have betrayed symptoms of degeneration, be it political, academic, cultural, economic, etc. Even a non-political cultural organisation like Axom Xahitya Xabha has been drawn into unhealthy controversies, including misappropriation of its funds and manipulating the results of its organisational elections. Such unhealthy developments have resulted in the resignations of a few ex-presidents of the Sabha from the AXX, including Homen Borgohain and Dr Nagen Saikia. In fact, personally I was also fed up with the intra-Sabha bickerings and deciding to remain far from such dirty ambience, I also resigned from the Sabha. Certainly, Borgohain's and Dr Saikia's resignations conveyed a very significant message for the cultural and the academic world of Assam. Anyway, I was silently observing the various developments and adverse fallouts resulting therefrom. The results of hoodwinking all concerned in the name of police modernisation scheme and the politicisation of the police were gradually showing up —particularly in respect of security of lives and properties, both public and private. The primacy of security matters had convinced the intelligentsia of the state that the insurgent outfits must be brought to the negotiating table if permanent peace was to return to Assam. The central and the state government also seemed to be keen on such a settlement. Thank God that the authorities concerned had realised that the strategy of negotiations would yield better results than the strategy of inhuman secret killings!

Meanwhile, anti-Indian regime of Begum Khaleda Jia was replaced in Bangladesh by Sheikh Hasina's government. Sheikh Hasina had not forgotten India's contribution to liberating her country from the colonial rule of Pakistan. Her friendly attitude towards India opened a new vista for controlling the problem of insurgency bedevilling the public life of Assam. Many insurgent outfits of the North-East had set up their camps in Bangladesh during Begum Jia's rule and been operating freely therefrom, aided by the ISI and other Muslim Fundamentalist Organisations (MFO). In this context, a report filed on 21 October 2002 by Alex Perry of *Time* is very illustrative:"— Bangladesh also has its fundamentalists. And its southern coastal hills and northern borders with India are lawless and bristling with Islamic militants armed by gunrunners". Having ascertained the emergence of Laden's al-Qaeda in Bangladesh, he has further reported: "-- The emergence of al-Qaeda in Dhaka is merely the latest sign that Bangladesh's more radical Islamic groups are coming out from the forests. On 9 and 10 May, 63 representatives of nine Islamic groups, Rohingya forces, The Islamic Oikya Jote and the ULFA met in Ukhia to form the Bangladesh Islamic Manch, a United Council under HUJI's leadership. So far the Manch has restricted itself to circulating speeches by Bin Laden and Mullah Masud Azhar, a Pakistani militant leader. But it has big plans, says the HUJI source: "The dream is to create a larger Islamic land than the territorial limits of Bangladesh to include Muslim areas of Assam, North Bengal and Burma's Arakan province. 'That dream if Islamic terrorists are allowed to continue, their operations in Bangladesh, could be a nightmare for the rest of the region." This should also explain the reason for emergence in Assam of so many underground militant units of immigrant stock.

Sheikh Hasina is known for her secular outlook and friendly attitude towards India. Her return to power rang the alarm bell for the insurgents from the North-East as she was determined to uproot them from their camps located within Bangladesh. Many of the insurgents camps were demolished and many insurgents including the top leaders of ULFA were arrested and handed over to the Indian authorities. Both the governments and the ULFA leaders expressed their desire to start negotiations afresh. Some of the ULFA leaders were released on bail so that they could set the ball rolling for activating the process of negotiations. It was also decided to hold a national convention at Guwahati for ascertaining the view-points of various organisations, both political and non-political, and representatives of a cross section of the people of Assam. Efforts were made earlier also for holding talks between the government and the ULFA; but the civil society was not associated with the process and possibly this was why such efforts proved to be abortive and a stalemate ensued. I was simply an onlooker while the stalemate continued, although I very much wanted an honourable settlement for all concerned so that peace could return to Assam. The people of Assam were really fed up with the inhuman atrocities unleashed by the armed forces in the name of controlling the insurgents under the protection of the **Armed Forces Special Power Act.**

It was under such circumstances that on a fine morning, two prominent ULFA leaders, namely Pradip Gogoi, the vice chairman and Mithinga Daimary, the publicity secretary of the organisation, since released on bail, turned up at my residence and requested me to be one of the conveners of the aforementioned national convention. They further explained that the proposed all-Assam Convention would succeed only if persons with credibility would convene it. They would not listen to my plea that I had already retired from public life. I was still hesitating to resume my public activities; but Dr Hiren Gohain, the renowned intellectual and a public activist for whom I entertained great respect and adoration, ultimately persuaded me to become one of the conveners of the said convention. A Steering Committee was formed for the purpose of facilitating the holding of the Convention. Members of the Steering Committee were the following:

Dr Hiren Gohain, Dr Mamoni Roisom Goswami, Hiranya

Kumar Bhattacharyya (the author of this book), Dr Nirmal Kumar Choudhury, ex-VC of Guwahati University, Harekrishna Deka, ex-DGP of Assam, Prof K Alam, ex-head of the Department of Economics of Guwahati University, Indibar Deuri, ex-Post Master General of North-eastern region, Dr Rohini Barua IAS (Retd), ex-Commissioner, Ratneswar Basumatary, an intellectual and reputed essayist; Dilip Patgiri and Lachit Bordoloi, both well known public activists. It was decided to hold the said convention at Guwahati on 24 April 2010.

To start with, the Steering Committee issued the following press note:

Press Statement on All Assam Convention for Resumption of Talks Between The Central Government and The ULFA on Longstanding Issues of Dispute.

A group of conscious and concerned citizens are convening an All Assam Convention on the 24 April at the Pragjyotika Auditorium of Machkhowa, Guwahati, with the objective of imparting fresh momentum to talks between the Government and the ULFA which seem to have reached a stalemate and clearing the hurdles before talks. It is conviction of this group of citizens that an honest effort can still be made to disentangle certain contentious issues in an All Assam Convention with representatives of different socio-political and cultural organizations from diffierent regions of Assam as well as from various all Assam organizations of similar nature. The idea is to find a broad consensus in the convention to be suggested to both the parties as a basis for resumption of talks. In the interest of restoration of peace and normalcy, and restoration of unhindered democratic political life, as well as removing the ever-present danger of gradual and imperceptible growth of military domination over ordinary life, such a step has been found an imperative necessity in the state.

It is hoped that since the media in general share this perception they will give the needed support to this earnest effort, and the general public will also help turn the proposed convention into a success.

Conveners

Dr Hiren Gohain, Dr Nirmal Kumar Choudhuri, Mamoni Roisom

Goswami, Dr Rohini Barua, Harekrishna Deka, Hiranya Kumar Bhattacharyya, Indibar Deuri, Prof Khorshed Alam, Ratneswar Basumatari, Lachit Bardoloi and Dilip Patgiri.

The response was tremendous--in fact, beyond our imagination. As many as 130 organisations and many prominent citizens from all over the state attended the daylong conference. We also subsequently visited the Guwahati jail to hold discussions with the top leadership of the ULFA. A press statement issued by the Steering Committee subsequently, as reproduced below, would speak for itself.

Press Statement
By
Delegation from All-Assam Convention for Revival of efforts to initiate Talks between the Government and the ULFA

A mammoth convention attended by delegates from 130 different ethnic, socio-political and cultural organisations from all over Assam as well as political parties and distinguished citizens, intellectuals and social workers of the state and numbering more than 2000 people was held in Guwahati on 24 April 2010 with the objective of reviving the process of initiating the dialogue between the Government of India and the ULFA which has now remained frozen for a long time. The massive and enthusiastic turn out reflected the sentiments of the people of Assam.

The Convention elected a Steering Committee which met the imprisoned ULFA leaders that included the majority of the top leaders of the insurgent organization, and received their assurance that if they are released to hold a meeting of their Central Committee in an atmosphere of freedom, and allowed to contact the other members of the Central Committee still at large, then it would be possible for them to adopt formal resolutions that might be acceptable to the Government and honourable to the leaders of the insurgent group.

It may be mentioned that the members of the Steering Committee do not believe in secession from India but hold that the basic problems and grievances of the people of Assam that originally provoked ULFA's demand for independence deserve serious consideration. They also hold that such basic problems must be addressed in the interest of permanent peace and normalcy in Assam.

Dr. Hiren Gohain, M.A., Ph.D (Camb.),

Former Deam, Arts Faculty, Guwahati University & Author

Dr. Nirmal Kumar Chaudhuri, M.A., Ph.D (Manchester),

Former Vice Chancellor, Guwahati University and Social Activist

Dr. Rohini Barua, IAS (Retd.), Social Activist and Author

Shri Hiranya Bhattacharyya, IPS (Retd.), Author

Shri Indibur Deuri, Retd. CPMG, North-East Circle, Author

Prof. Khorshed Alam, Retd. Professor of Economics, Guwahati University.

Despite the Convention being a runaway success, there were efforts galore for sabotaging the cause of the convention on one or the other plea. Ultimately, heated discussions took place on the issue of Paresh Barua's participation in the proposed negotiations. It may be noted that Barua had already made it clear that he would not come forward for any negotiation unless the issue of Assam's sovereignty was included in the agenda and New Delhi would never accept such condition while also making it clear that the centre was ready to offer as much concessions as were possible within the Constitution of the country, although we did envisage the need for amending the Constitution for accommodating many other demands of the ULFA. A very few young delegates went even to the extent of suggesting that there should be no negotiation without Paresh Barua. I am mentioning this only for the sake of truth and transparency. Their protest against holding negotiation without Barua, was simply indicative of how much a section of the youths of Assam were nursing extreme bitterness against the colonial and oppressive role of the central government! The resolution for reopening the negotiations with the centre was passed by overwhelming majority of the Convention. But the question of breaking the ice for removing the stalemate still remained which could be done only by the highest authorities of the land. As such, six members of the Steering Committee landed up in New Delhi with a view to confer with the PM, the union home minister and the chairperson of the United Progressive Alliance (UPA).

Dr. Manmohan Singh received us very warmly. I had met him earlier also while attending some seminars before he became the PM of India. In fact, in one of the seminars I had criticised him rather harshly for not ensuring proper safeguards to the small scale industries in the context of his policy of liberalisation. Obviously, his warm reception indicated that there was no ill feeling left behind because of the aforementioned bitter criticism. He treated us to a nice cup of tea and snacks. SS Menon, the National Security Adviser was also present with him. Dr Gohain was our spokesman and his submission of our viewpoints could not have been better. It was emphatically stated that none of us was secessionist and that our intention was to put an end to the stalemate which had prevented any meaningful talks between the Centre and the ULFA, I am appending below the full text of our memorandum submitted to the PM for favour of the reader's ready reference:

Hon'ble Dr Manmohan Singh,
Prime Minister of India
New Delhi

Subject : Memorandum to the Prime Minister on Resumption of Talks Between the Government and the United Liberation Front of Assam.

Sir,

We, the following members of a delegation, nominated by a state-level convention held in Guwahati on 24 April this year wish to represent to you in person the strong consensus of public opinion now emerging in Assam supporting the urgent need for resumption of talks between the government and the leaders for the principal insurgent Group of Assam, namely the ULFA. With your well-known concern for peace, progress and welfare of Assam you had earlier responded favourably to an initiative to facilitate talks with the ULFA. The long-drawn-out conflict between the security forces and the insurgents has not only inflicted great hardship on the common people of Assam in carrying out the daily business of life, but has also made them victims of prolonged social disorder and economic uncertainty, resulting in constant disruption of the rule of law. We are also constrained to state that in carrying out their mission of controlling insurgency, the army and the security forces have at times committed unacceptable excesses, causing widespread discontent. Thanks to the general atmosphere of insecurity and repression, anti-social elements have thrived, corruption has increased manifold, and there is a sense of despair among the common people about the prospects of peace and progress of the region.

It may be stated with regret that there has been for a long time a sense of alienation among the people of our state, from the nation at large owing to their perception of neglect and discrimination by the Centre and the resulting under development of the state. While the successive governments of the state must share the burden of the blame for economic stagnation and poverty of infrastructure, the Centre's policies have also contributed to the lack of development of this region, and the state government is lacking in powers to make bold departure from such policies for redressal of problems. Agitations were necessary to establish the first project of modern industry in the state designed to relieve acute unemployment after independence while natural resources were callously pumped out of the state for use elsewhere, and development has suffered from severe and chronic shortage of finance. Millions of cubic metres of natural gas have been flared for decades. Credit-deposit ratio of nationalized banks too has ben poor in comparison to more developed states. This vicious circle, generating intractable problems of employment and frustration among youths led unfortunately to an upsurge of secessionist sentiment which eventually drove a section of them to revolt against the Indian state and demand independence for Assam.

This deplorable situation can perhaps to some extent be brought under control by use of military action, but it is hardly a real and permanent solution of the underlying problem, and the present stalemate bodes ill for the future of the region. Because of the peculiar geo-political situation of the country and its North-Eastern region, insurgency in our opinion may once again gain ground if the international situation becomes less stable and imperil the security of the whole country. The rise of terrorism in different forms should sound an alarm among responsible circles.

We have now reason to believe that the great majority of the ULFA leaders have come to realise the futility of a dogmatic adherence to the line of armed struggle and are desirous of seeking a settlement on honourable terms through discussions with the Government of India. The state-level convention has been a popular response to this favourable climate of opinion, and it will be a grievous mistake on the part of the government to miss this opportunity.

We, therefore most respectfully bring to your notice the attached resolutions adopted at the state-level convention and earnestly request you to take statesman-like steps to deliver Assam and the nation at large from the danger from the unresolved political imbroglio in Assam favouring an early resumption of the stalled dialogue.

Guwahati the 21 May 2010

Yours faithfully,

Hiren Gohain
Chief Convener, Steering
Committee for All-Assam
Convention

Members of the Delegation To Meet the Prime Minister

Dr. Hiren Gohain, M.A., Ph.D. (Camb), Former Dean, Arts Faculty, Guwahati University & Author

Dr. Nirmal Kumar Choudhuri, M.A., Ph.D. (Manchester) Former Vice Chancellor, Gauhati University & Social Activist

Dr. Rohini Barua, IAS (Retd.), Social Activist and Author

Shri Hiranya Bhattacharyya, IPS (Retd.) Author

Shri Indibar Deuri, Retd. CPMG, North-East Circle, and Author

Prof. Khorshed Alam, Retd. Professor of Economics, Guwahati University.

The resolution passed by the Convention has been reflected later on in the Frame Work of Charter of Demands for negotiation. Hence not enclosed for avoiding repetition.

Besides being very cordial, Dr Singh gave us a very patient hearing and assured us that he would do all the needful for the resumption of negotiation to arrive at an amicable settlement of all the issues. He, however, advised us to meet P Chidambaram, the union Home Minister, for setting the ball moving. Meanwhile, he said, he would also talk to the Home Minister. Thus we met the union home minister next. To start with, Chidambaram seemed to be speaking the language of a stiff-necked bureaucrat but we could ultimately convince him that this was the last chance to both the parties involved for coming to an amicable and honourable settlement. He, ultimately, stated that all efforts would be made to cross the legal hurdles so that the ULFA leaders could be released on bail for starting the negotiation.

Next day, we met Mrs Sonia Gandhi, the chairperson of the UPA who was also the chairperson, National Advisory Council (NAC). Dr Gohain was very tactful in presenting our case before her. Dr Gohain recalled how her husband Rajiv Gandhi had brought the Assam Movement to an end by devising the Assam Accord and that this time she might also play a similar role for breaking the stalemate. This seemed to have pleased her and minutely went through the memorandum we had submitted to her. A copy of the same is reproduced below for ready reference. :

To

Hon'ble Shrimati Sonia Gandhi
Chairperson, National Advisory Council (NAC)
Government of India

Subject : Memorandum for Initiation of Peace Talks between the Government of India (GOI). and the United Liberation Front of Assam (ULFA) submitted on behalf of the All Assam Peoples Convention for dialogue between the Government of India (GOI) and the United liberation Front of Assam (ULFA)

Respected Madam,

We, the following signatories to this Memorandum, members of the Steering Committee authorised by the Civil Societies' Convention for resumption / initiation of peace talks between the Government of India and the United Liberation Front of Assam (ULFA) held on 24 April 2010 feel privileged to carry forward the earnest desire of the people of Assam expressed through the aforesaid convention for resumption of the much desired stalled talks, in the interest of restoring the normalcy, peace and progress of Assam bringing relief to her hapless people for whom endless suffering from the conflict has become the lot. In the context of the grave situation that Assam and her people find themselves in, we call to your urgent attention, the following facts:

1. It is well known that poverty, reinforced by perception of neglect and discrimination, is the breeding ground for crime, rebellion and insurgency. Assam well known as the storehouse of natural resources is an example of poverty in the midst of plenty. The insurgent group of ULFA and their clones like of NDFB, DHD, KLO, etc. have taken birth in the womb of under development at the perceived notion of neglect and discrimination. We firmly believe once these and other imbalances are wiped out insurgent groups would lose their ground.

2. The people of Assam have through the form of the massive State Level Convention attended by more than 2000 participants and 130 organisations, reflecting as it did the opinion of the educationist, intellectuals, literateures, lawyers, statesman as also the common man have expressed unequivocally and vociferously that what they need is not so much sovereignty or freedom from India but the freedom from hunger, ill-health, illiteracy, ignorance and injustice. The ULFA and the other insurgent organisations of the State have thrived and shall flourish so long as these conditions of stagnation and powerlessness are allowed to thrive. It is incumbent on the Government of India as custodian of the Indian democracy and welfare of the people to take the initiative to start the dialogue with ULFA and put the State of Assam on a speedy course of economic and industrial development based principally on her natural resources available locally.

3. The long drawn out conflict between the security forces and

the insurgent groups of the state including ULFA has not only inflicted horrifying hardships on the hapless common people of Assam in carrying out their daily livelihood but also had made them victims of a prolonged and endless social disorder and economic uncertainties further resulting in ever deteriorating law and order, loss of hundreds of innocent lives at the behest of both the ULFA and the security forces who have often been led to commit undue and inexcusable excesses, commission of crimes by the various antisocial elements taking full advantage of such a chaotic situation leading to further regression, frustration and suffering of the people. The sad story of socio-economic disorder and human tragedy does not end here. In addition to colossal amount of money that would otherwise have gone for development, loss of lives on both sides, has become an horrendous evil.

4. Of no less significance is the harsh truth that greater the army offensive and delay in holding talks more would be this sense of alienation of the people of Assam and therefore, greater the boost to the morale of the insurgent groups. Since economic packages have not always worked in our experience and have indeed sometimes led to corruption, it is necessary to think of proper constitutional measures to empower the state government so that it can act promptly and decisively to carry through necessary economic and other programmes in the larger interest of the people.

5. The people of Assam are long weary and frustrated of crimes, killings, extortion and disruption of development and earnestly desire almost in one voice peace and development. The moment of realisation of this truth has come to the great majority of the people and it is for the Government of India to seize this rare opportunity to marshal the support and cooperation of the people and build up a solid basis for future peace and progress. History will be harsh in judgement if the Government of India fails to seize this opportunity.

We, therefore, strongly urge that in tune with the sentiment and opinion of the civil society of Assam that conditions congenial for dialogue in the interest of peace and uninterrupted progress in Assam be created by the Government of India and the political leadership.

Yours faithfully,

(Dr. Hiren Gohain, MA., Ph.D. (Camb)
Chief Convener
Former Dean, Arts Faculty,
Guwahati University

1. Dr. Nirmal Kumar Choudhury, M., Ph.D. Former Vice Chancellor, Guwahati University.
2. Dr. Rohini Kumar Barua, IAS (Retd.)
3. Shri Hiranya Kumar Bhattacharyya, IPS (Retd)
4. Shri Indibor Deuri, Retd. CPMG
5. Prof. Khorshed Alam

The emergence of ULFA has been discussed earlier. Some of the issues highlighted by ULFA, centred round many longstanding grievances of the people of Assam and all the members of the Steering Committee were well aware of these grievances. We were entrusted with the job of reducing all the demands of ULFA into writing and articulate the same as ULFA's Charter of Demands for submission during the forthcoming negotiation. It was quite a difficult and time consuming exercise. Many weeks of deliberations, interaction with knowledgeable persons and experts backed up by real hard works ultimately took the shape of ULFA's Charter of Demands. During these deliberations, I was very much benefitted by the erudite reflections of most of my colleagues of the Steering Committee. Particularly, Indibor Deuri's deliberations on the tribal problems of Assam, not only helped me to have an insight into the tribal mindset but I also felt vindicated about my views on the tribal issues.

But all that glitters not being gold, we had to also put up with some high sounding utterances devoid of any perspective for the future and scholastic depth. Instead of entering into bitter, meaningless controversial exchanges, I decided to write a personal letter to Dr Gohain, the captain of the team for letting the whole team know my reaction to such barren discussions. Some excerpts from the letter will speak for themselves. :

"Dear Dr Gohain,

Before submitting views on Social Security, etc., kindly permit me to invite your attention to a very important point which has been agitating my mind since the days of the Assam Accord.

1. Our intellectuals have remained content with their words, written or spoken, without, however, bothering to translate their utterances into action. Nothing laudable can be attributed to the media either.

   -------- an action plan is being prepared. This has led me to deliberate within myself about the following :

   If our Charter of Demands remains confined to only economic/socio-political regeneration, etc., without proper and extensive articulation of a vision amongst new generations, then the journey is likely to be unending and the possibility of a fragemented setup cannot be ruled out; but the commitment to a vision may sustain our efforts on a strong basis. This will necessarily imply----

1. To rally the people under strong leadership—selfless, devoted and imaginative, a phenomenon perceived to be totally absent in the context of the Assam Movement (1979–1985); the leadership will have to create trust by examples. Complete loss of faith in leadership has been the bane of Assam's civil society.
2. Transparency and public accountability have been put on heavy premium. Apparently, a post-colonial mindset is perceived to be enslaving us.
3. To generate regularly new ideas for social and economic march ahead. You may kindly recall that in the 1970s, the French Communist Party, had generated such new ideas galore without even coming to power and being sub-servient to USSR. To be very precise, we must evolve a non-political 'Think Tank'.

4. Ground realities divide our people into haves and have-nots, educated-semi educated, literate-illiterate, superestitious and rational-minded. These realities have to be juxtaposed and then create a vision.

----

b Social Security & Insurance: With a population of more than 3 crores and undeveloped economy, it may not be wise for Assam to shoulder the responsibility of social security and allied matters. This scheme will entail huge financial burden. Besides, the matter has to be viewed in an all-India context and the Central govt. should be the nodal point for articulation as well as for bestowing equitable benefits.

However, in the state's periodic memorandum to the Finance Commission, the requirement for Assam in this respect must be focussed with full details.

A study of social security system of USA may prove beneficial.

Yours as ever

Sd. H.K. Bhattacharyya."

The Charter of Demands was given final shape and handed over to the ULFA leaders, presently holding negotiations with New Delhi. Unlike on previous occasions, total secrecy has been maintained in respect of both the Charter of Demands and the negotiations. I am, as such, not in a position to disclose the Charter of Demands which was, however, approved by the general council of ULFA. With permission from Aravinda Rajkhowa, I am reproducing below, "**The Frame Work Of Charter For Negotiation To Resolve The Issues Between Assam And India**": "Assam and its people were sovereign before the British imperialism snatched away the sovereignty of the people of Assam after the Yandaboo Treaty of 1826. Starting from the heroic struggle of Gomadhar Konwer, the people of Assam were part of the great anti-imperialist struggle against British imperialism which ultimately resulted in the independence of India on 15 August 1947.

Questions of negotiations between various constituent entities on mutual adjustment of their respective sovereignties through a written formal agreement therefore cropped up. The results were seen in the Constitution of India. Here naturally the question arises in a written Constitution with division of powers between the executive, legislative and judiciary at Central and state level with three lists enumerating fields of exercising the power, who is the sovereign or where does the sovereignty lie in the Constitution of India? Secondly, in an ever growing encroachment of each other's powers between the various constitutional entities in Indian scheme of governance is the sovereignty which was negotiated in 1947 still valid?

Whether the members of the Constituent Assembly from Assam adequately represented the people of Assam to defend and uphold the rights of Assam is also a question which is shrouded in jurisprudential ambiguity. The continued failure and disinclination of the Government of India to stop illegal immigration from Bangladesh into Assam, which even the Supreme Court, has declared to be a silent invasion, indicates the failure of Government of India to defend the land and the people which it claims to be representing under the agreement of sovereignty i.e., the Constitution of India. It is also evident that Assam was allowed to languish in backwardness as other states marched ahead. The people of Assam have suffered historic neglect and disdain at the hands of the Government of India. There were therefore real grounds for struggle to uphold Assam's inalienable rights, which had also led to the rise of the ULFA.

It is in this historical context that the United Liberation Front of Assam reiterates the ongoing issues between Assam and India can be honourably and meaningfully resolved peacefully only by a fresh look at the issues of sovereignty so as to ensure that the people of Assam can assert their inalienable rights to control their lands and their resources therein, which they inherit and occupy from their forefathers, for securing their honourable existence and for developing the economy and the society of their state according to their needs and aspirations and also to protect their own identity and develop themselves according to their genius. The people of Assam today feel insecure in their own traditional homeland and have been left far behind. To achieve such objectives, United Liberation Front of Assam proposes that negotiations be initiated between India and the People of Assam to bring in measures Constitutional and otherwise of wide scope and that certain urgent political, economic, social, cultural arrangements be undertaken and completed within a reasonable time-frame by the Government of India to ensure a peaceful democratic solution of the historical Indo-Assam question.

In the negotiations, the issues will be discussed under the following broad groupings:

a Grounds for ULFA's struggle and their authenticity.

b Constitutional and Political arrangements and Reforms—including protection of the identity and material resources of the local indigenous population of Assam.

c Financial and Economic Arrangements, including settlement of all royalties on mines/minerals including oil on a retrospective compensatory basis and rights of independent use for a sustainable economic development in future.

d Illegal migration—its effect/impact and required remedies including sealing of international borders, river patrolling, development of a native force to man the borders.

e Ethnic issues—problems and constitutional restructuring including settlement of border disputes and removal of encroachment.

f Education and Health—reforms as required to preserve the identity of the people of Assam and benefits.

g Agricultural and Rural Development.

h Land and Natural resources—including right of natives to the land, flood control and management.

i Industrial Growth—Development of infrastructure, removal of transport bottleneck, development of entrepreneurial skill and efficiency in labour, availability of credit, infusion of capital-leading to industrial take off.

j Restoration, protection, preservation and spread of indigenous culture of Assam in all its variety.

I have been informed that the progress of the negotiation is satisfactory and a final settlement should not take very long. Because of the secrecy maintained so far, the people have so far remained silent; but indefinite delay in working out a settlement, as has happened in case of NSCN, may again trigger off another round of unnecessary agitation. It will be wrong to assume that the people have forgotten all about it; they are simply waiting patiently for the final outcome. Of course, nobody from this part of the country would welcome another still-born baby like the "Assam Accord". But a settlement with Aravinda Rajkhowa and his colleagues accompanying him to the negotiation-table may not be the end of the matter as ULFA has split into two factions, viz, pro-talk faction under Rajkhowa and anti-talk-faction under Paresh Barua, although Barua's sphere of influence has been considerably reduced to few pockets in Upper Assam. Certain knowledgeable quarters, however, believe that Barua is surviving with strong patronage from some foreign powers ever ready to cause problems for India. His close links with China, ISI and NSCN (K) are too clear to be denied.

The emergence of ULFA should have been a matter of serious discussion at the national level but such efforts are yet to be in evidence. Though a constituent unit of the Indian Republic, Assam's political clout in New Delhi has not been something to write home about. Assam has 21 MPs—14 in LS and 7 in RS; but they have so far failed to present a united front. As a result, no pressure group operates cohesively for extracting Assam's dues unlike many other states of India. The absence of such a pressure group has been resulting not only in delay in initiating talks with various insurgent groups but also delay in achieving the target dates of many development projects. A significant reason may be that our Constitution-makers did not envisage the equality of all the constituent units with the result that states having more MPs, had been so far dominating political interaction at all levels. Our political system as reflected in the Directive Principles of the Constitution, though not justiceable, was intended, as it appears to me, to be a marriage between Gandhian humanitarianism approach with a rural bias and British liberal constitutional practices. Gandhiji was done away with long back and now for quite some time, constitutional requirements had been also ignored for promoting partisan interests as also the causes of vested interests.

The current political situation in Assam is still more demoralising. Assam has been virtually under one party rule for more than a decade now. There is no opposition worth the name whereas in days gone bye, Assam's Legislative Assembly used to boast of opposition leaders like Gaurishankar Bhattacharya, Khagen Barbora, Hareswar Goswami, Phani Bora, Dulal Barua, Hemen Das, Bishnu Rava, Dr Bhupen Hazarika, Atul Goswami and many other luminaries. In the present Assembly, Congress has 78 MLAs and active support of BPF with 12 MLAs while two independent MLAs also support the ruling party. Of course, in the wake of largescale communal disturbances in the Bodoland Territorial Areas District (BTAD), the BPF has in 2014 withdrawn its support to the Congress ministry, without, however, causing any threat to the continuance of the ministry. On the other hand, the Opposition is a divided house with AIUDF being the next largest party with 18 MLAs. AGP has nine MLAs and BJP five. All these three parties do not see eye to eye. That aside, even the quality of their deliberations both inside and outside the House does not leave much to write home about. Significantly, all the stalwarts of the Opposition mentioned above belonged to the left of the centre and as such, there was no question of any effort on their part for communalising the politics of Assam whereas the emergence of the UMF in 1985 and lately, of the AIUDF under the leadership of Maulana Badruddin Ajmal unmistakably point to reviving the communal politics of pre-partition days. AIUDF's promotion of minoritism under the cloak of secularism is certainly not aimed at furthering the interests of Assam's indigenous population. After the emergence of the AIUDF, a threat has been held out that all Assamese people would be driven out of lower Assam and demands made that there should be an autonomous Muslim Council and "Topi" and "Lungi" (dress commonly used by the immigrant Muslim) should be made the national dress of Assam! But surprisingly, such overt efforts for creating communal tension have escaped any punishment.

There being no organised strong Opposition in the Assembly, the media has been filling up the gap. The media has today in Assam assumed the role of the Opposition. Some of the powerful political leaders have their own newspapers and TV channels and their rivalries have been reflected in their respective newspapers and TV channels. As a result, objectivity and neutrality of the media have been put on very heavy premium on the one hand and on the other, the discriminating policy in respect of development and too much centralisation of political powers, have once more given rise to the need of a new regional political outfit as AGP has totally failed to cater for the aspirations of all the ethnic groups of the state. Few non-political prominent intellectuals have, therefore, given a call either for totally reorganising the AGP or form a new regional political party which should embrace all sections of the society. If the call materialises, it may be a new beginning for Assam which may augur well for the future of the state, provided the leadership proves to be dedicated and selfless. (*Amar Asom*, June 22/13.)

True, peace-talk between the Centre and the ULFA are in progress. But will New Delhi ever do a dispassionate study of the causes leading to the rise of ULFA? Why ULFA? A brief reference to some of the main causes of such militancy may be of interest to the reader. Contrary to the opinion generated by the detractors of the historic Assam movement, ULFA certainly was not an offshoot of the Assam movement. ULFA was born on 7 April 1979, many months earlier than the said movement took off the ground. In fact, some of the top ULFA leaders took active part in the agitation aimed at detection and deletion of alien names from the ERs and deportation of the illegal migrants. But gradually they lost faith in the non-violent nature of the Assam Movement and took to the path of violence.

The disillusionment of the ULFA leaders was total when the much vaunted Assam Accord proved to be still born. The non-implementation of whatever little there was in the Assam Accord, led the ULFA leaders to their firm conviction that New Delhi would never understand the language of non-violence. The long standing sense of deprivations thus engendered a sense of alienation which degenerated into secessionism. Three main factors appear to have exacerbated the situation: Anowara Taimur's brief rule of inhuman atrocities, adverse fallouts of the forcibly held elections of 1983 and the infructuous Assam Accord. Certainly, the neighbourhood of Manipur and Nagaland helped in accelerating the process.

The unfriendly neighbours of India took no time in extending a helping hand to ULFA. ISI stepped in. Pakistan was too eager to settle its account with India for holding on to Kashmir and causing her own partition. China did not lag behind either as she found a sure outlet for expanding illegal export of arms and explosives to an unprecedented extent. The credibility of New Delhi was never lower. Past experiences of deprivation and deceit comprising a long list, were haunting the new generation.

The weak leadership representing Assam failed to respond to the gradually emerging situation nor did it exercise any influence over the new generation of political activists who were groaning under serious grievances of deprivation and deception.

The discovery of new oil fields with rich potentials naturally led to the demand for setting up an oil refinery in Assam. But the so-called experts toeing the line of the Centre, turned down the demand on grounds of security. Splendid plea indeed! Oil fields are secure but not an oil refinery! Which is why, crude oil had to be pumped out to Barauni in Bihar and a huge refinery was set up there.

Bishnuram Medhi, known as the "Iron Man of Assam", was then the chief minister of Assam. Medhi, on tremendous popular demand and rousing pressure, wrote a personal letter to Pt Nehru who ultimately agreed to set up a refinery in Assam, but the deception was total when only a mini refinery was set up in Guwahati as mere eye-wash. However, the new generation did not take to this deception kindly and grievances kept on accumulating. Again, Assam had to resort to another agitation under the leadership of Hem Barua and other few leaders for constructing the first-ever bridge over the Brahmaputra, presently, known as the Saraighat bridge. It was so named because the famous battle of Saraighat was fought here in the 17th century against Mughal General Ram Singh sent by Aurangzeb to invade Assam. General Ram Singh lost to Assamese General Lachit Barphukan, a legendary figure of Assam's history. Now, of course, two more bridges have been constructed over this mighty river—one at Jogighopa and the other near Tezpur. The one at Jogighopa has been named as "Naranarayan Setu" after the name of Koch King Narayana and the other near Tezpur has been named after Kaliabhomara Barphukan, an Ahom General under the Ahom King Kamaleswar

Singha. Kaliabhomara had planned to construct a bridge over the Brahmaputra towards the later part of 18th century but he could not execute the plan. So, as suggested by Dulal Barua, the present bridge has been named after Kaliabhomara.

Anyway, New Delhi's slow response to Assam's legitimate demands created an impression that Assam never got her dues without an agitational approach. On the other hand, New Delhi spared no efforts to treat any movement for legitimate dues as a law and order problem only—a really very sad commentary on the political leadership and the bureaucracy. Take for example, the cases of Railway ministry, the P & T ministry, the LIC and many other Central Government agencies: Even the third and fourth grade employees of so many Central Government establishments, are imported from outside Assam. The Railway ministry, the largest employment generating channel, has been focussing only on the respective states of the incumbent ministers. Laluprasad and Mamata Banerjee are cases in point. The rest of the country also fails to appreciate why armed violence erupts here so frequently. Unknown to the rest of the country, thus the process of alienation gradually gets stronger and stronger, thereby making the emergence of insurgency and ultimately secessionism a reality.

As the peace-talks with ULFA have reached a crucial stage, the top leadership of ULFA, despite its dissident faction, must work overtime to change the mindset of their cadres into a democratic way of functioning. A massive economic programme on co-operative basis may facilitate this process. However, whatever ULFA intends to achieve, must be planned in the socio-economic context of the ethnically divided contemporary Assam, totally devoid of shallow, emotional fervour and lesser loyalties as was done in the case of Assam Accord.

All said and done, the ball is in the court of the Central Government. New Delhi, in all its powerful posture, must realise that here is a great chance for regaining much of its lost credibility. A change of attitude, particularly in respect of amending the constitution and the relevant laws, will stand out as sine qua non. Genuine goodwill and solid earnestness may be the stepping stone for clearing the desk.

The final results of the election held for Guwahati Municipal

Corporation was announced on 24.6.2013. AGP was wiped out as anticipated. Out of 31 seats for councillors, AGP has won only one seat, BJP 11 seats and Congress 19 seats. There is no doubt that BJP's gain has been at the cost of AGP—a phenomenon I had visualised way back in 2001 as already discussed earlier. But, I am afraid, that BJP cannot become a viable alernative to Congress in Assam, entirely depending on defection from AGP or any other party.

22

Trip to Bangladesh

I had mentioned earlier that 42 years back I had to train up some Bangladeshi guerillas in the wake of the liberation war of Bangladesh. I had already forgotten all the details about this. Now as I was about to end writing this chapter of the discourse, a letter from Dr Dipumoni, the Foreign Minister of Bangladesh, arrived. The letter as reproduced below will speak for itself :

Foreign Minister

Government Of The
People's Republic Of Bangladesh
Dhaka

MFA/HFF/102 24 January 2013

Dear Mr Bhattacharyya,

It is my privilege to write to you in my capacity as the Convener of the National Committee to Honour Foreign Friends of the Bangladesh Liberation War. The Committee has been especially constituted by the Government of Bangladesh to honour outstanding friends of Bangladesh who participated in, or contributed to, the process of our Liberation War.

The National Committee has particularly taken note of the support extended by our foreign friends to the Bangladeshi cause and also the moral and material support provided to our people during the War. We are mindful that your support came at a critical time when we stood up in the face of barbaric atrocities and the worst ever genocide in world history. Your support contributed to the eventual emergence of sovereign Bangladesh.

I take great pleasure in conveying to you that upon recommendation of the National Committee, the Government of Bangladesh has decided to formally recognize your contribution and to express gratitude on behalf of the people of Bangladesh.

We are cognisant of the fact that our decision to formally recognize your contribution has come forty years after our achieving independence. That omission, we feel, is set right today forever for our posterity and for the world.

The Government of Bangladesh has decided to hold an official ceremony on 24 March 2013 to honour friends of Bangladesh like yourself. I have great pleasure in inviting you to this State Ceremony as a guest of the Government of Bangladesh. In the event, you are unable to join us, we would be happy to welcome your representative. We shall arrange for your travel and extend full hospitality to you or your representative for this programme. The official programme will span over 23 and 26 March. We expect arrivals on 23 March midday with some side events planned for 25 and 26 March. A tentative programme is attached.

I look forward to receiving you in Dhaka.

Yours most sincerely,

Dr. Dipu Moni, MP

Foreign Minister
And Convener of the National Committee to
Honour the Foreign Friends of the
Bangladesh Liberation War

So, I arrived at Dhaka on 23 March 2013 accompanied by J P Saikia, a senior journalist of Assam who had retired as a senior IAS Officer. During Bangladesh's War of Liberation, Saikia was the staff correspondent of the *Times of India* at Agartala. He played a major role in exposing to the Western world the genocide committed in Bangladesh by the Pak army which created international concern. He has, therefore, been honoured by Bangladesh government with the same award as I have been. The citation for his award reads as follows:

"During the Liberation War, Shri Jyoti Prasad Saikia as the staff correspondent of *The Times of India*, provided regular reports on sufferings caused on the people of Bangladesh by the Pakistan Army and the success of freedom fighters. As a prolific writer and dramatist, he wrote a play titled 'Titasher Osru', which was aired from Assam Radio and Akashvani. This became a popular programme. Other than providing news, he used to assist foreign journalists by providing them with information on Liberation War. For this great contribution, Shri Jyoti Prasad Saikia is awarded Friends of Liberation War Honour."

The citation for the award given to me is also reproduced below:

"During the Liberation War, Shri Hiranya Kumar Bhattacharyya was a senior police officer of 5 Assam Armed Police Training Center at Kahilipara. He was entrusted with the training of Mukti Bahini guerillas and commanders. He performed the task with utmost sincerity. Later, he was the security in-charge and administrator of refugee camps at Haflong with two lakh refugees where he accomplished his task with efficiency. For his great contribution, Shri Hiranya Kumar Bhattacharyya is awarded **Friends of Liberation War Honour.**"

I really felt flattered when I found that some of the recipients of Bangladesh's national awards in the same context were very prominent personalities of the world like Dr Fidel Castro Ruz, Lord Harold Wilson, Tomio Mizokami, Shri Jyoti Basu, Lady Ranu Mookerjee, etc.

During our visit to Dhaka, the law-and-order situation there was very grave with the fundamentalist elements and Begum Zia's party (BNP) trying their best to destablise Sheikh Hasina's nationalist government. Obviously, they had to take very strong measures for our security. Even then, we had ample opportunities for interacting with a cross section of educated people like the teachers and students of Dhaka University, advocates, retired army ofifcers, etc. It was evident that the clash was between linguistic nationalism represented by Sheikh Hasina's camp and religious fundamentalism represented by Begum Zia, well aided by Jamiat, Zehadis and Pak-sponsored agencies. The minorities of Bangladesh are feeling safer today under Sheikh Hasina's regime. That she is secular minded is evident from the speech she delivered to welcome us—the foreign guests. Following excerpts from her speech may be of interest to the reader:

"--- When Bangladesh is making remarkable advancement, when the long standing process of the trial of the war crimes is at the juncture of desired culmination, the defeated forces once again are out to mar the process through misusing people's religious sentiments and militancy."

"People of Bangladesh never accepted such design in the past and will not allow so in the future. Because, people of this country are religious-minded; but not bigots. The spirit of liberation war always keeps them awakened; they are committed to building a prosperous and non-communal Bangladesh free from hunger, poverty and literacy.

------------------------------"

It appeared to me as if the whole city of Dhaka had been converted into a university for promoting patriotism. Most welcome was the finding that the young generation had been developing a secular outlook and they were very confident about a bright future of Bangladesh. We, both the guests and the hosts, could not conceal our moist eyes at the time of leaving Dhaka for home.

23

Discernible Social Changes

Astounding changes have taken place over the last few decades. My mother was not very happy when I was one of the pioneers in introducing co-acting into Nalbari's Natya Mandir's stage whereas today, many girls from Assam, nay, the entire North-east, have earned many laurels even at national levels in performing arts, including acting in feature films and in the state as well.

Earlier, in the caste-Hindu families, particularly in the Brahmin families, daughters were married away before they attended the age of puberty. My mother was given in marriage before she completed the age of 10; two of my sisters were married away before they appeared in their matriculation examination; but my third sister was in her post-graduate class in the Guwahati University when her marriage was solemnised. To be precise, the practice of child-marriage has totally disappeared.

Inter-caste marriage was a taboo in Assam's Hindu society until the other day. In fact, anybody indulging in such venture used to be socially boycotted. Now, inter-caste marriages are accepted without any murmur. I even know instances of conservative Brahmin families welcoming their Muslim daughters-in-law, let alone non-Brahmin Hindu girls. Even marriages of widows and divorcees donot cause a ripple in the society. Of course, late marriage amongst the highly educated boys and girls has brought in its train some unforeseen problems, the details of which may be too cumbersome to dwell upon for the purpose of this discourse. But the evil of dowry has surfaced in Assam also, accompanied by concomitant atrocities.

The most significant change has been in the gradual breakdown of the joint family system. The breakdown of this system has cetainly imperilled the economic security of the unemployed members of the family, who used to find safe shelter during the period of their unemployment and such a system must have prevented them from taking to the path of criminal activities for sustenance as many were doing now.

Still the most perceptible change has been in respect of garments used by the girls and the working women. The traditional Assamese female costume of 'Mekhela-Chadar' is practically on its way out excepting on ceremonial occasions like Bihu, Saraswati puja and few religious/social rituals. Of course most of the housewives, particularly in the rural areas, are still using the traditional dress. "Mekhela-Chadar" and "Sari" have been replaced by "Salwar-Kamiz". However, the colourful female costumes of the tribal people are still very much in vogue, although sizeable percentage of tribal girls are also fond of the "Salwar-Kamiz". It seems that the working convenience and the cost factor tilted the scale in favour of this change. Of course, the exposure of the female figure whether in reel or real life, still causes quite a few ruffled feathers. Even the daily use of certain domestic vocabularies is undergoing changes in defiance of the age-old tradition. An example may be in order: In Assamese, the father is addressed as "deuta" or "pita" and the mother as "'ma" or "ai". By and large, particularly in the upper middle class, these have been changed into "papa" and "mummy". This is now catching up even with the lower strata of the society. Obviously, this has resulted from the preponderance of missionary convent and English medium schools. Thus the exposure to the West has dragged the traditional society into a transitional stage. Unfortunately, most of the evils of the West are also gradually surfacing. The advent of the computer, TV, cell-phone, internet, the system of SMS and Facebook, etc., has certainly upgraded the communication system; but at the same time, all these modern facilities have been promptly followed by what is known as "cyber crime". Assam Police also has not lagged behind; today Assam Police boasts of an "investigation squad" for investigating "cyber crime" and it has been successful in detecting quite a few such sensational cases,which was simply inconceivable during my time.

It is obvious that the traditional sense of values has been under tremendous pressure with concomitant fallouts—both beneficial and adverse. A rational attitude is certainly developing toward the human existence despite superstitions galore still holding their sway. In other words, we are trying to be modern without ceasing to be mediaeval. The saddest part is that material comforts are claiming precedence over humane commitments. Obviously, human relations at all levels are likely to undergo unimaginable changes in days to come. Briefly speaking, it may take time for integrating past heritage with neo-modernism of the cyber-age. No doubt, to prove Hegel right once more, there is bound to be a synthesis in due course.

24

ENVOI

That “some mirth, some sorrow” (not literal translation) composes one’s life, is the main theme of a very popular number sung, possibly composed also, by Dr Bhupen Hazarika. The song not only impressed me immensely but also persuaded me to look back as to how much I had enjoyed ‘mirth’ and how much ‘sorrow’ I had suffered. I am happy to find that I had taken everything in my strides. But that was not the end of the story. Some more anxious days full of unforeseen crises were in store for the family:

My youngest son, Rajeev Bhattacharyya, is a journalist. He had already worked in *The Times of India*, *The Telegraph*, *The Indian Express*, *The Bengal Post* and also as the bureau chief of the TV channel, *Times Now* for the North-east. His preference has always been the print-media. Ultimately, he landed up at Guwahati as the executive editor of the newly started English daily, the *Seven Sisters Post*. Over the years, he has been trying to specialise in insurgency in the North-east. He was nursing for long a desire to personally meet the rebel leaders of various outfits including Paresh Barua, the c-in-c of ULFA, SS Khaplang, the chairman of NSCN (K) and few others from Manipur and Kachin. So he embarked upon a plan to visit these leaders.

The arduous journey was supposed to be a very secret mission for obvious reasons. He had to be extremely cautious as he had to dodge the Intelligence agencies and the security forces of both India and Myanmar. But his own editor betrayed him by publicly claiming that he had sent his executive editor on this mission for collecting first hand information and he even wrote two editorials about it, with the sole purpose of exposing Rajeev to serious threat to his life. All my friends and well-wishers were very upset for divulging such an essential secret after they read the editorials. But why did this garrulous editor do this?

Rajeev left home on 11 October 2011 and crossed the Indo-Myanmar border in the wee hours of 13 October 2011. He took about 40 days to reach one of the main camps of Paresh Barua in Eastern Nagaland of Myanmar through dense forest, hills and torrential rivers. Of course, he was escorted by armed guides deputed by Paresh Barua. Rajeev and his cameraman stayed in this camp little over a month and it was from this camp that he visited many other rebel camps and interviewed quite a number of rebel leaders of other militant outfits, including SS Khaplang of NSCN (K), Sangbijit of NDFB, etc. He also visited the camp of UPKK, a rebel outfit from Manipur.

Meanwhile total confusion and worries overtook our mental state of affairs as we did not hear anything from him. The matter took a serious turn because of two news items published on the matter in the local media. Firstly, it was published that two journalists from India had been arrested in Myanmar. As if that was not sufficient to rattle us, another news item was caused to be published by Rajeev's detractors that NSCN (K) had demanded a ransom of rupees five crores for safe release of Rejeev. Thank God, promptly came a denial by the NSCN (K) to our great relief. Even my daughter-in-law, Rajeev's wife, was threatened with such an enventuality by one of Rajeev's detractors who was a retired Colonel of the army.

Our worries were endless. It was simply impossible to get in touch with Rajeev. It was already more than three months that we had not heard anything about Rajeev. All sorts of rumours compounded our anxieties and worries. Finding no way out, I wrote two personal letters—one to Dr Manmohan Singh, the PM and the other to Tarun Gogoi, the CM of Assam, with the request to help us in ascertaining the wherabouts of Rajeev. The Indian embassy of Yangoon could not be of much help. But certainly both Dr Singh and Gogoi had done their best to do the needful. Then suddenly in mid-December, I received a telephonic call from Arunodoy Dahotia, the assistant publicity secretary of ULFA, who informed me that Rajeev was doing well and there was no need to worry for his welfare whereupon I requested him to arrange for Rajeev to talk to us.

Meanwhile, one of Khaplang's representatives also informed me over telephone that there was no cause for any worry and that Rajeev would reach home safely in due course. Arunodoy had complied with my request, obviously with Barua's approval and ultimately Rajeev talked to us on 26 December apparently from ULFA's camp. Again there was no information about him for more than a month. I consoled the family everyday that being on his return journey home, he had no access to any telephonic network. Ultimately, he telephoned me in the late evening of 31 January 2012 to inform us that he had safely crossed over to Assam few minutes back after covering 800 kms on foot and that it would take few more days to reach home as he would have to wait for the arrival of his luggage and accoutrements.

Ultimately, he landed at home in the late evening of 8 February 2012 after spending three months and 20 days in the jungles for interviewing some of the top rebel leaders of the North-east. He has already published a pictorial book of 52 insurgent groups of the North-east while his travelogue is in the press. We are all happy. All well that ends well.

But what about the editor who had dragged Rajeev to such a difficult situation and placed his family in a state of tremendous mental anxieties and worries? It did not take us long to trace the motive behind.

This man had so far survived and earned quite a few laurels entirely because of his unending capacity to bluff his way out. His past association with an international TV news channel had also helped him in his bluffing campaign.

Sometime in the month of December 2011, he even went to the extent of telling me that he had spoken to Baruah who had asked him to assure me that Rajeev would reach home safely. All this turned out to be sheer bluff. So, instead of his bluff getting exposed, why not facilitate Rajeev's outright elimination by publicising Rajeev's secret mission?

His prejudice against the Assamese and bias in favour of his own community also stood exposed in due course. Anyway, he had burnt his boat so far Assam was concerned and had been practically compelled by the turn of events to leave Guwahati—possibly for good.

Further, Col G Srikumar of Military Intelligence filed a case against *Seven Sisters Post* for a false report published by the editor. Then, failing in his sexual advances, he compelled a young female journalist to resign. All these developments did not augur well for the future of *Seven Sisters Post.* So ultimately, the management of the newspaper removed him from Guwahati. His bluffing habit and scheming strategy thus failed to sustain him. But I am yet to forgive myself for being allowed to be totally fooled by this past master of bluffing. Candidly speaking, I had never in my life entertained any intention to cause any slander to anybody but I simply could not put up with such white lies. I had never imagined that at the fag end of my life's journey, I would have to confront such rogueries. Once again, I had to take this also in my stride. Still I feel that his is a case for psychological analysis.

At the end of the day, I cannot help anticipating that the inherent sense of social order and justice is gradually collapsing. I wonder how long the application of the Panchayat system will take for filling up the resultant vacuum. A whole lot of new concepts are emerging. To quote Jaswant Singh: "-- In our age, issues of international concern are being redefined, national sovereignties and boundaries downgraded, human rights, environment, globalisation gaining primacy. We have to recognise this new agenda and work together to meet the challenge. ---" (*A Call To Honour*-- page 186)

Though this has been written in a different context, this is equally applicable to the new emerging socio-political order of Assam also. In the wake of the globalisation, the emergence of new socio-cultural nuances, the indigenous socio-cultural patterns may get obliterated and I have personally seen symptoms of such revolutionary changes in most interior rural areas of Assam.

Throughout my life's journey, I had occasions to feel that some unseen super power controls the happenings of our lives. The Baptist fatalism seemed to have come alive during the time I had left behind: "Nothing can hinder the execution of the designs of Providence. What is to be will be and we can do nothing about it". But certainly I did not remain content with fate alone and had tried my best to confirm that life was worth-living. I entirely agree with Pt. Nehru when he wrote to his sister Vijaya Lakshmi Pandit on 12 September 1934 from Naini Central Prison, Allahabad: " ----- Not to reject life but to accept it in all its fullness, and yet to go through it finely and with light steps and refusing to allow it to besmirch us. That is a worthwhile ideal, a difficult undertaking, and the very few who may have the good fortune to approach it can never regret the choice. Success, if it comes, comes worthily, with no tinsel or vulgarity; failure itself approaches with noble and tragic mien. ---------

---- We have all to face nervous strains which are more difficult to bear often enough than actual physical pain. **We must be tolerant of each other's failings and help to lighten each other's load.**" (Emphasis mine) (Quoted from Indira Gandhi by Nayantara Sahgal, page 41/42.)

I have really tried throughout my life to imbibe what Nehru wrote to his sister. Hence the quotation.

Even then at the end of the day, I find that occasions of 'sorrow' have outnumbered the occasions of "mirth". Still I feel, I have lived a full life with its quota of ups and downs. I am left with only one grievance (do not remember who said it): "The greatest tragedy of life is to be guilty without true guilt, " ---- a statement applicable to my personal, official and public life.

Index

Abdul Momin, 220
  Eminent Person of Bangladesh, 220
Abida Ahmad, 136
Abu Parbat, 45
Adivasi, 152
  Prisoners, 152
Administration, 52, 76, 78, 84, 86, 88, 99, 126, 145, 146, 150, 162, 163, 179, 231, 233, 235
  People Oriented, 76
Administrative System, 18
Advani, Lal Krishna, 99, 255, 257
Advent of Christianity, 29
Afforestation, 31
African Countries, 78
Age Old Settlement, 248
Agitation Leaders, 169
Agricultural
  And Industrial Production, 24
  Labour, 88, 264
AIUDF, 294
Ajmal Maulana Badrudin, 294
Al Qaida in Dhaka, 277
Alam, Prof. Khorshed, 280, 287
Alcoholism, 233
All Assam
  Bandh, 183
  Bank Employee Parishad, 112
  Convention—ULFA, 279, 280
  Gana Sangram Parishad (AAGSP), 111, 112, 117, 120, 182-185, 215, 218, 219, 221, 224, 228
    Leaders, 120, 183
  Minority Students Union (AAMSU), 84, 117
  State Karamchari Parishad, 111
  Students Union (AASU), 52, 76, 99, 110-112, 114, 117, 135, 138, 140-142, 169, 181, 183, 186, 199, 207, 208, 215, 216, 220, 222, 225, 226, 228, 230
    And AAGSP, 121-123, 126, 185, 205
    Delegates, 116
    Demands, 116
      Salient Features, 116
  Executive Committee, 119
  Leaders, 108-110, 116, 119, 149, 183, 219, 221
  Leadership, 116, 132, 218, 219, 223, 226, 228

Tribal Sangh, 111
All India
Congress Committee, 93, 96, 98
Police Meet, 76
Services, 48, 50
Sikh Students Federation, 112
Allahabad
Days, 34
High Court Judgement, 84
University, 27, 36, 38, 39
Alliance With BJP, 267
Amalgamation of Sylhet, 52
Amarnath, Lala, 81
Amrit Bazar Patrika (newspaper), 41
Ancient and Medieval India, 36
Anglo-American Approach, 43
Anil Bora of Nagaon District, AASU Leader, 76
Anowara Taimur's Ministry, 112
Anti-
Assam Act, 128
Election Rallies, 185
India Stance, 234
Indian Regime of Begum Khalida Zia, 277
Infiltration Measures, 66
Insurgency Campaign, 55
Insurgency Measures, 26
Naga Insurgency, 55
National Politicians, 71
Smuggling Measures, 66
Armed
Dacoities, 73
Forces (Special Powers) Act, (AFSP), 118, 278
Outfits, 131
Police Training Centre, 77, 86
Struggle, 284
Arora, Gopi Krishan, 40
Assam, 18, 20, 21, 22, 31, 34, 36, 40, 41, 51, 52, 54, 55, 66, 78, 88, 95, 96, 199
A Multiracial and Multilingual State, 231
Accord (AA), 1985, 119, 120, 128, 133, 183, 220-229, 231, 232, 236, 289, 293, 297
Implementation of-, 222
Stillborn Baby, 220
Agriculture University (AAU), 139
And Bangladesh, 17
Atmosphere of-, 50
Bandh, 112
Blockade, 117
Composite Society, 82, 209, 223
Distinct Identity of-, 263
Disturbed Area Act, 204
Hills, Forests and Rivers, 20
In Pakistan, Inclusion of-, 65
In Post-Colonial Hangover, 41
Jagrati Mahila Parishad, 112
Jails, 171
Jatiyatabadi Dal, 127, 203
Jatiyatabadi Yuva Chhatra Parishad, 111
Leaders, 169
Legislative Assembly, 251, 294
Movement, 72, 105-131, 138, 142, 165, 195, 196, 203, 207, 208, 220-222, 225, 228, 235, 236, 255, 256, 268, 275, 289, 295
Activists, 125
Petrochemicals, 216
Police, 54, 100, 126, 144, 241, 305
Police Housing Corporation, 86
Policy, 154
Politics, 82, 187, 242, 273
Population, 187
Social Development in-, 75
Tea, 81
Tribune Group, 218
Valley, 49, 91, 112, 123
Yuva Parishad, 241
Assam's
Administration, 144
Civil Society, 289
Crude Oil to Bihar, 116
Economic Development, 23

Economy, 24-25, 26
Flora and Fauna, 47
Geographical Isolation, 24
Land Mass, 25
Muslim Population, 214, 215
Natural and Water Resources, 27
Policies, 233
Rich Potential, 20
Rich Potential, For Developing International Tourism, 20

Assamese
And Bengalis, 164
And Bengali Communities, 141
Dailies, 161
Amar Asom, 161
Dainik Agradoot, 161
Game Plan, 229
Hindu Villages, 121
Journalist, 165
Dharendranath Bezbarua, 165
Kanaksen Deka, 165
Kirtinath Hazarika, 165
Prafulla Barua, 165
Language, 50, 52, 73, 249
Medical Schools, 76
Medium Schools, 133
Movement, 165, 176
Muslims, 204, 228
Society, 248, 249
Villages in North Kamrup, 207

Assamese-Bodo Relations, 72
Assemblies Constituencies, 206
Association of Jatiyatabadi Dal, 110
Ataur Rahman of Titabar, 210, 231, 247
Atta Khan, Afghan Citizen, 167
Atwar Rahim
IGP, 164
Addl IGP, 77
Australia, 78, 80
Author,
Accused of Communal Prejudices, 68
Address to meetings all over Brahmaputra Valley Sponsored by AASU, 182
Allotted Assam Cadre, 49
Anupama Devi, Younger Sister, 15, 16
Appeared in IPS Examination in 1957, 39
As AIGP Administration, 82
As DIGP Border, 101
ASP in Nagaon District, 161
Associates,
Dr. Birendra Kumar Bhattacharya, 218
Kiritinath Hazarika, 218
Professor Jogesh Das, , 218
Association and Legacy (with Sanskrit), 16
At Dergaon Police Training College, 48
At Dhubri, 58, 65
Attended Management Course in Australia, 76
Awarded Friends of Liberation War Honour, 301
Book (*Fagunar Kopili*) in Assamese, 20
Book-*The Silent Invasion*, 275
Camped at Fort Largin in Australia, 81
Close Association with Lalit, 272
Conducted Departmental Proceedings Against--, 51
Confinement in Hazaribagh Jail, 217
Detained under NSA, 168
DIGO (border), 168, 260
DIGP Southern Range, 140
Father,
A Great Humanist, 28
Late Devendranath Bhattacharyya, 15
Got Meritorious Scholarship, 35
Guest Kalpana Azmi, 90
Habeus Corpus Petition, 172
Habit of Reading Books, 17, 167
Held Charge of Three Offices, (AIGP, TAPTW) 5APBN, APTC, 77
Hostel-mate, Dr. Murli Manohar Joshi, 255

In Allahabad in 1954, 20
In Semi-finals of All Assam Tennis Champion Tournament, 49
Interest in Football, 37
Intimate R'elations with Capt. Williamson Sangma, 55
IPS Examination, 37, 39, 40
IPS days, 45-53, 75
Letter to Prafulla Kumar Mahanta, CM, 245
Love for Dogs, Flowers and Gardening, 19
Married Deepika Sharma, 48
Met Hiten Goswami, Student Leader, 186
Met Prafulla Goswami from Nalbari, 37
Met Sir Donald Bradman, 81
Mother Chandraprabha Devi, 15
Nalbari Days, 19
Police Career, 45
Posting in Halflong, 64
Published 'Jail Diary', 217
Refused Electioneering Campaign in 1952, 18
Resignation from Party, 268
Retirement and Back to Public Life, 274-298
Returned from Australia, 82
Role in Films, 90
SDPO at Golaghat, 104
Selection to IB, 76
Serious Charges on link with Assam Agitation, 168
To Silchar for Practical Training in Police Work, 48
To Train up Bangladesh's Guerrillas, 299
To Tura as SP, 54
Transfer from AIGP (A) as SSP CID, 85
Trip to Bangladesh, 299
Turning Point in Academic Career, 34
Visit to
  Agra, Mathura, Brindavan and Benares, 36
  Australia, UK, Philippines, Hong Kong, Thailand, 58
  Brisbane, Melbourne and Sydney, 78
  Kokrajhar, 72
Worshipped AB Vajpayee, 275
Wrote
  Detective Novels, 218
  Short Stories and Articles on Socio-Political Problems, 217
  Three Novels, including Detective Novel, 275

Axom Gana Parishad (AGP), 124, 177, 183, 190, 219, 222, 224, 233, 239, 242, 244, 266-268, 270, 271, 295, 298
  Betrayal, 256
  Dominated Seats of Guwahati, Nagaon, Mangaldoi, 268
  Downfall, 266
  Government, 205, 215, 224, 230-251, 256
  Infamous Second Tenure, 235
  Leaders, 227, 231, 235
  Leadership, 213, 274
  Ministry, 128, 131
  MLAs and MPs, 225
  Out of Power in 1996, 233
  Rule, 224, 237, 239
  Split, 235, 247
Axom Jatiyatabadi Dal, 111
Axom Xahitya Xabha (AXX), 110, 182

Babri Masjid, 99
Bachan, Amitabh, 38
Bachan, Haribans Rai, 38
Backward
  Communities, 248
  Ethnic Tribes, 248
Bagley, Desmond, Novelist, 276
Bahuguna, HN, 124
Barthakur, Dr. Anandeswar, 255, 258

Bakul Nath, 149
Balance of Power, 43
Balmiki, 16
Baloka, 31, 32
Banabhatta, 16
Bandung Conference, 41
Banerjee, AK, Justice, 40
Banerjee, Mamta, 297
Banerjee, Prof. AC, Vice Chancellor, 35
Banga Bhasiya Assamiya Samaj, 111
Bangladesh, 77, 78, 88, 101, 212, 213, 221, 228, 229, 276, 277, 278, 300, 301, 302
(*See also* East Pakistan)
  Citizens, 214
  Flag, 121, 207
  Infiltration, 108, 117
  Infiltrator from-, 26
  Islamic Manch, 277
  Liberation, 299
  Lobby, 123, 126
  Miscreants, 125
  Mukti Bahini, 77
  National Awards, 301
  Nationals, 112, 125, 212, 214, 225, 228
    Enrolled Voters in Assam, 185
  Origin, 254
  Refugees, 77
  Voters, 110, 113, 125
  War of Liberation, 187, 301
Bangladeshis, 208
Banks of Rivers, 20
  Buroi, 20
  Jiyabhoroli, 20
  Kopili, 20
  Manas, 20
  Subansiri, 20
Banned Inter-District Movement--, 89
Baptist Fatalism, 310
Bar Association, 176
Barak Valley, 49, 52, 114, 126, 141, 204
Barauni, 115
  Refinery, 122
Barbara,
  CM, 109, 110, 111
  Ministry, 96
Barbara, Golap, 107
Barbara's Socialism Program, 97
Barbarian Atrocities, 300
Barman, Bhumidhar, 124
Barpeta, 121, 136
  Curfew Orders, 121
Barua, Anjan, 176
Barua, BK, IGP, 55, 59, 74
Barua, Brig. ML, 77
Barua, Devakanta, 93, 136
Barua, Dr. Rohini, IAS, 279, 280, 281, 288
Barua, Dr. S, 141
Barua, Dulal, 101, 103, 297
Barua, Girin, 203
Barua, Hem, MP, 19
Barua, Indrajit, 127, 196, 203
Barua, Khanindra Chandra, 120
Barua, Nagen, Minister of Assam, 36
Barua, Nem, 21
Barua, Paresh, 281, 293, 307
Barua, PG, 216, 218
Barua, Raju, ULFA Second in Command, 241
Barua, Sricharan, 252
Basu, Jyoti, CM West Bengal, 117, 301
Basumatari, Ratneswar, 280
Batubabu, 49
Begam Abida Ahmad, 114
Begum Zia, 302
Begum Zia's Party (BNP), 301
Bengal Muslims, 117
Bengali
  Dramas in Assamese, 29
  Hindus, 68
  Language, 52
  Refugee at Matia, 74
  Refugees, 74
  Society of Assam, 164
  Speaking Muslims, 147
  Speaking Officers, 51
  Speaking People, 49
Bhagalpur Jail, 121

Bhakra Nangal Dam Project, 22
Bhagavad Geeta, 77
Bharat Ratna Gopinath Bordoloi, 82
Bhartiya Janata Party (BJP), 52, 124, 130, 183, 209, 227, 233, 266-273, 294, 298
  And AGP, 267
  Constitution, 268
  Days, 255-264
  Five Principles, (BJPF), 255
  In Assam, 266
  Led Union Government, 232
Bhattacharya, Birendera Kumar, 182
Bhattacharya, JP, Author's Advocate, 170
Bhattacharya, Ramendra Narayan, 216
Bhattacharya, SK, AASU Adviser, 227
Bhattacharya, Tushar, 79, 80
Bhattacharyya, Rajeev, Journalist, 306-309
Bhattacharyya, Anil, Author's Younger Brother, 147
Bhattacharyya, Hiranya Kumar, 279, 280, 281, 284, 288
Bhindranwale, 84
Bhramyaman Theatre, 29
Bhutan, 31, 234
Bhutanese Army, 234
Bhuyan, Ajit, 238, 241
Bhuyan, Amity, AASU President, 227
Bhuyan, Dr.Manesh, Cardiologist, 133
Big Projects, 22
  Bhakra Nangal, 22
  Damodar Valley, 22
Bihar
  And Uttar Pradesh, 27
  Armed Police, 151
  Assembly, 156
  Police, 154
Bihari Muslims, 212
Bihu, 304
Bihu Vacation of High Court, 172
Bill of Rights, 99
Bin Laden, 277
Biosphere Degradation, 31
Biraj Kumar Sarma, Kumar Deepak Das, etc, AG Pleaders 239
Bishnu Rava, 72
Black
  Law, 128
  Money, 31, 232
Bodo
  Dacoits, 73
  Gang, 73
  Land, 72, 73
  Militants, 250
  State, 66, 131
  Youth, 31, 66
Bodo, Karmalal, 73
Bodoland, 250
  Territorial Area District (BTAD), 294
  Territorial Council (BTC), 250
  Violence in-, 74
Bodos, 72, 131, 248, 265
Boko Police Station, 124
Bora, Anil, Assamese Student Leader, 52
Bora, Atul, 120, 247, 256
Bora, Nibaran, 120
Bora, Prabin, AASU President, 226
Border
  Of Dalu, 58
  Organization, 168
  Outpot, 91
  Police Organization (BPO), 101, 102, 169
  Road Organization (BRO), 108, 110
  Security Force (BSF), 69, 70, 77, 128, 209
Bordoloi, 21
Bordoloi, Lachit, 284
Bordoloi, Gopinath, Bharat Ratna, 20, 32, 82, 236
  Death, 20
Bordoloi, Kanak, 91
Borgohain, Homen, 217, 218
Borjhar
  Airport, 185, 205
  Meeting, 266
Borkotoky, Dr. Dulal Chandra, 63, 64, 257

Borkotoky, SN, Commissioner, 59
Boro Xahitya Xabha, (BXX), 111
Borpujari, Utpal, 242
Bose, Subhash, 145
Botanical Garden of Adelaide, 80
Bradman, Sir Donald, 81
Brahma, Rupnath, 248, 250
Brahma, Upen, 131
Brahmaputra, 49, 73, 74, 91, 107, 126
  Bridge, 137
  Bridge at Saraighat, 70
  Known As 'Sorrow of Assam', 24
  Life Line of Assam, 24
  Valley, 49, 50, 52, 114, 141, 146, 181, 210, 259, 268
British
  Companies, 248
  India, 99
  Liberal Constitutional Practices, 293
  Policy of Divide and Rule, 52
  Tea Planters, 248
Brittamanjory, 16
Buddha, 100
Burma's Arakan Province, 277
Burmese Invasion, 112, 208
Burney, Union Home Secretary, 150, 151
Burnihat Meghalaya, 197, 201, 203
Bus Diplomacy, 263

Cabinet
  Mission, 249
  Muslims, 68
    Fakhruddin Ali Ahmed, 68, 69
    Moinul Haque Choudhury, 68
Cachar, 169
Capt. Sangma, 56, 60
Catastrophic Elections of 1983, 119
Central
  Industrial Security Force (CISF), 133
  Intelligence Agencies, 268
  Police Academy, 45
  Police Training College, 46
  Reserve Police Force, 115, 123, 125, 126, 128, 143, 144, 205, 209, 210
Chagla, Justice, 269, 271
Chakraborty, Bijoya, 235
Chaliha, Bimal Prasad (Late), 21, 62, 65, 82, 85, 107, 250
  CM, 50, 55, 56, 59, 61, 62, 63, 64, 72
  Death, 65
Chaliha, Paragdhar, 231
Chaliha, Paresdher, 257
Chandrasekhar, 40, 233, 247
Charan Singh, 124
Charter of Demands, 222, 289, 290
  of ULFA, 234
Chaturvedi, IGP UP, 47, 48
Chaturvedi, TN, Home Secy., 255
Chaudhury, Mahendra Mohan, 82
Chidambaram, P, 285
Chief Election Commissioner (CEC), 106, 109, 113, 123, 130, 146, 186, 187-192, 193, 194, 195
  Guidelines, 193, 194
Child Marriage, 303
China, 293
Chinese
  Aggression in 1962, 41, 54, 56, 67, 70
  And Pakistan, 263
  Invasion, 42
Choudhury, Abdul Gani Khan, 186, 206
Choudhury, Dr. Nirmal Kumar, 142
  Ex-VC Guwahati Univ., 279-281, 284, 288
  Principal, Assam Engineering College, 142
  Vice Chancellor, Guwahati University, 142
Choudhury, Mahendramohan, Punjab Governor, 21, 91, 102, 250
Choudhury, Tarun, 91
Christian
  Medical College, Vellore, 134
  Planters, 29
  Refugees, 60
Civic Peace, 253
Civil

Administration, 78
Defence, 93
Liberties, 210
Society, 56
Close Quarter Battle (CQB), 77
Coal Mines, Bihar, 158
Coalfields, 25
Colonial
Day, 161
Exploitation, 247
Imperialism, 44
Rule, 22
Rule of Pakistan, 277
System, 160
Communal
Politics, 65, 294
Problems, 32
Riots, 50, 115, 120
Communication
Network, 24
System, 305
Communist Party of India (M), 233
Congress (I), 98, 108-110, 113, 121-123, 125, 127, 128, 142, 183, 186, 187, 203, 207, 209, 210, 224, 233
In Assam, 236
Leaders, 213
Conservation, 17
Constitutional Rights, 160
Conveners, 279
Cooperative Movement, 177
Corrupt Practices, 154
Corruption, 224, 235
Cotton College, 50, 179
Counsel and Guidance Class, 36, 41
CPI (Communist Party of India), 21
And CPM, 239
MLA, 156
Jogendra Sharma, 156
Ramendra Kumar, 156
CPM's Support to Barbara, 96
Criminal Administration of Australia, 80
Criminals in India, 159
Cultural Organizations, 276
Culture of Bhaona, 30
Cut-Date for Detection of Illegal Migrants, 221
Cyber Crimes, 305

Dahotia, Arunodoy, 308
Daimary, Mithinga, ULFA Publicity Secretary, 241, 278
Dainik Basumati (Newspaper), 164
Dainik Janambhumi, 165
Daka, Tarunsen, 21
Dalgaon Legislative Assembly Constituency, 142
Dalu, 62
And Tura, 63
Police Station of Garo Hills, 58

Damodar Library, 17
Damodar Valley Project, 22
Dams, 93
Dandavate, Madhu, 124
Das, Bipin Pal, Union Deputy Minister, 88, 250
Das, Hemen, 124
Das, Dharmananda, 91
Das, Nripen, Registrar High Court, 170, 171
Das, Omeo Kumar, 250
Das, Parag, Journalist, 239
Das, Pradip, IGP, 103, 144
Das, Prof. Hariprasanna, 138
Das, Prof. Jogesh, 182
Das, Samar, 144, 149-151, 158, 162, 246
Das, TK, Jail Doctor, 157
Dasgupta, Pannalal, 21
Dasgupta, Santiranjan, Cabinet Minister, 138, 139
Data Karma, 18
Death Penalty, 154
Defence of India Rules, 71
Deforestation, 92
Deka, Harekrishan, Ex-DGP Assam, 279, 280
Deka, Kaushak, 242

Daka, Manoj, CPI Leader, 161
Deka, Ramen, BJP MP, 258
Delgam Legislative Assembly Constituency, 105
Demand Day, 207
Denmark, 177
Deporters, 190
Desai, Morarji, Janata Party, 84, 95
Detection of Foreign Nationals, 168
Deuri, Indibar, 280, 281, 288
Deuri, Late Bhimber, 248, 249
Dev, Satindera Mohan (Sateebabu), 48, 49
Devdasa, 17
Development of Entrepreneurship, 25
Development of International Tourism, 240
Dey, LBK, Retd. IGP of Assam, 134
Dhaka University, 302
Dhireshwaracharya, Mahamahopadhyaya, 16
  Sanskrit Scholar, 16
Dhubri, 64, 66, 67, 68, 69, 71, 75, 162
  Days, 58, 65-74, 85
  River Port, 70
  Troup, 30
Dhupdhari, 74
Dichotomic System of Control, 269
Digboi, 115
Digboi Oil Refinery, 22
Dilwara Jain Temple, 45
Dimasas, 250
  Homeland-Domaraji, 250
Dipomoni, Foreign Minister of Bangladesh, 299
  Convener of National Committee, 299
  Letter to Author, 299
Directive Principles of State Policy, 293
Dispur, 86, 87, 91, 103, 126, 140, 162, 208, 221, 228, 229
District
  Goalpara, 61
  Administration, 59, 62, 74
  Bongaigaon, 58
  Council Authority, 60, 61
  Council of Garo Hills, 60
  Darrang, 210, 264
  Dhubri, 58, 264
  Garo Hills, 54, 55, 58
  Goalpara, 58, 72
  Goalpara, Nagaon and Barpeta, 121
  Hazaribagh, 152
  Kamrup, 32, 124, 259, 271
  Kokrajhar, 58, 265
  Lakhimpur, 22
  Lushai Hills (Now Meghalaya), 56
  Nagaon, 52, 53, 77, 122, 125, 207
  NC Hills, 117
  Sylhet, 52
  Tinsukia, 22, 248
Disturbed Areas, 117
Donald, 82
Dorendra Singh, RK, CM Manipur, 169
DONER Ministry, 263
Dowry System, 30
Dr. Kalwar, Jail Doctor, 170, 171
Drainage of Economic Resources, 26
Dulaijan Mission, 115
DUNSTAN, PM of South Australia, 82
Dwijoo Valley, 91

Earthquake
  Of 1950, 92
  Prone Areas, 92
East Bengal, 211
East Goalpara Legislative Assembly Constituency Area, 270
East Pakistan, 55, 58, 59, 64, 66, 67, 72, 212
  Border, 58
  See also Bangladesh
East West Corridor Concept, 263
Eastern
  Europe, 43
  Nagaland, 307
Economic
  Development, 24, 25

Growth, 75, 84
Problems, 213, 297
Sector, 40
Security, 304
System, 82
Warfare, 44
Economy, 26, 232
Enclave, 26
Mercantile, 26
Of Assam, 233
Education
And Health Reforms, 292
Elementary, 18
Primary, 251
Egypt, 43
Eklavya, 18
Election
Campaigning, 127, 186
Commission (EC), 105, 108, 110, 191, 195, 196, 198, 199, 203, 206
Commission of Bangladesh, 214
Commission of India, 187, 188
Elections
In Assam, 119
Of 1983, 185-216, 219
Electoral
Registration Officers (ERO), 185, 191, 193 199-202
Of Bangladesh, 214
Rolls (ERs), 104, 193, 198
Rolls of Assam of Foreign Voters, 188
Elementary Education, 18
Embankments, 25
Emergency
Days, 145
Of 1975, 82
Enclave Economy, 25
Encroachment by Arunachal, 91
Enforcement Agency, 253, 254
Entrepreneurship in Assam, 27
Environmental Degradation, 25
Epical Characters, 16, 18
Bhisma, 16
Moidanab, 18
Ram, 16
Sri Krishna, 16
Epics, 29, 30
Essential Services Maintenance Act, 126
Ethnic Communities, 249
Ahoms, 249
Chutias, 249
Koch Rajbongshis, 249, 250
Mataks, 249
Morans, 249
Tea Tribes and Adivasis, 249
Ethnic
Groups, 20
Of Assam, 50
Issues, 292
Tribes, 248, 249
Tribes of Assam—Demands, 251
European Masters, 29
Evils of Dowry, 304
External Affairs Ministry, 213
Extra-Judicial Killings, 242

Faculty of Arts, 36
Fakhruddin Ali Ahmed, 88, 90, 114, 136
Famous Social Activists, 269
Atul Goswami, 269
Bijit Saikia, 269
Charan Narzary, 259
Dulal Barua, 269
Fascism, 184
Federal Constitution, 47
Female Refugees, 61
Feudal System, 18
Fifth (5) Assam Armed Police Training Centre Kahilipara, 301
Firaque Gorakhpuri, 38, 39
Incharge of English Tutorial Class, 38
Private Secretary to Mahatma Gandhi, 38
Flood
And Erosion, Problems of-, 25
Problem, 27
Prone Areas, 25, 91

Foreign
  Infiltration, 190, 208
  Infiltration Problem, 119
  Labour, 261
  National Problem in Assam, 210
  Nationals, 126, 191, 193
    Silent Invasion, 227
Foreigners
  Act 1946, 88, 128, 129
  Population, 194
Forest Land, 31
Freedom
  Fighters, 252
    Association of Assam, 204
  Movement, 65, 75, 77, 145, 164, 248
  Of Expression, 271
  Struggle, 163
Fresh Hideouts, 234
Friends of Bangladesh, 300
Fundamentalism, 213
Fundamentalist Forces, 78, 212

Gandhi, Mahatma, (Gandhiji), 21, 293
  Non-Cooperation Movement, 163
Gandhi, Mrs. Indira, 72, 78, 93-95, 109, 124, 116-121, 125-128, 136, 146, 186, 195, 203, 207, 208, 209, 210, 228, 236, 256, 263
Gandhi, Rajiv, 221, 228, 230, 285
Gandhi, Rajmohan, 100, 165
Gandhi, Sanjay, 84, 93
Ganganath Jha Hostel, 255
Garo Hills, 55, 55, 59, 61
Gazetted Police Officers, 85
  Age Old Procedure of Transfer, 85
General Elections, 1952, 19, 20
  Of 1977, 72
  Of 1991, 257
General Medical College (GMC), Vellore, 149
Geographical Isolation, 107
Ghost Stories, 31
Gill, KPS, 136
Gills from Punjab, 86
Gitanjali, 17
Globalization, 309
Goalpara, 126, 259, 264
Gogoi, Akhil, 92
Gogoi, Jibeswar, 70
Gogoi, Majumdar, 97
Gogoi, Munin, DC, 59
Gogoi, Pradip, 278
Gogoi, Promod, CPI, 237
Gogoi, Tarun, 92, 130, 308
  CM of Assam, 308
Gohain, Dr. Hiren, 165, 209, 278, 279, 284
Gohain, Rajen, 268
Golap Barbara, 95
Gopal Khura, 31
Gossip Club, 17
Goswami, Dinesh, Congress MP, 88, 231, 235, 247, 257
Goswami, Mamoni Roisom, 278, 279, 281
Goswami, Sabita, Journalist, 196
Goswami, SP, 252
Goswami, TN, 19
Goswami, Viswadev, 19
Great Earthquakes of 1950, 24
Grouping Scheme, 249
Growth of Population since 1951, 25
Guhpur, 206
Gujarat High Court, 172
Gujral (IK), PM, 271
Guwahati
  Central Jail, 179
  High Court, 130, 151, 162, 172-174, 244, 253
  Jail, 144
  Legislative Assembly Constituency, 260
  Legislative Assembly Seat, 258, 259
  Medical and College Hospital, (GMCH), 125, 133, 134, 179
  Mission, 120
  Refinery, 234
Refinery Employees Union, 271
University, 303

Habeus Corpus
  Cases, 172, 173, 174
Habibur Rahman, 269
Hailakandi, 141
Hajong, 63
Handique, Ghanikanta, Police Inspector, 124
Harijan, 28
Hazare, Anna, 84
Hazare, Vijay, 81
Hazaribagh
  Central Jail, 145, 146
  Jail, 151, 152, 177, 179
  St. Xavier School, 158
Hazarika, Bhupen, Legendary Bard of Assam, 72, 90, 94, 155, 306
Hazarika, Jatin, 230
Hazarika, Jogen, 96
Hazarika, Kirtinath, 127, 217
Hazarika, Makhan, 104
Healthy Democratic Traditions, 18
Heinous Crimes, 254
High-Tech Culture, 25
Hill
  State Movement, 55
  Tribes of Assam, 55
Hilsa Fish, 58
Himalayan Blunder, 42, 163
Himmat Journal, 164
Hindi Chini Bhai Bhai, 42
Hindu
  And Muslims, 32
    In Assam, 269
  Muslims Unity, 147
Hinduism, 99
Hira's Suicide, 162
Hitler, Adolf, 176, 184
Hmars and Zemi Nyas, 250
House Chores, 15
House Sparrow, by DS Smith, 156
HUJI, 277
Hungarian Crisis, 43
Hungary, 42
Hydel Power, 93
Hydel Project at Gerukamukh, 92
Hyderabad, 42, 45

Identification Process, 194
IGPs From UP, MP, Bihar, 47
IIT, 220
Illegal
  Export of Arms, 296
  Human Trafficking, 61
  Infiltrators, of Foreign Nationals, 181
    From Bangladesh and Nepal, 181
  Infiltrators, Problem of-, 182
  Migrants, 40, 66, 67, 68, 69, 104, 105, 165, 214, 220, 221, 262, 292
    Detection and Deportation, 69
    From Bangladesh, 104, 275, 186, 193, 237, 256
    From Nepal, 105
    Prone Districts, 264
    Trans-Border Migration, 218, 220
IMDT Act, 119, 128, 130, 223, 227, 235, 237, 257, 261, 262
Immigrant Muslims, 52, 186, 187, 203, 207, 208, 250
Immigration of Bengal Hindus from Sylhet, 52
Imperial Police, 46
India
  And Assam, 61
  Multiethnic, 47
  Multilingual, 47
  Multiracial, 47
  Multi-Religious, 47
India's
  Defence Preparedness, 42
  National Life, 84
  National Life and Its deficiencies, 18
Indian
  Army, 56, 234
  Citizens of Assam, 188
  Embassy at Yangoon, 308
  Heritage, 17, 18
  Police, 62
  Voters, 190

Indigenous People of Assam, 221
Indira Gandhi's
 Administration, 120
 Electioneering Campaign, 210
 Naramedha Yojana, 206
 Reign, 203
Indira-Mujib Pact, 118
Indira Gandhi and Sarat Sinha—Unconstitutional Functioning, 83
Indo-Bangla Border, 227
Indo-Pakistan
 Border, 55, 227
 Border Management Policy, 55
 War, 1985, 66, 69
Indo-US Relationship, 263
Industrial
 Development, 26
 Growth, 292
Infamous
 Election of 1983, 203, 204
 Emergency, 80
Infiltration
 From Bangladesh, 181, 207
 In North East from Bangladesh, 211
 Lobby, 115, 116, 203, 207
 Of Alien Citizens, 27
 Prone Constituency, 189
Influx of
 Foreigners, 227
 Refugees, 66
Infrastructure, 24
 Facilities, 26
 Inadequacy, 59
Inhuman Activities in Jail, 155
Insurgent
 Groups, 280, 293
Camps, 278
 Group (ULFA) Clones, (IGC), 286
  DHD, 286
  KLO, 286
  NDFB, 286
Outpost, 120
Intelligence
 Bureau, (IB), 45, 63, 64, 45, 74, 77
 Report, 58
International
 Border of Dalu and Purakhusia, 59
 Colonial Exploitation, 44
 Media, 60
 Politics, 43
Inter-State Boundary Disputes, 186
Irrigation
 And Infrastructure, 28
 System, 25
ISI (Inter Services Intelligence-Pakistan), 229, 234, 277, 293, 296
Islamic
 Fundamentalists, 213
 Kikya Jote, 277
 Militants, 277
 Terrorist, 277
  Operates in Bangladesh, 277
Issue of Infiltration, 231

Jacob, MM, Minister, 212
Jalan Group, 97
Jalukbari, 137
Jamiat, 302
Jan Sangh, 146
Janata
 Curfew, 127, 136
 Dal, 124, 209
 Legislative Party, 142
 Party, 146, 233
 Regime, 142, 143
Jaswant Singh, 124, 255
Jatin Babu, 19
Jha, Dr. Amarnath, 38
Jinnah, 32, 65, 270
Joint Family System, 304
Jorhat Legislative Assembly Constituency, 101
Joshi, Dr. Murli Manohar, 40, 255, 257, 261
Joy Bangla, 121
Judiciary, 82, 171
 Cell, 170
Justice Saikia Commission, 271

Kadir Ali, 210
Kaliabhomara, Bridge, 297
Kalidasa, 16
Kalita, Ananta, 241, 242
Kalita, Ganga, 124
Kalita, Kamda, Minister, 239
Kamrup, 115
  And Darrang, 61
  And Nagaon, 50
Karbi Anglong, 113
Karbis, 250
Kargil, 263
Karimganj District of Sylhet ,Transfer to Assam, 52
Karmee Devi, 153, 154
Kashmir, 296
  Problem, 42
Kasim Ali of Laluk, 88
  Notorious Dacoit, 88
Katigara Police Station, 141
Katiram Rabha, Freedom Fighter, 270
Khanna, Meharchand, Union Min for Relief & Rehabilitation, 62
Khargeswar Talukdar, 137, 138
  Death in Police Station, 136
Kharupetra, 104
Khushwant Singh, 17
King Nero, 206
Kole, Ranjit, 152
Kolkatta High Court, 150
Kopiti Dam in Central Assam, 92
Krishna Iyer, VR, Retd. Justice, 168
Kureshi Dam in Bhutan, 92
Kusak Mukti Sangram Samiti (KMSS), 92

Labour Class, 29
Laden's Al Qaida, 277
Lahiri, K. Justice, 173
Lake District of England, 33
Lakhimpur, 87, 88, 91, 93
Lal, Prof. AB, 36, 37, 43, 46
Lalit Mech of Boko, 270, 273
Lalu Prasad, 297
Laluk, 89
Land Alienation, 250
Landless Peasants of UP, 40
Language Movement, 50
Law and Order, 59, 74, 76, 162, 197, 232, 287
  At Hajoi, 1972, 53
Leadership, 19, 21
Left Parties, 186, 237
Leftist Leaders, 124
Legal Act, 151
Legislative Assembly (LA), 84, 105
  Constituencies, 221, 266, 268, 270
Letter of Credit, 90
  Scandal, 232
Liberalization of Administration, 248
Liberation
  Of Bangladesh, 78, 299
  War, 301
Life Oriented Politics, 21
Line of Communication, 27
Lingua Franca, 50, 73
LMGs Mortars, 69, 70
Lohia, Ram Manohar, 258
Lok Dal, 124, 146, 209, 233
Lok Sabha, 21, 95, 110, 112, 199, 204, 247, 261
Loka Parishad, 110
Lolit Doley, 250
Look East Policy, 263
Lower Assam, 30
Lushai Hills, 56

Magna Carta, 99
Mahanta, Prem Kanta, 109, 119
Mahanta, Profulla Kumar, 108, 110, 120, 196, 221, 222, 230, 231, 237, 247, 267, 268, 272, 274
  Chief Minister, 131, 231, 233, 235, 238-242, 245, 256
  Character, 242
  Extra-Marital Relations, 267
  Hidden Agenda, 228
  Second Ministry, 237, 242

Mahapurush Sankerdeva, 30
Maintenance of Internal Security Act (MISA), 83, 85, 86
Mairabari in Nawagaon District, 206
Manoj Deka, CPI Leader, 161
Majumdar, Abdul Muhim, 237
Mallick, BN, 46, 67, 76
Mallick, BP, IPS, 62
Mandal Committees, 259
Mangaldoi, 21, 124
Mangaldoi Legislative Assembly Constituency, 108, 110, 164
Manikpur, 74
Manmohan Singh, PM, 282, 308
Mann, SS, 246
Marlow, 38
Marshall Tito, 42
Marwaris and Bengali Hindus, 22, 23, 71
Marxists, 157
Massacre of Nellie, 187
Matrimonial Practices, 31
Mazumdar, Abdul Muhim, 128
Medhi, Bishnuram, 20, 296
Medhi, Sri Surendranath, 245
Medium of Instructions Movement, 1972, 131
Meghalaya, 55, 56, 208
  State Electricity Board, 196
Mehta Commission, 124, 206, 207
Mehta, TU Justice, Retd. Chief Justice of India, 204
Mekhala Chadar, Traditional Assamese Female Costume, 304
Members of Delegation to Meet Prime Minister, 284
Menon, SS, NSA, 282
Menons from Kerala, 86
Mid Term Poll, 115
Middle East, 43
Migration of Muslim Farmers, 211
Militancy, 226
Militant
  Bodo Youth, 73
  Immigrant Muslims, 115
Ministry of Home Affairs, 87, 105, 106, 191, 247
Minorities
  Commission, 211
  In Bangladesh, 211-212
Misra, AK, Justice, 150
Misra, Shyamanandan (of Lokdal), 124
Mitra, Dr. Rahi, 115
Mixed Economy, 41
Mobile Polling Centre, 206
Modern
  Day Circus, 30
  Democracies, 161
  Education, 248
  Management System, 26
  Sanitary System, 28
  Technological Base, 27
Modernization, 30
  Of Agriculture Sector, 177
  Scheme, 54
Modi, Marak, Chief Executive Member, 60
Moirabari, 187
Montgomery, Field Marshall, 64
Mookerjee, Lady Ranu, 301
Movement, Assam
  Activists, 125
    Chitra Barua, 125
    Prahlad Sharma, 125
    Tapan Basu, 125
  Leaders, 207
  Leadership, 126, 127, 222, 224
  See also Assam Movement
Mt Abu, 46, 48, 454
  Hill Station in Aravali Ranges, 45
Mufti Muhammad Syeed, HM, 247
Mukherjee, Otima, 40
Mukherjee, Subroto, Youth Congress Leaders, 117
Mukti Bahini, 77
  Guerrilla, 301
Mullah Masud Azhar, 277
  Pakistan Militant Leader, 277

Muslim
  Autonomous Council, 265
  Citizens of Assam, 186
  Council, 294
  Fundamentalist Organization (MFO), 273, 277
  League, 65, 66, 68
  Majority—Districts, 52
  Militant Outfits, 117
  Political Leaders, 68
  Population, 61, 128
Muslims in Assam, High Growth Rate, 211
Myanmar Border, 307
Mymensing, 58

NAC (National Advisory Council), 285
Naga
  Rebels, 55
  Student Federation, 208
Nagaon, 264
  And Kaliabor Legislative Assembly Constituency, 261
  Jail, 179
Naini Central Jail, 310
Nalbari, 16, 21, 22, 23, 30, 31, 41
  Areas, 19, 28, 29, 31, 41
  As Nabadweep of Assam, 16
  Caste Ridden Society, 28
  College, 18, 19
  Days, 15, 19, 31, 41
Natya Mandir, 303
  No Water Supply System, (1940), 16
Narain, Jay Prakash, 84
Narasimha Rao, PM, 211
Naresh Kalita of Agradoot Group, 238
National
  Committee. Bangladesh, 299, 300
  Convention, 278
  Emergency, 51, 53, 192
  Emergency of 1975-77, 21
  Leaders, 118
    Atal Behari Vajpayee, 118
    Chandrasekhar, 118
    George Fernandes, 118
  Political Parties, 209
    Bharatiya Janata Party, 209
    Lok Dal, 209
  Register of Citizens (NRC), 117
  Security, 86, 87, 179
  Security Adviser, 149, 170, 186, 238, 242, 246
  Security Act, 143
  Trust Fund, 182
Nationalism, 43
NATO, 42
Naxalites, 19
NC Hills Districts, 113
NDA Government, 232
NEFA (Now Arunachal), 42
Nehru, Pandit Jawaharlal, 20, 38, 39, 41, 42, 44, 48, 50, 62, 91, 263, 310
  Modern Temples of Progress, 41
  Modern India Concept, 42
  Socialistic Pattern of Society, 41
Nehru's Kashmir Policy, 42
Nellie, 186, 206, 207, 208
  Massacre, 121, 125, 208
Nepali Migrants, 260
NHPC, 92, 93
No Oil No Food, 117
Non-Assamese Voters, 206
Non-Cooperation Movement, 38
Non-Muslim People of East Pakistan, (NMPEP), 58
  Buddhists, 58
  Christians, 58
  Hindus, 58
Non-Violent Movement, 162
North East
  Congress (I), Cabinet Committee, 211
  Council, 261
  India, 182
  Region, 174
  States, 193
  Students Organization (NESO), 186
North Kamprup, 51
North Lakhimpur, 73
Norway, 177

NSCN, 293
NSCN (K), 293, 306, 307
Nurul Amin, 49
Nurul Hasan, 241

Oil
- Blockade, 114, 115, 120
- Fields, 25
- Refinery, 107

Om Mehta, Union Minister of State, 88
Opera System, 29
Operation
- All Clear, 234
- Bajrang, 234
- Rangapani, 73
- Rhino-1, 234, 240
- Rhino-2, 234, 241

Opposition Leaders, 294
- Gauri Shankar Bhattacharyya—Atul Goswami, etc. opposition leaders, 294

Paine, Robert, Biographer of Hitler, 184
Pakistan, 21, 70, 71, 77, 78, 212
- Army, 69, 71, 77, 78, 301
- Infiltrations, 67
- Inter-Services Intelligence (ISI), 78, 227
- Steamers, 70

Pakistani Muslims, 73
Palestine Problem, 43
Panchayat Elections, 267
Pandit, KC, 261
Pandit, Mrs. Vijaya Lakshmi, 42, 310
Paramilitary Forces, 186
Partition of Bengal, 52
Patel, Sardar Vallabhbhai, 42
Patgiri, Dilip, 280
Pathak, D Justice, 173
Patna
- Jail, 166
- Medical College, 166, 170

Patwari, Chandramohan, Minister, 239
Patwari, Hiralal, 108
Paul, Swaraj, 232
People's Republic of Bangladesh, 299
Phizo, 55
Phukan, Bhrigu Kumar, 120, 108, 196, 235, 245, 256
Phukan, Ganesh Chandra, 204
Plains Tribal Council of Assam, 111
Planned Development, 26
Planning, 27
- Commission, 27
- For Assam's Development, 24

Pokhran Experiment, 263
Poland, 43
Police
- Academy, 45
- Administration, 51
- Budget, 80
- Modernization Scheme, 277
- Welfare Fund, 80

Policies on Industrial Location, 28
Policy of
- Economic Liberalization, 263
- Liberalization, 282
- Non-Alignment, 41
- Self-Aggrandisement, 82

Polish
- Communist Party, 43
- Proletariat, 43

Political
- Affairs Committee, 209
- Agitations, 74
- And Economic Powers, 18
- Parties, 194, 280
- Philosophy, 19

Politicisation of Police, 277
Polling
- States, 206
- Stations, 186

Population Growth of Assam, 211
Post State Languages Act, 66
Press Censorship, 127
Prevention of Infiltration (PIP) Scheme, 67, 101-103, 119, 190, 211
- From Pakistan Scheme, 66

Primary Education, 251
Princely Nature States, 42
Principle of Accountability, 224
Prominent Assamese Muslim
  Personalities, (PAM), 207
    Abu Sama, 207
    Fazlul Rahman, 207
    Hamidur Rahman, 207
    Nusen Ali, 207
Prominent National Leaders, 209
    AB Vajpayee, 209
    Jaswant Singh, 209
    Charan Singh, 209
    HN Bahuguna, 209
    Karpuri Thakur, 209
    Raj Narain, 209
    Madhu Dandvate, 209
    Shyamanandan Misra, 209
Pro-Pakistan Muslims, 71
    CM, 68
Pro-Pakistan Politicians, 65
Pseudo-Patriotism, 133
Public Funds, 18
Punjab and Haryana, 90
Puranas, 29, 30
Purbanchaliya Loka Parishad, 111

Quit India Movement, 1932, 113

Radcliff Awards, 52
Radical Islamic Groups, 277
Ragamani, 40
Raj Narain, 40, 124
Rajagopalachari, C, 100
Rajasthan
    Armed Constabulary, 126
    Desert Climate, 45
    Police, 205
Rajendra Prasad, 145
Rajkhowa, Arabinda, ULFA
  Chairman, 241, 293
Rajkhowa, Lalit, 110
Ram Singh, Mughal General, 296
Ramendra Kumar, Labour Leader,
  158, 159
Ranchi
    Jail, 151
    Medical College, 151
Ranga, Miss, 36
Ranganadi Dam in Arunachal, 92
Ravi Kesari, Adivasi Youth, 154
Ravi, RN, Spl Director of IB, 223
Ray, SS, 178
RCPI
    Activists, 19, 21
    Leaders, 21
Red
    Light Area, 37
    Tapism, 25
Reforms, 292
Refugee (s), 59-61, 77, 78
    Camp, 63
    Camps at Halflong, 301
Regional Politics, 247
Relief Camp, 207
Religious
    Fundamentalism, 273, 302
    Minorities, 212
    Minority Community, 190
Religious/Social Rituals, 304
Representation of People Act (ROP), 192
Resistance Movement, 128
Reva, Bishnu Prasad, 21
Revenue Circles, 66
Right to Information (RTI) Act, 99
Rioting and Arson, 206, 212
River (s), 20
    Police, 70
    Police Organization, (RPO), 109, 113,
      130, 187, 196, 198-200, 202, 262
    Semen, 91
    Subansiri, 91, 92
Robbery Cases, 89
Rohingya Force, 277
Roy, Nicholas, 250
Roy, Niranjan, 66
Roy, Phani, 149
Roy, SS, CM West Bengal, 19